CURRENT ENGLISH USAGE

Frederick T. Wood

Revised by R. H. Flavell and L. M. Flavell

First published 1962
This edition first published 1981

Published by
THE MACMILLAN PRESS LIMITED
London and Basingstoke
Associated companies in Delhi, Dublin, Hong Kong, Johannesburg, Lagos, Melbourne, New York, Singapore, and Tokyo.

Typeset in 10/12 pt Times by Santype International Ltd., Salisbury, Wilts
Printed in Hong Kong

ISBN 0 333 27840 2

INTRODUCTION

The aim of this book is a practical one: to provide an easy work of reference for those who wish to write good English. The entries deal with points of grammar, punctuation, style, idiom, spelling and modern usage generally. As the focus of the book is on good *written* English, pronunciation has not been dealt with.

Given the wide range of the book's subject matter, it is obviously impossible to be comprehensive. Indeed, there is no attempt to be so, for a comprehensive treatment of grammar would turn this handbook into a fully-fledged grammar book, and a comprehensive treatment of vocabulary would turn it into a dictionary. The entries have been selected in the light of the difficulty they offer to the learner. The selection has been made on the basis of the author's and revisers' considerable teaching experience in England and overseas, on the basis of reference to many other authorities' publications on usage, and on the basis of the mistakes actually made in a wide variety of written sources. We are also very grateful to the friends who have passed on to us common confusions of their pupils or who have commented on parts of the manuscript. The entries, then, come from a wide range of sources, but they can never hope to be complete. Further suggestions will always be welcomed.

It is worth pointing out that a work of this nature is necessarily prescriptive. The aim is to give guidance as to what is accepted as good written English by educated users of the language. Our task was not that of the linguist – simply to record what people do – but rather to give a faithful account of what people consider standard written English to be. The question of standard is important since the labels 'correct' and 'incorrect' only make sense in relation to a norm. What is Standard English? To find out, you might look up the entry **Standard English** where we have narrowly defined it as prose (not verse); it is neutral in style (not very formal or informal); it is non-specialist in subject matter (to avoid the technical vocabularies of law, engineering, etc); it is contemporary (not the standards of earlier years); it is educated usage (the work of careful writers, thoughtful about the language they use).

Having said that, we must admit there must still remain a grey area as to what constitutes Standard English. Language, in all its aspects, is permanently changing and it always has done so. A usage which is informal to one generation, to be used primarily in speech with one's friends, may well become accepted Standard English to the next, to be used in all written contexts. Furthermore, it is amazing how the experts themselves differ in their opinion as to what is good English and what is not. In England there is no body which conveniently decides on the acceptability of a word, as does the Academie Française in France, so it has been left to the judgement of the revisers to provide answers in these difficult areas of changing usage and divided opinions. Fortunately, only a relatively small number of entries are in this class!

On the trials of a reviser, we can do no better than quote Sir Bruce Fraser who was responsible for the revision of the classic *Complete Plain Words* by Sir Ernest Gowers:

> This tempts me into moralising about the duty of anyone who writes about the use of English for the general practitioner. He must, as I see it, have the courage of his convictions, but must not express them too dogmatically on points which fairly admit of a different opinion. He must avoid pedantry, and must also recognise that what seems obviously right to one man seems pedantic to another. He must offer resistance to undesirable innovations, but must not assume that every innovation is sure to be undesirable. He must respect the genius of the language, which includes a wonderful capacity for change. All this requires personal judgment, and every man's judgment is fallible.

As one small illustration of the difficulties, we use *judgement*, yet Fraser prefers *judgment*!

In another respect we share Fraser's problems as a reviser. Dr Wood had strong views on English usage and did not hesitate to make them plain by using labels such as 'vulgarism' and 'uneducated usage'. We are aware of the different value accorded to varieties of English today, yet felt we wanted to retain something of the forthright nature of Dr Wood's views. Consequently we have at times left in some of his strongly-worded opinions where they warn the reader that people might frown upon such a usage in writing.

An effort has been made to keep the explanations and comments as simple as possible, without the obscure technical vocabulary of grammarians. Whether the learner speaks English as his mother-tongue, as a second language or as a foreign language, it seems reasonable to assume a knowledge of basic grammatical terminology (traditional terms, rather than modern linguistic terms, have been retained as they are widely known and used throughout the world). Less known items receive their own explanation, listed alphabetically in the body of the work (eg **euphony**, **tautology**).

In general, the entries of the first edition have been simplified and often abbreviated. Other changes have also been made. Much older material has been removed and a large number of new entries have been inserted. Some deal with points of grammar; most deal with problems of vocabulary, punctuation and style. The format is clearer, and cross-references are much more extensive. Many are for quick reference (Is it *focused* or *focussed*?), with a cross reference to the general principle involved. These innovations make the book easier to refer to. There are also a lot of illustrative quotations from newspapers, etc. Some of these come from the *This English* column of the *New Statesman*, who have kindly allowed them to be used here. American usage has also received comment wherever it seemed appropriate, although the emphasis is on British English.

In short, our aim has been to provide a source of interest and even amusement for the browser, a practical tool for the learner to help him with his studies and a handy source of reference for anyone in need.

We hope this book will serve you well.

Roger and Linda Flavell

Abbreviations used

COD	The Concise Oxford Dictionary of Current English
DNB	The Dictionary of National Biography
LDOCE	The Longman Dictionary of Contemporary English
OALDCE	The Oxford Advanced Learner's Dictionary of Current English
OED	The Oxford English Dictionary
TLS	The Times Literary Supplement

a

AD

See **dates 5**.

a-an

(indefinite article)

1 General rule Use *a* before consonants: *a tree*, *a flower*, *a hotel*, etc. Use *an* before vowels: *an article*, *an ear*, *an iron*, and unsounded *h*: *an hour*, *an heir*. The only members of this last class are, in fact, *heir*, *honest*, *honorary*, *honorarium*, *honour*, *hour* and their derivatives.

2 The terms 'vowel' and 'consonant' are phonetic: they refer to sounds, not letters (see **vowel**). Words which have the initial letters *u* or *eu* pronounced like an initial *y* do not begin with a vowel sound and take *a*: *a university*, *a unit*, *a European*. The same principle applies to *a one-man business*, where the initial sound is *w*.

3 An initial *h* is silent when it is followed by an unstressed syllable. Compare *a heretic*, *an heretical opinion*.

4 Whether *a* or *an* is used before initials depends on how the initial is pronounced. *A*, *E*, *F*, *H*, *I*, *L*, *M*, *N*, *O*, *R*, *S* and *X* all begin with a vowel sound: hence *an LEA school*, *an MA*, *an MP* but *a BBC production*, *a BA*, *a PhD*, etc.

abbreviations

1 Punctuation English is in a state of change with respect to punctuation. The new style is simpler and more informal. The general trend is to reduce as much as possible the use of punctuation marks with abbreviations. Some people, however, like to retain a more formal style. It is a matter of taste and the choice is yours, but once you have adopted a particular style, you must be consistent. In the following notes, it is made clear where punctuation marks *must* be used by all writers, whatever their style. Similarly, it is indicated where some writers may still prefer to use them, though others may not.

2 Full stop

a When the abbreviation consists of capitals, the full stop *may* be omitted: *MP*, *TV*, *BA*, *PTO*. If a stop is used, it is placed after a letter that stands for a complete word, hence *M.P.*, *B.A.*, *P.T.O.* but *TV.*

In the same way, stops *may* be omitted with points of the compass:

NW, SE, E or *NW., SE., E.* and with London postal districts: *SW10, WC1* or *S.W.10, W.C.1.* Because of the widespread use of postcodes in recent years, it is now usual to omit the full stops: *WC1H 0AL, SW1A 2BN.*
b Stops are usually omitted in acronyms: *UNESCO, SALT, OPEC.*
c A full stop *may* follow a person's initials: *F T Wood* or *F. T. Wood, Messrs T J Jones & Co* or *Messrs T. J. Jones & Co.*
d Omission of stops If the abbreviation ends with the last letter of the word, it is now common practice to omit the stop: *Mr, Mrs, Dr, Maths.* Some publishing houses omit all full stops when punctuating abbreviations. The *OALDCE* follows this policy. However, Simeon Potter in his book *Changing English* still includes the stop if the last letter of the abbreviation is not the last letter of the word. The student must decide for himself whether to write *eg, Prof, ref, Jan* or *e.g., Prof., ref., Jan.*
e The abbreviations *1st, 2nd, 3rd,* etc should never be followed by a full stop.
3 Apostrophe It *must* be used to indicate the omission of letters from a word: *o'clock, can't, isn't.* Care should be taken to place the apostrophe correctly in contracted forms. In *could not,* the *o* is omitted and replaced by an apostrophe, and the contracted form is therefore *couldn't.* If there are two omissions in a word, only the second is normally indicated: *shall not = shan't.*
4 Plurals Some single-letter abbreviations double the letter in the plural: *pp.* or *pp* (pages), *vv.* or *vv* (verses), *ll.* or *ll* (lines). Usually, however, the plural is formed by simply adding an *s*: *M.P.s* or *MPs, TV.s* or *TVs.* The second form is to be preferred. It is wrong to form the plural by adding *'s* to abbreviations: *MP's, TV's.* This may lead to confusion with the possessive.
5 Possessive The possessive of abbreviations is formed by adding *'s* or *s'*: *an MP's speech, both JPs' qualifications.*

aborigines

The singular is *aboriginal* not *aborigine* or (worse still) *aboriginee.*

about/on

These prepositions are used after a wide range of verbs and adjectives with the meaning of 'concerning, on the subject of'. *On* is more formal and refers usually to a thoughtful expression of views:
☐ He talked *about* his new lawnmower when he came to see us
☐ He talked *on* Evolution versus Creation to the invited guests.

It is not, therefore, appropriate to use *on* with colloquial verbs dealing with inconsequential daily events (*bicker, natter, moan*, etc). The same difference is also found after nouns: *a tale about a frog and a donkey, a report on colonialism in Africa.*

Other less common formal alternatives for *about* and *on* are *of* and *concerning*. They are somewhat literary or formal:

☐ He told *of* fear and futility, yet healing and holiness

☐ There was a lengthy debate *concerning* the financial provisions of the Budget.

above/over

Both prepositions are used to express a vertical relationship between one thing and another: *There was a picture above/over the door.*

Over may suggest closeness, as in *The dog stood over the pups to protect them.*

Above tends to suggest 'on a higher level than': *The headland was above a beautiful sandy beach.*

Note: Similar general remarks apply to *below* and *under*, the converses of *above* and *over*.

It is pedantic to think that *above* should not be used before a noun: *see the above quotation.* It may also equally well be used as an adverb: *see the quotation above.* An alternative to the adjectival use is to write *above-mentioned*: *see the above-mentioned quotation.*

abscess

Note the *sc* in the spelling.

absence

See **lack/absence**.

absorb

This is often used incorrectly, as in:

☐ His work absorbs him completely. He doesn't notice time pass.

Where *absorb* is used in the sense of 'holding one's attention' it should be in the passive only, followed by the preposition *in*. The correct construction is *He is completely absorbed in his work . . . .*

Absorbing work is very interesting work which holds one's attention.

Absorbent is the adjective from the other meaning of *absorb* (= 'to soak up'). A sponge is *absorbent*; it soaks up water.

abstract language

Sometimes objections are raised to the use of abstract terms. However, if the abstract style is concise and clear, there seems no objection to it; a change to the concrete may be a change for the worse:

□ The Chairman expressed his appreciation of the loyalty of the staff and the workpeople

is much to be preferred to:

□ . . . said he appreciated the way that the staff and the workpeople had been loyal,

and:

□ There is no denying the seriousness of the situation

is no more objectionable than:

□ There is no denying that the situation is serious.

But of recent years there has grown up, especially in official documents and in journalism, a vague kind of style which uses circumlocutory abstractions which are clumsy in construction and which say rather ineffectively what could have been said much more clearly in far fewer words. This should certainly be avoided by anyone who wishes to write good English. Below are a few examples. A simplified version is given in brackets after each one.

□ What is the position with regard to the availability of a house? (*Is a house available?*)

□ There is no likelihood of an early finalisation of the plans. (*It is unlikely that the plans will be put into a final form for some time.*)

□ The implementation of the scheme would involve the expenditure of a large sum of money. (*It would be very costly to carry out the scheme.*)

□ The situation with regard to the export of cars has shown a slight improvement. (*Rather more cars have been exported.*)

□ In the eventuality of this being the case. (*If this is so.*)

□ In view of the fact that. (*As.*)

□ If the weather situation permits. (*If the weather permits* or *weather permitting.*)

(See also **-ese**.)

accentuate

Here are two examples of misuse, both from *The Financial Times*:

□ The steel shortage has been *accentuated*, and will particularly hit the motor industry

□ In America cotton, hessian and paper share the important bagging market. With the first two in short supply, the trend towards paper sacks is *accentuated*.

This misuse has become very common in the last few years. *Accentuate* means 'to throw into relief or into prominence': *The microphone accentuates certain defects of intonation.* It does not mean 'to increase, aggravate, make more acute', and the several related meanings which modern usage (or abusage) gives it.

accessary/accessory

Note the spelling: double *c* and double *s* in both words. *Accessary* is a legal word meaning 'a person who helps in something, especially a crime'. One becomes an *accessary to* a crime. An *accessory* is an extra but not essential part of something:

☐ 'The bride's going-away outfit was a cream suit with brown *accessories* (brown hat, gloves and handbag)'

☐ The more expensive car comes with several *accessories* (a clock, a cigarette-lighter, a radio, etc).

The American spelling is *accessory* for both meanings.

accommodate

Note the spelling, double *c* and double *m*.

accord/accordance

Of *one's own accord*, not *on one's own accord*: *I did the work of my own accord* (meaning 'without being forced or asked').

When the sense is 'following out' or 'obeying' *in accordance with* is required:

☐ *In accordance with* your instructions we have suspended work on the heating apparatus.

according

Followed by the preposition *to*.

1 Meaning 'on the authority of': *According to my newspaper, the Chancellor is going to increase taxes.*

2 Meaning 'in proportion to': *He earns between £550 and £620 a month, according to how much overtime he does.*

3 *According* cannot be used as an adverb: *We will find out what they need and act* accordingly – not *according.*

acknowledge

Note the *c* in the spelling.

acoustics

The acoustics of the hall are *not all that could be desired*, but *Acoustics* is *an important subject in the training of an architect.* In the first case, *acoustics* means the physical properties of the hall and takes a plural verb; in the second case, it is the study of the science which is in question, and the verb is therefore singular. (See also **mathematics** and **politics**.)

acquaint

1 We acquaint a person *with* (not *of*) a fact. The expression, however, is best avoided, since it is usually no more than a piece of pretentious English for the simpler *inform, tell* or *let know*.

2 Note the *c* in the spelling. Similarly *acquaintance, acquit, acquiesce, acquire*.

3 Acquaint/acquit Here the wrong word is used:

□ They *acquainted* themselves creditably in both tests. (*The Times*)

There is confusion of *acquaint* and *acquit*; the latter means 'conduct oneself'. Amend to *They acquitted themselves* . . . .

acquaintance/colleague/friend

An *acquaintance* is a person one simply knows; a *friend* is someone with whom one has a deeper relationship; a *colleague* is a person one works with.

See **colleague**.

acquiesce

Acquiesce means 'to accept something without a protest'. Followed by the preposition *in*:

□ Although he would rather have made alternative arrangements, the Secretary of State *acquiesced in* the plans his host had made for him.

(See also **acquaint** for similar spellings.)

acquit

See **acquaint 3**.

acronym

See **abbreviations 2b**.

act

See **bill/act**.

add up to

What it adds up to is . . . . A piece of modern jargon for *amounts to, comes to* or sometimes simply *means*. Allowable colloquially, but should not be used in serious writing.

addicted

The sentence *He is addicted to drink* has perhaps given rise to the unidiomatic use of an infinitive after *addicted. To drink* is here not an infinitive, but a noun preceded by a preposition. *Addicted* is always followed by *to* plus a noun or a gerund: *addicted to drugs*, *addicted to gambling*, but not *addicted to gamble.*

adequate

1 Adequate for Where *adequate* is used immediately before a noun and means 'sufficient for the purpose', it is followed by *for*, not *to*:

□ They fortunately had *adequate* money *for* the cost of the journey.

2 Adequate to Where *adequate* is used as a complement after a verb and means 'with the necessary qualities', it is followed by *to*, not *for*:

□ He seems quite *adequate to* the task that faces him.

3 Other phrases Since *adequate* means 'just sufficient', *adequate enough* is incorrect, as is *more adequate.* Logically, there is no objection to *more than adequate*:

□ The time you were allowed for the work should have been *more than adequate*,

but *more than enough* or *more than sufficient* is to be preferred.

adherence/adhesion

Adhesion means 'sticking to' in the literal sense: the *adhesion* of a stamp to an envelope, or of flies to a fly-paper; *adherence* is 'sticking to' in the figurative sense, as *adherence* to a plan, to one's principles, etc.

The verbal counterpart of both is *adhere*: wallpaper *adheres* to the wall, and a person *adheres* to his plans.

Adherence gives the adjective *adherent*, and *adhesion* the adjective *adhesive* (as *adhesive tape, an adhesive plaster*). Both adjectives may be converted to nouns: *adhesives* (paste, gum, etc), a person's *adherents* (meaning 'supporters').

adjacent

Note the unpronounced *d* in the spelling. Similarly *adjourn.*

adjective or adverb?

See **adverb or adjective?**

adjourn

Note the unpronounced *d* in the spelling. Similarly *adjacent.*

admission/admittance

When *admit* means 'to confess', the noun is always *admission*: *the admission of one's guilt*; *the admission that one was to blame.* When it means 'to allow in' *admission* is also the more usual word: *Admission one pound, Admission by ticket only. Admittance* is more formal or official, and means 'right to enter': *No admittance except on business.*

admit

1 Admit/admit of *Admit* may take a personal subject, and indeed usually does, but *admit of* (meaning 'to allow of, leave room for') cannot:

☐ I *admit* breaking the window

☐ She *admitted* having read the letter,

but:

☐ The position *admits of* no delay

☐ The regulations *admit of* no variation.

Wrong use: *I cannot admit of your doing that*; amend to *I cannot allow you to do that*. But *The regulations do not admit of your doing that* is perfectly good English.

2 Admit to

☐ In spite of all the evidence against him, he refused to *admit to* the allegation.

Admit to something that is charged against one (perhaps on the analogy of *confess to a crime*) is occasionally to be found in modern writing, but it is not yet fully established as idiomatic. The simple form *admit* is preferable. (See also **allow/allow of**.)

admittance

See **admission/admittance**.

adopted parents (father, mother)

Strictly speaking, the following is incorrect, though it is sometimes heard in speech, and occasionally seen in print: *The Reverend Joseph Evans, the adopted father of Peter Evans*. It is the child who is adopted by the parents, not vice versa. Substitute *adoptive parents* (*father, mother*). *Adopted child, son, daughter* is, of course, correct.

advance (noun)/advancement

Advance means 'progress' or 'going forward' (or sometimes 'coming on'): *the advance of an army, the advance of science, the advance of medical knowledge, the advance of old age*.

Advancement means 'promotion' or 'helping forward': *to seek advancement, to work for the advancement of a cause, the Royal Society for the Advancement of Science*. We say that with the *advance* (not the *advancement*) of winter the days grow shorter.

adventitious/adventurous

Adventitious means 'coming by accident or by chance'. *Adventurous* means 'ready for adventure':

☐ The *adventurous* boy would have drowned but for the *adventitious* arrival of the life-boat.

adverb or adjective?

1 There are a number of adjectives which can have an adverbial function. Consider the following:

☐ Don't speak so *loud*

☐ Speak a little *slower*

☐ The bus will get you there as *quick* as the train

☐ She sells her goods *cheap*

☐ We got back *late/early/fast* yesterday.

These uses are quite idiomatic. In all cases except the last (where no corresponding adverb exists), however, it is permissible to use an adverb: *Don't speak so loudly*, etc.

2 Some verbs connected with the body's senses are commonly followed by an adjective rather than an adverb.

☐ That pie tastes *marvellous*

☐ The rose smells *superb*

☐ She looked *very pretty* on her wedding day.

3 Combinations such as *new-laid eggs, new-won freedom, a new-born baby* and *new-mown hay* are correctly adjective plus participle. Do not write *newly-laid eggs*, etc. (See also **quicker**, **hardly**, **high/highly**, **tight/tightly** and **different(ly)**.)

adverse/averse

Adverse means 'unfavourable, hostile': *adverse criticism*, *adverse weather conditions*, etc.

Averse means 'unwilling, opposed'. Followed by *to*: *The Government is not averse to raising the tax.*

advice/advise

Advice is the noun; *advise* the verb. For the general rule, see **practice/practise**.

affect/effect

The verb corresponding to the noun *effect* is *affect* ('to produce an effect upon'):

☐ The climate *affected* his health

☐ The increased tariffs recently announced by the Australian government are bound to *affect* our exports to that country.

Affect also means 'to pretend to have or feel':

☐ She *affected* surprise

☐ He *affected* a superior air.

Effect, when used as a verb, means 'to bring about', or 'to achieve': *to effect an escape, to effect a change*. The plural noun *effects* may mean 'results': The full *effects* of the measures have yet to be felt, or it may mean 'personal property or belongings', as in the expressions *one's household effects, one's personal effects*.

affinity

There is an affinity *between* two things, or one has an affinity *with* (not *to*) the other. *Affinity for* is recognised in scientific language. One substance is said to have an affinity *for* another when it has a tendency to unite with it. Outside this rather specialised use, *an affinity for* is considered incorrect by some writers, but it is becoming progressively more common in modern English.

afflict/inflict

Afflict is regularly found in the form *afflicted*, as the adjective or past participle. It is followed by the prepositions *with* or *by*, and it suggests a passive suffering from something:

□ Mr Simmonds is *afflicted with* arthritis

□ Her mother was sadly *afflicted by* the news of her ill health.

Inflict means 'to cause bodily or mental suffering, usually deliberately': *His attacker inflicted severe wounds on him*. The preposition is *on*.

aforesaid

Except in the language of legal documents, an archaic word, which has a slightly absurd or humorous effect: *the aforesaid Mr Smith*. Do not use it in ordinary English. (Compare **said** and **above/over**.)

after

On *after the manner* or *style of* and *named after*, see **named 2**.

age

(verb) There is an increasing tendency to write *aging* rather than *ageing* as the present participle. See **spelling 4**.

agenda

Through strictly a Latin plural (meaning 'things to be done'), in English this word is treated as a singular. Say *The agenda has not yet been drawn up*. Plural: *agendas*. (Compare **data**.)

aggravate

Commonly misused in the sense of 'to annoy or irritate':

□ Don't *aggravate* your aunt in that way

□ It is very *aggravating* to be constantly interrupted when you are engaged on an important piece of work.

The mistake is a very old one. Jerry Cruncher, in *A Tale of Two Cities*, it may be recalled, referred to his wife as 'an aggrawater'.
The only legitimate meaning is 'to make worse something that is already bad':
☐ The measures designed to remedy the situation only *aggravated* it.

aghast

Note the unpronounced *h* in the spelling.

ago

It is ten years ago since his father died. This sentence illustrates a very common mistake. *Ago* normally takes the past tense; it refers to a point of time in the past, and reckons backwards from the present. It cannot, therefore, be combined with *since*, which reckons *from* a point of time in the past *up to* the present: *I have not seen him since last Christmas.* The alternative constructions are:
☐ It was ten years ago that his father died
☐ It is ten years since his father died
☐ His father died ten years ago.
(See also **since**.)

agree

1 Agree with/agree to To *agree with* a suggestion or a course of action is to regard it with approval; to *agree to* it is to give consent to it. Thus we may *agree to* something without *agreeing with* it:
☐ He was forced to *agree to* the proposals, though he did not like them.
2 Transitive use of agree *The Inspector of Taxes has now agreed your claim for expenses.* This transitive use of *agree* has now become firmly established in accountancy, and it should not be criticised there. The accountants are entitled to use the idiom of their profession.
It is now also beginning to creep into the newspapers and into official announcements, where it is not recognised:
☐ The committee have *agreed* wage increases for nurses and hospital staffs.
If they have accepted increases that were already proposed, then they have *agreed to* them; if they have discussed them with representatives of the nurses and the hospital staffs, and have

finally reached agreement, then they have *agreed on* them. The passive *wage increases have been agreed* or *the terms have now been agreed* is more acceptable than the active.

agreement of verb and subject

The rule is that a verb must agree with its subject in number and person. The following points should be noticed:

1 Plural subject with plural verb When a subject consists of two singular words co-ordinated by *and*, it normally becomes a plural subject and must take a plural verb: *Your aunt and uncle have arrived.* But combinations like *bread and butter, fish and chips, whisky and soda* are singular. The agreement in the following sentence taken from *The Times* is obviously incorrect:

□ 10.30 *Word for Word*: Robert Robinson and Vicky Payne looks at the uses and abuses of the English Language.

2 Alternative subjects Alternative subjects to the same verb each apply to it separately; if each of the alternatives is singular, therefore, the verb is singular:

□ Either John or James *is* the culprit.

But if the alternatives are each plural, the verb is plural:

□ Neither the boys nor the girls *have* done well in the examination.

When there are alternative subjects which each demand a different verb form, the form used is that which is appropriate to the subject which comes immediately before it:

□ Either you or I *am* to go

□ Neither Sheila nor her parents *were* there.

3 Singular verbs with plural complements Care is necessary when a singular subject is separated from its verb by a plural enlargement (as *a bunch of grapes*) or when the verb is followed by a plural complement. The verb must still be singular, though there is a tendency for it to get attracted into the plural. The following example of misuse comes from the *Birmingham Post*:

□ The price of easier-flowing and safer traffic *are* the sights of the Old Bull Ring – the hawkers, the orators, the flower-bedecked stalls and fascinating crowds.

And in this headline from *The Times*, the verb has been made to agree with *riots* where it should have agreed with *inquiry*:

□ Inquiry Into Anti-Muslim Riots *Are* To Go Ahead.

(See also **singular or plural verb?**, **there** and **of 1**.)

aim

Either *aim at doing something* or *aim to do something.* The former construction is preferable: *This book aims at giving a general outline of the subject.*

airplane

An American word not accepted in British English.
Use *aeroplane.*

aisle

The centre passage in a church. *The bride walked slowly up the aisle.* Note the unpronounced *s* in the spelling. In a clever pun a bride, when asked what plans she had for her marriage, answered, 'Aisle-altar-hymn' (I'll alter him).

alias

In Latin *alias* means 'at another time'. In English it is used to indicate an assumed name by which a person is known for a certain part of his life or in certain circles: *William Arthur Jenkins alias Samuel Henderson.* It may also be used as a noun, with the plural *aliases*: *He had had several aliases.* It must, however, be confined to names: it cannot be used of a disguise or an assumed character, as in:

☐ He gained admission to the premises under the *alias* of a police officer.

Amend to *under the guise of* or *by posing as.*

alibi

Alibi is a Latin adverb meaning 'elsewhere'. In legal language an accused person proves an *alibi* when he is able to show that at the time when the crime with which he is charged was committed he was elsewhere. The word does not mean 'an excuse, justification, extenuating circumstances' or the various related ideas that popular misuse has given it in the past few years. The following are examples of this misuse:

☐ The Government is entering on a new phase. Up to now ministers have been carrying on where Labour left off, and have been able to plead various *alibis* as a result. (*The Observer*)

☐ It is unfortunately true . . . that directors couch their dividend forecasts in terms which provide them with a complete *alibi* if profits go sour, and they cannot fulfil their forecasts. I am getting a trifle fed up with these *alibis*, which must confuse unsophisticated shareholders. (*The Stock Exchange Gazette*)

☐ The *alibi* of an awful lot of people asked to judge the late Pope Paul VI is that only history will tell. (*Spectator*)
The legal sense is the only legitimate one, but that is certainly not the sense that the writers of the above sentences intended.

all/all of

1 Though *of* is used when a simple pronoun follows: *all of it, all of us, all of them,* it should be omitted if the pronoun is itself followed by a noun in apposition: *all you boys.*

2 Before a noun, or a noun qualified by an adjective, *all* is more usual, though *all of,* in contrast to *some of, few of,* etc, is allowable if the reference is to number:

☐ *All* his children are now grown up, or:

☐ *All of* his children are now grown up;

but it should not be used for amount, quantity, distance, length of time, etc: *all the milk, all the morning, all the way* – not *all of.*

all ready

See **already/all ready.**

all together

See **altogether/all together.**

all ways

See **always/all ways.**

allergic

In the literal sense a medical term, meaning 'highly sensitive, so that the slightest amount of a certain substance produces a violent reaction'. It does not mean 'having a strong dislike', and the recent use of it metaphorically in this sense is to be deprecated:

☐ I am *allergic* to people who are always thrusting their politics or religion upon others.

In the medical sense a person may be *allergic* to something of which he is very fond, eg strawberries.

alleviate

Alleviate means 'to make something (pain, grief, etc) easier to bear'. Note the double *l* in the spelling.

allow/allow of

Allow means 'to permit', *allow of* means 'to give scope for, leave room for':

☐ The regulations do not *allow of* any variation.

Allow of cannot take a personal subject; we cannot say *He would not allow of my going.* (See also **admit.**)

allow/enable

Allow means 'to permit', 'to let someone do something':

□ Non-residents are not *allowed* to park their cars behind the hotel.

□ Are the boys *allowed* to play by the river?

Enable means 'to give someone the power or means to do something':

□ The small legacy enabled them to take a much-needed holiday.

allude

Allude means 'to make reference to something indirectly'. The word is often incorrectly used as a synonym of 'mention', as in:

□ The Minister *alluded* to the low pay of Health Service employees.

A correct use of *allude* would be:

□ The Minister spoke of low-paid workers. Although he did not mention them directly, he was obviously *alluding* to National Health Service employees.

allusion/delusion/illusion

Allusion means 'a passing, indirect reference':

□ In the course of telling us his recent adventures, he made several *allusions* to his childhood.

Delusion means 'a false belief with no basis in fact':

□ He is under the *delusion* that little green men from Mars have landed on earth.

Delusions of this type are often a first stage of madness, and cannot be removed by reasoning or explanation.

Illusion means 'a false mental conception or image, the result of imagination or misinterpretation':

□ Because of his own emotional state and the poor lighting in the old house, he was under the *illusion* that he had seen a ghost.

The adjectives are *allusive*, *delusive* and *illusory*.

almighty

Although this word is a combination of *all* and *mighty*, it is spelt with only one *l*. For other examples see **spelling 3**.

almost/nearly

1 In many contexts *almost* and *nearly* are, for all practical purposes, interchangeable: *It is almost ten o'clock*; *it is nearly ten o'clock*. Which we use depends on our attitude of mind towards the fact concerned. *Almost* is what we might call a 'minus' word; it subtracts from the idea of the word it modifies. *Nearly*, on the other hand, represents an approach towards it, and therefore gives it more emphasis. *Almost* is a genuine adverb of degree; *nearly* is not. The tendency seems to be to use *nearly* rather than *almost* when some special significance is implied. If someone asks us the time we might reply that it is either *almost* or *nearly* ten o'clock; but we should probably use *nearly* to the exclusion of *almost* if we wished to express surprise at the fact, or if someone had asked us to tell him when it was ten. *It is almost eight kilometres to the next village* is a simple statement of distance. If we wish to suggest that it is too far to walk, or that it is farther than one would think, then we are more likely to say that it is *nearly* eight kilometres.

Similarly, *It cost me almost twenty pounds* is a mere statement of price, but *It cost me nearly twenty pounds* suggests that it was more than might have been supposed, or more than I wished to pay.

2 When we wish to say that we come near to doing something, but then refrain from doing it, or avoid it, *nearly* is used in preference to *almost*:

☐ I *nearly* ran over that dog
☐ We *nearly* called to see you last Saturday
☐ I *nearly* offered to give them a lift.

3 Verbs and adjectives denoting feeling or state of mind take *almost*, not *nearly*:

☐ I *almost* wish I had taken his advice
☐ You could *almost* imagine you were in Switzerland
☐ I *almost* dread going
☐ I am *almost* glad that the project has failed.

alone

For its position in a sentence, see **particularly 3**.

already/all ready

When *ready* has the meaning of 'prepared', two words are required:

☐ We are *all ready* to start
☐ They came *all ready* for a day in the country.

Note the difference between *The meal is already on the table* and *The meal is all ready on the table.*

alright

A very common misspelling. The only correct form is *all right*.

also

Also is an adverb, not a conjunction; it should therefore not be used: (a) at the beginning of a sentence or of a clause, and (b) after a comma, to co-ordinate two nouns, unless it is preceded by *and* or *but*. Examples of wrong usage:

□ He had spent a good deal of his life on the Continent. *Also* he had lived for a year or so in India. (Correct to *He had also lived* . . . .)

□ She sold her diamond ring, *also* a pearl necklace. (Correct to *and also a pearl necklace.*)

The following sentence, from a published report, is a particularly glaring example of careless style:

□ Preparation of the book was deferred so that an account of the opening proceedings could be included, *also* photographs of the new building. (Correct to . . . *so that an account of the opening proceedings and photographs of the new building could be included.*)

Some defence of the initial *also* is possible, however, in sentences like the following:

□ *Also* on the platform were the Mayor, the Town Clerk and the Borough Librarian.

By bringing forward the phrase that would otherwise stand at the end, we given greater prominence to the names of the persons in question by leading the reader up to them as a kind of climax.

altar/alter

Altar means 'a table where offerings are made to a god'. *Alter* means 'to change': *alter a dress to make it fit, alter arrangements.*

alternate/alternative

Alternative implies a choice between (strictly) two things (either one or the other); *alternate* means 'first one, then the other, in turn', as:

□ We play football and hockey on *alternate* Saturdays,

ie football one Saturday, hockey the next. Note also:

1 Though, as stated above, *alternative*, strictly speaking, implies only *two* things or courses, it is no longer limited to that number. Only the strictest grammarian will object to our speaking of *several alternatives.*

2 The term *alternative accommodation* (as applied to housing) is now so strongly rooted in the vocabulary of officialese that it is probably useless to object to it, though usually the accommodation offered is not an alternative, since the unfortunate householder is not free to choose whether he accepts it or remains where he is.

3 The construction *no alternative but* (*I had no alternative but to do it*), is used to mean that only one course was open. It is illogical, but usage has established it as an accepted idiom.

although

See **though/although**.

altogether/all together

The first spelling should be used only when the sense is 'completely'. When *all* has a separate meaning, denoting number or quantity, it must be written as a separate word. Examples:

□ He took several pieces of string and tied them *all together*

□ Now we will say the poem *all together* (ie in chorus)

□ I found the missing papers *all together* in a drawer of my desk, but

□ The letter that I thought was with them seen to have vanished *altogether*.

always/all ways

Always means 'at all times', *all ways* 'in every possible way': *We have tried all ways to get the information, but without success.*

amateur/amateurish

This word has a French ending. Note the *eur* in the spelling. An *amateur* is a person who dedicates much of his free time to sport, music, photography, etc just for pleasure and without receiving payment. A *professional* does these things for a living, to earn money. The noun *amateur* gives the attributive adjective *amateur*. *Amateur golf* is played for pleasure whereas *professional golf* is played for money. *Amateur golf* may also be of a very high standard. *Amateurish*, however, is a derogatory word implying a very poor standard:

□ I'm afraid the golf I play is very *amateurish* – I never have time to practise.

amenable

Followed by the preposition *to* plus a noun: *amenable to discipline*, *amenable to reason*, etc. An infinitive, whether active or passive: *amenable to learn*, *amenable to be taught*, is incorrect.

amend/emend

Amend means 'to alter (usually for the better)'; *emend* means 'to correct an error'. Nouns: *amendment*, *emendation*.

amiable/amicable

Amiable means 'good-natured', 'friendly' and is used of people: *an amiable fellow, an amiable smile, an amiable character*, etc. *Amicable* means 'in a peaceful or friendly way'. We try to settle arguments in an *amicable* way, we make *amicable* decisions and reach *amicable* agreements.

amok/amuck

Amuck is preferred. The word is only used in the phrase *to run amuck* meaning 'to run around wildly':

□ During the riot, bands of armed civilians *ran amuck* in the streets.

among/amongst

1 There is no difference of meaning, and no rule as to which should be used in particular circumstances, though some authorities suggest that *amongst* is more usual before a vowel. The deciding factors are really **euphony** and the rhythm of the sentence. *Among* is more common.

2 Both must be followed by a plural noun or pronoun, or by one which though singular in form, has a plural sense (such as *clergy, staff, family*). *Amongst a pile of rubbish* is incorrect.

3 At one time grammarians insisted that a thing is shared *between* two people, but *among* (or *amongst*) more than two; but this distinction is no longer observed. Modern usage permits *between* where the purist would insist on *among*, but not vice versa. (See also **between 4**.)

amoral/immoral

Immoral means 'contrary to morality, wrong, evil'. *Amoral* is not a synonym, although it is often used in that way, but means 'not related to morality, unconcerned with morals', as in:

□ This is an *amoral* subject, so it would be quite wrong to introduce questions of morality into the debate.

amuck

See **amok/amuck**.

an (indefinite article)

See **a/an**.

anæmia

In Britain, one suffers from *anæmia* (poor condition of the blood), and in America from *anemia*. The adjectives are *anæmic* and *anemic* respectively.

anarchy/anarchism

Anarchy is a state of political disorder. *Anarchism* is a political philosophy which would reduce laws to a minimum and allow the individual the maximum of liberty to follow his own reason and conscience.

ancillary

So spelt, not *ancilliary*.

and

1 Syntactic units joined by and must be of same kind *And* is a co-ordinating conjunction, and must therefore join two syntactic units *of the same kind*, whether the units are single words, phrases or clauses. The following sentences are therefore incorrect:

□ It was decided that all books must be returned promptly, *and* a fine of six pence per day to be imposed on defaulters

□ He had with him a friend from somewhere in the Midlands, *and* whom I had never seen before.

2 Subjects of clauses co-ordinated by and Care is necessary with the subjects of clauses co-ordinated by *and*. Normally each will have its own subject. The subject may be omitted from the second only if it is the same as that of the first, so that the one can serve for both. There is thus no objection to the sentence:

□ There are some people who rest during the day *and* work at night,

since *who*, the subject of the first subordinate clause, is understood in the second. The construction:

□ Children whose parents are badly off *and* are unable to provide them with sufficient clothing

is also quite idiomatic, since *whose parents* is the subject of both verbs. But the following, from *A Guide to Bath Abbey*, is clearly incorrect:

□ For visitors whose time is limited *and* are unable to learn the history and examine the building in detail on the spot, it is suggested that the following itinerary be followed.

Who is required before *are unable*. As the sentence stands we must understand *whose time*, from the previous clause, and this would make nonsense. *Whose* and *who* always need watching. Sometimes, as in the above sentence, *who* is required after *whose*, but sometimes it would be wrong to insert it. There is, for instance, a great temptation to write:

□ Children whose parents are badly off and *who* are unable to provide them with sufficient clothing;
but it would be incorrect, for the antecedent of *who* would be *children*, not *parents*. It would mean that the children were unable to provide the parents with sufficient clothing.

3 And beginning a sentence Contrary to a very widespread belief, there is no rule against beginning a sentence with *and*; in the Bible hundreds of sentences begin with it. It is also extremely common in advertisements and journalese. Often it is the most appropriate word to begin with, as it links what is to follow to what has gone before; but this does not mean that it can be used arbitrarily. Two principles at least must be observed:

a The second sentence must introduce a new idea; it must not be just an extension or continuation of the first. The following should clearly have been written as one sentence, not as two:
□ After we had finished tea my wife settled down to sew. *And* I read the newspaper.

b The second sentence must have its own subject. If one subject has to do service for two verbs, then both verbs must go in the same sentence. The following (from *The Observer*) is an example of a violation of this rule:
□ Johnny lives alone in two rented rooms. He's been in the district all his life. *And* is prepared to live it out there.
The last two sentences should have been written as one.

4 And preceded by comma Should a comma be used before *and*? If *and* joins two words or two short phrases the comma is best omitted, but if it joins two clauses, or two phrases of some length, then it should be used. It should never be omitted if its absence might lead to misunderstanding, or cause the reader to follow a false scent:
□ He shot the landlord, and the barman only escaped by ducking behind the counter.
(See also **comma**.)

anecdote/antidote

An *anecdote* is a short story told about a real person or event. People from the world of classical music, for instance, delight in *anecdotes* about Sir Thomas Beecham.
An *antidote* is a medicine used to counteract the effects of a poison or disease:

□ This injection contains the *antidote* to the poison.
The writer of the following sentence from the *Evening Standard* has confused the two words:
□ With the Chamber Orchestra, he has now recorded Rossini String Sonatas Nos 2–5 which are just the *anecdote* to a gloomy summer day.
Here, the word *antidote* was required.

anemone
This word is spelt with a medial *m*, not *n*.

annihilate
Note the spelling with a double *n* and unpronounced *h*.

another
1 For alternatives, where only two things are concerned the correct idiom is *one or the other*, where more than two *one or other*, though *one or another* is also found.
2 *Some way or another* is incorrect. The alternatives are *one way or another* and *some way or other*. Similarly the compounds with *some-* as their first element (*someone, somehow, somewhere*, etc) must be followed by *other*, not *another*: *We shall have to do it somehow or other* – not *another*.
3 One another/each other Strictly speaking, *one another* should be used of three or more, and *each other* of two only, but the distinction is no longer rigidly observed.

antecedent
An *antecedent* is a word that is grammatically related to a word that comes later in the sentence. It most often refers to the noun or pronoun that relates to a relative pronoun. For example, in:
□ The curtains, which we bought in Liverpool, are new,
curtains is the antecedent of *which*.

anticipate
This verb has been so long misused, as though it meant *expect*, that it is perhaps useless to protest, especially when the error appears in a publication of a university examining board:
□ We do not *anticipate* that many candidates will enter for the paper.
Its strict meaning is 'to forestall' or 'to foresee, and take action against': *The enemy had anticipated our move.*

antidote
See **anecdote/antidote**.

antipathy

Wrong use:

□ Nigel is the *antipathy* of everything that people would expect the Post Office to be like. (*Campaign*)

If the writer means that Nigel is not the sort of person we would expect to find working for the Post Office, then the word he should have used is *antithesis*, (meaning 'the direct opposite'), not *antipathy*. *Antipathy* means 'strong dislike'. We speak of antipathy *between* two people, *to* a place, an idea, a person, etc.

antithesis

See previous entry.

any

1 Than any *London is more densely populated than any city in the world.* This is an example of a very frequent mistake. *Any city in the world* includes London. Correct to *any other city in the world.*

2 Of any Incorrect:

□ Dickens was the most widely read *of any* of the nineteenth-century novelists.

The alternatives are *more widely read than any other* and *the most widely read of all.*

3 *Any* used adverbially in interrogative and negative sentences is American: *I didn't like it any*; *does the radio disturb you any*? It is not recognised in British English. Use *at all.*

anyone

Anyone is singular and should therefore be referred to by a singular pronoun or possessive adjective: *Has anyone a dictionary he can lend me?* – not *they. Anyone who does that is risking* his *life* – not *their*. But in contexts where *anyone* is used in a general, and not an individual or specific sense, so that it has the force of 'all, without exception', a plural is allowable, since the singular would sound incongruous:

□ Anyone can enter for the competition, can't *they*?

NB – The above observations also apply to *anybody.*

anyone or any one?

1 The compound *anyone* can be used only of persons. When the reference is to things, two separate words must be used:

□ Which screwdriver do you want? – Any one will do.

2 Even for persons, if *one* has a numerical sense two separate words are necessary:

□ It took two of them to do the work that *any one* of us could do.

aplomb

Aplomb is cool assurance (in behaviour or speech). Note the unpronounced *b* in the spelling. The letter *b* is also unpronounced in *comb, lamb, limb, plumb* (as in *plumb-line*) and *climb*.

apostrophe

There are three uses:

1 In omissions To indicate the omission of one or more letters from the spelling of a word, see **abbreviations 3**.

2 In plurals For the plural of words which, not being nouns or pronouns, do not normally have a plural form: *if's, and's* and *but's*; *he gets mixed up with his will's and shall's*. It is also used for the plural of letters of the alphabet; *Mind your p's and q's*; *how many l's are there in travelling?*

An apostrophe may also be used for the plurals of numbers when they are written as figures: *He makes his 8's like 3's*; *the 1970's*, but the modern tendency is to omit the apostrophe here: *8s like 3s*; *the 1970s.*

It is quite wrong to form the plural of nouns with 's, as is seen on some signs.

3 In possessives To indicate the possessive (or genitive case) of a noun. (See also **possessives.**) On the use of the apostrophe in phrases with an *-ing* form, such as *I object to my son being punished* or . . . *to my son's being punished*, see **-ing 4**. The following points should be noted:

a The apostrophe is placed before the *s* for the genitive singular: *my father's car* and after the *s* for the genitive plural: *a girls' school, a dogs' home.*

Some writers become too enthusiastic when using apostrophes. This journalist from the *Daily Express* has punctuated the possessive correctly (*a man's man*) but has also punctuated plural words in the same sentence as if they were singular possessives – which they are not:

□ Jones at 37 remains, in the *word's* of the *valley's*, very much a *man's man.*

b Those nouns which do not make their plural in *s* (eg *child/children, woman/women, man/men*) add an '*s* to the singular and the plural forms:

	Singular	*Plural*
□	a child's toys	children's toys
□	a woman's hat	a women's college
□	a man's overcoat	men's clothing

c For personal names ending in *s*, add an *'s* if an additional syllable is pronounced for the possessive: *Jones's*, *James's*, *Charles's*, but if no extra syllable is pronounced, then place the apostrophe after the existing *s*: *Mr Humphreys' house.* (It would be very difficult to say *Humphreys-iz.*) For euphonic reasons names which sound like the plural of a common noun (*Masters*, *Stones*, *Fields*, *Knights*, *Vickers*) do not add an extra syllable, so the possessive should be written *Masters'*, etc.
d When two names are to be taken together as a 'joint' possessive, the possessive ending is added only to the last: *Gilbert and Sullivan's operas* (joint authorship), *William and Mary's reign* (they were joint sovereigns), but *Trollope's and Thackeray's novels* (the novels of Trollope and Thackeray considered separately).
e Note the 'free' or independent genitive in *St Paul's*; *she was staying at her aunt's*; *I am going to the butcher's/baker's/barber's.* It is helpful to think of these as short for . . .*'s cathedral*, *church*, *house*, *shop*, etc.
Many houses with names that are genitive by origin omit the apostrophe (eg *Mascalls*); so do some place names (*St Ives*, *St Helens*) but others do not. If in doubt, consult an atlas or a gazetteer.
f The names of companies, commercial firms and business houses which actually are singular were often given an *s*:
□ This book is published by *Macmillans/Harraps/Heinemanns.*
This is a specialised use of the ordinary plural and requires no apostrophe. Modern practice is to omit the *s*:
□ This book is published by *Macmillan*, *Longman*, etc.
g Use the *'s* or *s'* in phrases such as *an hour's time*, *a day's journey*, *two weeks' wages*, *three months' notice*, *three weeks' holiday*, etc.
h Note the 'post-genitive' in such expressions as *a friend of my father's*, *a poem of Shelley's*, *a relative of her husband's.* This usually occurs only in the singular, but a plural is possible, and care must be taken to recognise it and to place the apostrophe correctly: *that*

car of Smith's (belonging to Mr Smith), *that car of the Smiths'* (belonging to Mr and Mrs Smith or to the Smith family).
i Finally, note that there is no apostrophe in the possessive adjective *its*. *It's* is short for *it is* or *it has*. (See **its/it's**.) Similarly there is no apostrophe in the possessive pronouns *hers, ours, yours, theirs*. The indefinite pronoun *one* has the genitive *one's* (*to do one's duty*), but there is no apostrophe in *oneself*.

appendix
Plural: *appendices* (to books, documents, etc), *appendixes* (anatomical)

apposition
In apposition to (not *with*).
As a grammatical term, it means an explanatory word or phrase immediately following the headword. There is usually a comma before and after:
□ President Carter, a practising Christian, was very concerned with moral issues.
In this example, *President Carter* is in apposition to *a practising Christian*. Note that there is no comma where individual words are in apposition: *You boys ought to be more polite*.

appropriate
Appropriate to (not *for*) the occasion, etc.

approve/approve of
Approve means 'to give consent to': *approve a scheme*. *Approve of* means 'to think well of, regard with favour':
□ He did not *approve of* his daughter's marriage.
Approve is often used in the passive:
□ The plans have been *approved* by the local authority;
approve of is usually found in the active voice, though a passive is not impossible.

approximately
Very approximately, in the sense of 'roughly', when intended to suggest a greater margin of possible error than *approximately* alone would suggest, is colloquial, but illogical, English used for emphatic effect:
□ The area is *very approximately* 100 square kilometres.
Since *approximately* means 'approaching near to', *very approximately* should mean 'approaching very near to', and suggest a greater degree of accuracy.

apropos

The word comes from the French *à propos* which means 'to the purpose'. *Apropos of* is used when the speaker wishes to introduce a subsidiary remark or question only loosely connected with the topic under discussion:

□ A: 'Tourists want plenty of sunshine and low prices.'

B: 'Well, it's easy to see why so many British tourists go to Malta and Spain.'

A: 'Apropos of Malta (*while we're on the subject of Malta*), I believe the teaching of Arabic is now compulsory in schools there.'

Arab(adj)/Arabian/Arabic

Arab refers to race (*Arab tribesmen, Arab warriors*), *Arabian* more specifically to *Arabia* (*the Arabian desert, Arabian perfumes*), *Arabic* to the language, either as spoken or as written (*an Arabic dialect, Arabic characters, Arabic numerals*). Note, however, *gum arabic*. *Arabian* is much less frequent than the other two words.

archaisms

Archaisms are words and expressions, like *eftsoons, verily, peradventure, anent, vouchsafe,* which were at one time current English but are no longer part of the living language. They may still have their place in verse, or in prose written for devotional purposes (eg prayers and collects), where they have an evocative value, and a few of them may not be altogether out of place in other kinds of prose of a serious or elevated character, but generally speaking they should be avoided.

More strongly to be condemned than genuine archaisms, however, are what we may call 'spurious archaisms', where quaint spellings are supposed to represent 'old English'. It is nothing but affectation that prompts a cafe to call itself *Ye Olde English Tea-Shoppe*. And why must churches and chapels hold a *Christmas Fayre* (or, even worse, an *Xmas Fayre*), instead of a *Christmas Fair*?

aren't I?

The recognised negative interrogative form of *I am*: *I'm going to be late, aren't I?*

arise

See **rise/arise**.

around

□ He spent the whole afternoon sitting *around* doing nothing

□ The papers were left lying *around*
□ I shall be home *around* five o'clock.
This use of *around* is an Americanism. *About* is more common in British English. Both are colloquial.

arouse
See **rouse/arouse**.

artful/artless
Artful means 'cunning; deceitful'. An *artful* businessman is one who, by clever tricks and few scruples, gets his own way.
Artless means the opposite: 'natural; innocent'. Children are often described as *artless*.

article
See **a/an** and **the**.

artist/artiste
Artist means 'a painter of distinction'. It can also be applied to other distinguished practitioners of the arts:
□ Yehudi Menuhin, the violinist, is a great *artist*.
Artiste means 'a professional entertainer'. It is principally applied today to singers, music hall performers, etc, but is going out of favour.

artless
See **artful/artless**.

as
1 Case of pronouns *You seem to dislike him as much as . . . I* or *me*? It depends on the meaning. If it means 'as I do', then *I* is the correct word; if it means 'as you dislike me', then *me* must be used. The same principle applies to *he/him, she/her, we/us, they/them.* The test is to complete the sentence.
(See **pronouns**.)
2 The misrelated phrase Wrong:
□ *As* a heating engineer, your readers may be interested in my experience of central heating of large premises. (letter to *The Financial Times*)
But were the readers of *The Financial Times* a heating engineer? Recast to read: *As a heating engineer I think your readers*, etc, or better still, *As a heating engineer I have had considerable experience of central heating*, etc. Wrong:
□ *As* Chairman of the TUC, may I ask you . . . ? (from a BBC interview)

But the person who put the question was not Chairman of the TUC, as the sentence suggests he was. The question was put *to* the Chairman of the TUC.

Descriptive phrases of this kind, introduced by *as*, must be followed by the noun or pronoun to which they are intended to refer. But when *as* carries a meaning similar to *for*, the same rule does not apply (see **because, for or as?**); the phrase may legitimately be brought forward for the sake of emphasis: *As an example of a prose satire we may take* Gulliver's Travels.

(See **-ing**.)

3 As . . . as/so . . . as *As* is always correct, whether used with positive or negative statements; *so* is more usual with negative ones:

☐ That story is *as* old *as* the hills

☐ He is not *so/as* old *as* he looks.

4 Equally as In *equally as good, equally as cheap*, etc, *as* is redundant. The alternatives as *just as good* and *equally good.* One thing is *as good as* another or the two are *equally good.*

5 Comparative clauses Care is needed with comparative clauses introduced by *as* or *than* where the normal subject-verb order is inverted. The verb must agree with the subject which follows it, irrespective of whether a singular or a plural noun precedes: *as was the case, as was our intention, as were our intentions, than were the effects.* (See also **inversion of verb and subject** and **singular or plural verb?**)

6 Elliptical comparative clauses When the comparative clause is elliptical, the number of the verb can be determined only by completing the sentence:

☐ There were not so many tickets available *as were* asked for (an ellipsis of *as tickets were asked for*).

☐ There were not so many tickets available *as was* expected (an ellipsis of *as it was expected there would be*).

☐ There were not so many casualties *as was* feared (not *as were feared*, since it is short for *as it was feared there would be*).

7 Conjunctive pronoun When *as* is a kind of conjunctive pronoun (meaning 'and this', or 'but this') functioning as the subject of a verb and referring back to the whole of a previous statement, the verb must be singular: *Objections were raised by a number of Opposition members, as was to be expected.*

8 Intrusive as Similar to the redundant *as* noticed under **4** above, is the intrusive *as* exemplified in such sentences as the following:

☐ *As* much as I admire him, I cannot excuse his faults

☐ *As* poor as they are, they never refuse to give to charity.

The first *as* should be omitted: *Much as I admire him*; *poor as they are.* The introductory clause is not comparative, but concessive, meaning 'Though I admire him much', 'Though they are poor'.

9 On *as* and *like*, see **like**.

10 On *as* used to introduce a reason, see **because, for or as?**

as follows

Invariable in form, whether accompanied by a singular or a plural: *The chief points are* as follows (not *as follow*).

as if/as though

1 There is no difference in meaning. One form is used as frequently as the other.

2 Where they express an imaginary case, *as if* and *as though* must be followed by a subjunctive, not by an indicative verb. There is a distinction between *He walks as if he were drunk* (implying 'but he is not'), and *He walks as if he is drunk*, (meaning 'He is drunk judging from the way he walks').

as to

1 There are legitimate uses of *as to.* It is, for instance, used correctly when it introduces an infinitive construction denoting result:

☐ I am not such a fool *as to* believe that.

Again it is used correctly at the beginning of a sentence to draw attention to the subject with which the sentence is to be concerned:

☐ *As to* the allegation that he deliberately concealed the information, it has been investigated, but no evidence can be found to support it.

2 It should not be used merely to replace a simple preposition, as in the sentences:

☐ We have no information *as to* his present employment

☐ They could tell us nothing *as to* the probable cost of such a scheme.

Substitute *about*, *concerning* or some other suitable preposition, according to the context.

3 In the following sentences *as to* is wholly superfluous, and should therefore be omitted:

□ You had better inquire *as to* whether they will need lunch
□ There is some doubt *as to* whether he will come
□ I have often wondered *as to* where it [*some money*] had vanished. (W. H. Davies, *The Autobiography of a Super-Tramp*)
4 *As to* (when used correctly) 'picks up' something which has already been mentioned or which is presumed to be already in the mind of the speaker and of the person to whom the remark is addressed. When we wish to introduce something new, or an issue that has not already been raised, *as for* is used:
□ Much pasture land is under water; and *as for* the grain, most of that has been ruined
□ The substance of his lecture was quite good, but *as for* the delivery . . . !

as well

For its position in a sentence, see **particularly 3**.

as well as

1 Introducing a parenthesis Both the following sentences are incorrect:
□ The mother, *as well as* her three children, were taken to hospital
□ The mother, *as well as* her children, all perished.
As well as does not co-ordinate the two nouns; it introduces a parenthesis. In the first sentence, therefore, a singular verb is required (the subject is *the mother*), and in the second *all* should be omitted.
2 Followed by verb Care is necessary when *as well as* is followed by a verb. If an adverb clause of comparison is involved, a finite verb must, of course, be used:
□ You know that *as well as* I do
□ She does not play tennis *as well as* she used to.
But when *as well as* has the force of a compound conjunction, meaning 'in addition to', and joins two verbal forms, it *cannot* be followed by a finite verb. The following is therefore incorrect:
□ He spent all his money, *as well as* wasted his time.
If the first verb is a simple tense form, as it is here, then *as well as* must be followed by a gerund (*as well as wasting his time*). This can be seen if we imagine it transferred to the beginning of the sentence:
□ *As well as* wasting his time, he spent all his money.

3 Case of the following pronoun There is often a temptation to use a pronoun in the objective case after *as well as* when one in the subject case is required. The case depends on whether the pronoun is a subject or an object:

□ They have invited you, *as well as* me (objective case because it is the object of *have invited*).

□ You agreed to his suggestion, *as well as* I (subject case, because it is the subject of *agreed*).

You helped him, as well as I means 'You and I both helped him'. *You helped him as well as me* means 'You helped both him and me'. (See also **pronouns**.)

aside/a side

Aside is an adverb (*turn aside, put aside, set aside, stand aside*, etc). When the sense is 'on each side' two words (*a side*) are necessary:

□ The passengers sat four *a side*

□ They played seven *a side*.

When the expression is used as a compound adjective, two hyphens are needed: *a seven-a-side competition.*

asphalt

Note the spelling.

assemble

The pupils were all assembled together in the main hall. Assemble means 'to come together', so the word *together* is redundant. The same applies to *gather*. It means 'to come together' or 'to bring together', so we should not say *gather together.*

assent/consent

Both verbs take the preposition *to*, and both mean 'to agree to'. The difference between them is the spirit in which agreement is given. One usually *assents* readily to something, but if one *consents* it may be after deep consideration or even with a certain reluctance.

assist

Here is an example of incorrect use:

□ Let our sales staff *assist* you to make your decision.

We *assist* someone *in doing* something. Rewrite as *Let our sales staff assist you in making your decision.*

assure/insure

In commercial usage there is a technical difference; one *assures* against something that is bound to happen (eg death), and *insures* against something that may or may not happen (eg fire, burglary, etc). In ordinary English, however, we need not trouble ourselves about this distinction. We may speak of insuring our life, our house, our car or our luggage, irrespective of what the insurance (or assurance) companies call it. Of course, in writing to a company we must use the word by which it describes itself. Most call themselves *assurance* companies, but some have the word *insurance* as part of their name.

The verb meaning 'to make sure or certain' is *ensure*, not *insure*: *to register a letter, to ensure that it reaches its destination.* (See also **ensure/insure.**)

asthma

Note the unpronounced *th* in the spelling. The adjective is *asthmatic.*

astrology/astronomy

Astrology means 'the art of predicting future events by studying the stars'. *Astronomy* means 'the science of the stars and planets'. Many people do not take *astrology* seriously and say that it is based on guesswork. *Astronomy*, however, is a recognised science.

at

See **in/at.**

at home

See **home/at home.**

aural/oral

Aural means 'to do with the hearing'. *Oral* means 'by means of speech, by mouth': *an oral examination, oral medicine, oral hygiene.*

authoress

A needless feminine form. A woman who writes a book should be referred to as *an author*, not *an authoress*. Similarly *poet*, *poetess.* (See **gender in nouns 1.**)

authoritarian/authoritative

Authoritarian is generally used in a negative sense of a person or a system which demands instant, unquestioning obedience. Orders come from the top, and they must be followed. *Authoritative* is a positive word, meaning 'given with authority, commanding respect, to be trusted'. Examples of their usage:

□ He was very *authoritarian* in his dealings with his daughter. Not surprisingly, she rebelled in her teens and left home

□ It was a very *authoritative* report, convincing nearly everybody who read it.

autumn (adjective)/autumnal

Wrong use:

□ The *autumnal* social will be held on 3 October.

Change to *the autumn social.* When the sense is merely that of 'occurring or falling in the autumn' the adjective is *autumn*: *an autumn day, the autumn term* (in a school). *Autumnal* means 'having the qualities or characteristics that one associates with autumn'. We may say that the countryside looks quite *autumnal* even though it is not yet autumn, while we may have *autumnal* weather in late summer. *Autumnal* is to *autumn* what *wintry* is to *winter.*

Note that the American English for *autumn* is *fall.*

avail

1 Notice the idioms:

□ All his efforts were *of no avail* (adjectival).

□ He made repeated attempts, but *to no avail* (adverbial).

2 As a verb, *avail* is used either intransitively:

□ All his efforts did not *avail,*

transitively, with a personal object:

□ All his efforts *availed him* nothing,

or with a reflexive object followed by *of*:

□ You should *avail yourself of* this opportunity

□ I shall *avail myself of* your offer.

It cannot, however, be used in the passive voice as here:

□ The opportunity was not *availed of*

□ I am sorry that your kind offer cannot *be availed of.*

These are incorrect.

avenge/revenge

Avenge means 'to repay a wrong done to another'. *Revenge* means 'to repay a wrong done to oneself':

□ He *avenged* the death of his father

□ I *revenged* myself for his insulting behaviour towards me.

Avenge gives the noun *vengeance* and *revenge* the noun *revenge.*

averse

Followed by the preposition *to.* The only part of the verb that can follow *averse* is the gerund: *I am not averse to* gambling, not *I am not averse to gamble.* (See also **adverse/averse.**)

await

See **wait/await.**

awful/awfully

Strictly, *awful* is a word that should be used rarely, since the occasions or situations when it is really applicable are rare. *An awful scene* is a scene that fills one with awe. When the hymn-writer spoke of God's *awful purity* he was using the term correctly, to signify purity before which a mere mortal stands in awe; but popular usage has emptied the word of its real meaning, so that it has come to take its place with *nice*, *terrible* and *frightful* as an example of debased currency. It should not be used merely as an intensifier (*an awful headache, an awful cold*) or in a derogatory sense (*an awful bore, awful weather, an awful journey*) in serious writing. A similar warning is necessary about the adverbs *awfully, terribly* and *frightfully*. To describe a lecture as *awfully boring*, the weather as *terribly cold* or a person as *frightfully clever* is to degrade words to the point where they really express nothing at all. The late Aneurin Bevan once told a rally of Labour Party supporters that the Socialist experiment in the nationalisation of basic industries was *of frightful importance to the whole world*. If he really meant what he said, it was an example of unusual candour on the part of a politician.

Interestingly, *awfully* and *frightfully* (though not their corresponding adjectives) now have a dated and rather affected air. The vogue for using them is past. *Terribly*, however, remains in common colloquial use.

awhile/a while

See **while/whilst 4**.

BC

See **dates 5**.

back of

Back of, in the sense of 'behind' (*Back of the house was a small garden*) is an Americanism, and not a very elegant one at that. It is not accepted as British English. Even in America, according to Margaret Nicholson (*A Dictionary of American English Usage*), it is deplored by scholars and avoided by careful speakers. Say *at the back of* or *behind*, whichever is the more suitable to the context.

bacteria

A plural noun. Do not speak of *a bacteria*, but *a bacterium.* (See also **phenomenon** and **data**.)

baleful/baneful

Baleful means 'evil':

□ He gave her a *baleful* look, full of hatred and animosity.

Baneful means 'harmful; destructive':

□ Rasputin exercised a *baneful* influence over the Czar's wife.

balmy/barmy

Balmy means 'fragrant; sweet-smelling', as: *the balmy air, the balmy breezes.* The slang word meaning 'crazy' is spelt *barmy.*

baneful

See **baleful/baneful.**

banister

The word is spelt with only one *n.*

bar

Everything bar the clock was silent is a colloquial use. Apart from a few traditional expressions like *It's all over bar the shouting*, use *except* or *but.*

barbarity/barbarism

Barbarity is an act of savageness and cruelty. We might speak, for instance, of the *barbarity* of terrorism or of nuclear warfare.

Barbarism means the living of an uncivilised life:

□ The Amazonians live in *barbarism.*

More commonly, it means a misuse of language:

□ *Ain't* is a *barbarism.*

A *barbarian* lives an uncivilised life.

There is little difference between the adjectives *barbaric* and *barbarous.*

bare/bear

As an adjective *bare* means 'naked; uncovered'; as a verb it means 'to expose'. *Bear* (noun) is a large animal; *bear* (verb) means 'to carry' or 'to endure'.

barmy

See **balmy/barmy**.

bath/bathe

Bath, transitive, means 'to wash in a bath': *bath the baby. Bathe*, transitive, means 'to wash an injury': *bathe a wound* or, intransitive, 'to swim in the sea'. The present participle of both verbs is *bathing* and the past tense of both verbs is *bathed.*

bear

See **bare/bear**.

because

Incorrect use:

□ The reason he is absent from work is *because* he is ill.

The alternatives are *He is absent from work because he is ill,* and *The reason he is absent from work is that he is ill. The reason is because* is a mixture of the two. Other incorrect uses:

□ *Because* another person cheats is no reason why you should

□ *Because* you don't like a person is no excuse for being rude to him.

In these an adverb clause is made the subject of the verb *is.* Amend to *The fact that* . . . .

because, for or as?

The evenings were getting chilly, because it was late September. Because is quite correct in this sentence, although *as* and *for* could also be used. It is really a question of emphasis and formality. With *because* the emphasis is on the reason, which is presented as the important fact, it being assumed that we already know the fact given in the main clause. With *for* it is the first fact that is important and which we are really concerned to state; the second is added by way of explanation, almost as an afterthought. *As* is informal, *for* is formal and *because* can be used in any context.

become

See **come 1**.

beg

I beg to inform you . . . ; *I beg to state* . . . . A meaningless cliché, apologetic in tone, adopted by some letter-writers under the impression that it is a mark of courtesy. Avoid it. It is particularly out of place when attached to verbs like *acknowledge, thank,* etc – as though one needed to apologise for thanking a person, or for acknowledging a letter or a cheque.

beg the question

Not 'evade the question', or 'skilfully avoid answering the question', but 'base an argument upon the assumption of the truth of the very thing that has to be proved'.

For example:
□ We must believe that God exists, since it says so in the Bible, and the Bible is God's infallible word.
Here our 'proof' of the existence of God is based upon an assumption of his existence; hence it amounts to no proof at all.

begin/commence/start

1 Wherever possible, use *begin* or *start. Commence* is the formal word used for the announcement of meetings, concerts, etc.
2 *Begin* and *start* may be followed by either the gerund or the infinitive: *begin/start doing something* or *begin/start to do something.* The infinitive is more usual when we are concerned only with the inception of an activity, without any reference to its possible continuance:
□ It *began* to rain
□ He *begins* to look old.
The gerund is more usual when the inception is thought of as initiating a process that continued or is to continue:
□ Don't *begin* writing until I tell you
□ They have *begun* building the house.
Commence takes only the gerund.
3 *Start* should be used in certain contexts:
a Where the sense is 'to make begin': *start a car*; *the official started the race.*
b Where the sense is 'starting out': *John started the vigil, then I took over later* (took the first turn); *we started at six o'clock* (began our journey).

behalf

The British idiom is *on behalf of*, not *on the behalf of* or *in behalf of.* American English uses *in behalf of.*
On behalf of means 'acting for, as the representative of':
□ I am writing to you *on behalf of* my mother,
and in the passive:
□ A telegram of congratulation was sent to him *on behalf of* the Queen.
The following sentences exemplify errors which do sometimes occur:
□ I am writing to you *on behalf of* your family to express my sympathy in your bereavement. (If the writer was acting on behalf of anyone's family it was his own, not that of the bereaved person.)

☐ At the end of the lecture the Chairman moved a vote of thanks *on behalf of* the speaker. (He moved a vote of thanks *to* the speaker, *on behalf of* the audience.)

☐ Much of the delay is due to inefficiency and bad organisation *on behalf of* the railways. (Here *on behalf of* is wrongly used for *on the part of*.)

being

Often used incorrectly, as here: *Being as we were strangers, we had to ask our way*. The idiomatic alternatives are (a) *Being strangers*, (b) *As we were strangers*.

below

See **above/over**.

benefit

The past participle and present participle are spelt *benefited* and *benefiting* with only one *t*. For the general rule, see **spelling 6**. Note the middle *e*, not *i*. Similarly *benefactor*, *beneficial*.

bereaved/bereft

Bereaved by death; *bereft* (meaning 'deprived of something not material') of speech, one's senses, love, hope, etc. *Bereft* does not mean 'without', and is therefore used incorrectly in this sentence from a newspaper's sports page:

☐ Villa . . . adopted a defensive game, which involved a lot of back-pedalling, but they were not completely *bereft* of aggressive intent. (*The Times*)

beside/besides

Use *besides* only when the meaning is 'in addition' or 'moreover':

☐ She had five cats and a small brown puppy *besides*

☐ It wasn't a good hotel – *besides* it was very expensive.

For all other senses *beside* is the word:

☐ He sat *beside* the driver

☐ She was *beside* herself with joy.

better

1 I have not been well, but I am *better* now

☐ He got *better* very quickly.

This use of *better* in the sense of 'well' may be accepted as sanctioned by usage (strictly speaking, of course, a person may be better, but still far from well).

2 The negative of *you had better* is *you had better not*. *You better hadn't* is dialectal.

between

1 As preposition followed by objective *Between* is a preposition, and any pronoun that follows it must therefore be in the objective case: *between you and me*, not *you and I*. (See **pronouns**.)

2 Between each Here are two examples of incorrect use:

☐ A space of one metre must be left *between each* of the desks

☐ There will be an interval of ten minutes *between each* act.

Each is singular, and we cannot have 'between' one. Amend to *between one desk and the next*, and *between the acts*.

3 We have to choose between one thing *and* another, not *or* another.

4 Between or among? The rule, at one time insisted upon, that *between* is used of only two things or persons, and *among* of more than two, is no longer strictly observed:

☐ We shall do the work more quickly if we share it *between us* may refer to more than two people, and so may the expression *between ourselves*, meaning 'in confidence'.

☐ There does not seem much difference *between the three* of them is quite acceptable English. Even if *among* is used when the sense is distributive, *between* is always required when group activity or co-operation is expressed:

☐ The three children saved over a hundred pounds *between* them

☐ *Between* them the passengers managed to push the bus to the side of the road.

(See **among/amongst 4**.)

beverage

There is rarely any justification for this word, which is usually a piece of official jargon:

☐ Hot *beverages* are provided with the midday meal for those who require them.

Use *drink*, unless the word would be ambiguous or misleading (which is seldom).

bevy

Do not use this word in too wide a sense to mean 'flock' or 'crowd' as in *a bevy of taxis, a bevy of demonstrators*. It should only be applied to a flock of birds (especially quails) or a gathering of women: *a bevy of ladies, a bevy of beauties*, where it is now something of a cliché.

(See **collective nouns 5**.)

beware (of)

1 Despite Shakespeare's *Beware the Ides of March* and Lewis Carroll's *Beware the Jabberwock, my son*, the modern tendency is to use *of* before a noun or a gerund:

☐ *Beware of* the dog
☐ *Beware of* flatterers
☐ *Beware of* falling into bad ways.

Before a clause *of* is never used:

☐ *Beware* that he does not deceive you.

As an alternative to *that . . . not*, the much more formal *lest* may be used:

☐ *Beware lest* you take a false step.

2 Since it is made up of the verb *be* and an old adjective *ware* (meaning 'careful, cautious'), *beware* can be used only where the simple *be* would be possible, ie as an imperative, as an infinitive and after *shall, will, should, would, must, may, can, ought*. There are no participles, no past tense and no perfect or continuous forms. We cannot say *They bewared of the dog*. Nor is a passive voice possible; we may say *You should beware of flatterers*, but not *Flatterers should be bewared of*.

bi-annual/biennial

Bi-annual means 'twice a year'. *Biennial* means 'once every two years'.

biased

Spelt with a single *s*, not a double. For general rule, see **spelling 6**.

Bible

No inverted commas should be used, and in print the word should not be italicised. The first letter should always be a capital. The same applies to individual books of the Bible. (See also **titles 5**.) The adjective *biblical* always has a small letter: *a biblical reference, a biblical scholar*.

biennial

See **bi-annual/biennial**.

big-headed

It should only be used in informal speech; in more formal contexts use *swollen-headed* or *conceited*. A *big-head* ('a conceited person'), like a *big-mouth* ('a talkative, boastful person'), is slang.

bill/act

A proposed law under discussion in Parliament for approval is called a *bill.* It is an *act* as soon as it is approved and becomes the law.

billion

Until recently in British usage, *billion* meant the number 'one million million'; but the American sense of 'a thousand million' is becoming increasingly current. It is best to state clearly which is meant.

blame

He blamed it on to me. Acceptable colloquially, but in writing (except when reproducing dialogue) and in more formal speech say, *He blamed me for it* or *He put the blame on me.*

blond(e)

Though it is not impossible to describe a man, his complexion or his hair, as *blond* (adj), a *blonde* (noun) always means a woman. The adjective *fair* may be safely used for a man or woman.

blueprint

A very much overworked piece of official jargon or journalese, which is best avoided: (. . . *a blueprint for success*). Use instead *plan, scheme, project, diagram, design, sketch* or whatever the appropriate word is for the context.

There is, of course, a correct literal use for *blueprint* in drawing offices and in engineering and constructional work. (See **-ese** and **clichés**.)

blurb

Every modern book has a *blurb* on its dust jacket (if it is a hardback book) or its cover (if it is a paperback edition). A *blurb* is the information a publisher prints on the book's jacket to describe its contents and persuade people to read it. The word originated in the publishing world and is now fairly widely accepted.

bona fide/bona fides

Bona fides (from the Latin, meaning 'good faith') is singular: *His bona fides* is *in doubt* (not *are*).

Bona fide means 'in good faith'; that is to say, it is, strictly speaking, adverbial in sense, though in English it is more often used adjectivally: *bona fide enquiries, a bona fide applicant*. It should never be used as a noun; do not say *I should question their bona fide*. Here *bona fides* is required.

born/borne

The normal past participle of the verb *to bear* is *borne.* Thus a burden, an insult, a good character, responsibility, the brunt, etc is *borne.* In other words, if the idea to be expressed has no connection with birth, use the spelling *borne.*

A child is *born* (comes into existence as a separate being), and is *born to* its mother; but *A woman has borne a child.* Note also *born of* to denote origin (*born of lowly parents, born of a sick mother*) and the same word used metaphorically:

☐ Some people believe that crime is *born of* poverty.

borrow/lend

1 *Borrow* means to take something for one's own use for a limited period of time on the understanding that it will be returned:

☐ He lost all his money and had to *borrow* some for his train fare home.

Lend means to give someone something on the understanding that it is to be returned:

☐ I've *lent* my lawnmower to Mr Darrel – his has broken down.

The constructions are: *lend something* to *someone* or *lend someone something* and *borrow something* from *someone* (not *off* someone).

2 Misuse Sometimes *lend* is used where *borrow* is required. It is quite common to hear:

☐ Can I *lend* your pen for a moment, please?

Correct alternatives are *Will you lend me your pen for a moment, please*? and *Can I borrow your pen for a moment, please*?

3 Loan The noun from *lend* is *loan.* American English uses *loan* as a verb. Although this is sometimes heard in British English, it is not recognised as standard. (See also **loan**.)

both

Should one say *both his sons* or *both of his sons, both the men* or *both of the men, open both doors* or *open both of the doors*? Neither is incorrect, though the omission of *of* is more usual. Keep *of* with pronouns: *both of them, both of us*, etc. Incorrect use:

☐ Such a remark is *both* offensive, untrue and likely to cause trouble.

Both should not be used if more than two terms are involved. For *both . . . and*, see **correlatives**. On the repetition of the article, as in *both the boys and the girls*, see **the 2**.

bottleneck

A useful metaphor, but do not speak of *reducing* the bottleneck when you mean reducing the obstruction. A reduced bottleneck causes more obstruction, not less. Remember, too, that *severe* and *acute* are not suitable adjectives to apply to a bottleneck. Nor does one overcome, solve or iron out a bottleneck. One can, however, get rid of it. (See also **mixed metaphor**.)

brackets

Two types are in use, the round and the square, though the former are far more frequent.

1 **Round brackets** Apart from their use with numbers or letters of the alphabet in enumerating a series of subjects, sections or paragraphs, as (i), (ii), (a), (b), (c), etc, round brackets are employed to enclose a parenthesis. This, however, does not mean that they are appropriate for every kind of parenthesis; sometimes dashes or commas are to be preferred. (For details, see **parenthesis**.)

Care is necessary in punctuating a sentence which includes a parenthesis in brackets. The words within the brackets belong, grammatically, to the part of the sentence which precedes them; thus any stop which would have been placed, had the parenthesis not been there, after the word which immediately precedes the first bracket, is transferred to a position immediately following the second. At the same time the words within the brackets are punctuated according to their own meaning:

□ The new production of *Love's Comedy* (Is it really a comedy?), in which Mr X Y takes the part of the hero, opened last night.

The parenthesis is a question; hence the question mark is placed within the brackets. If there had been no parenthesis the name of the play would have been followed by a comma. This is now transferred so that it follows the second bracket. Similarly, when a parenthesis in brackets occurs at the end of a sentence the full stop will go *outside* the final bracket.

2 **Square brackets** These are used to enclose wholly extraneous matter, chiefly an insertion of the writer's own within a quotation from another writer:

□ He [Heathcliff] stubbornly declined answering for a while.

The name *Heathcliff* has been inserted in square brackets because it has been supplied by the present writer to explain *He*. To put it in round brackets would have implied that it was Emily Brontë's

parenthesis, and therefore part of the quotation.
3 In the language of printing, round brackets are called *parentheses*, and the word *brackets* denotes square brackets.

brake/break
There are three pedals – the middle one is the brake *which stops the car. Be careful with my glasses – if you* break *them I won't be able to see a thing.*

brimful
So spelt. The sense is 'full to the brim'. The word can be used metaphorically: *She was brimful of good intentions.*

bring
See **fetch/bring.**

Britisher
American, not British usage. Even in the USA it is avoided by careful writers and speakers. Use *Briton*. The abbreviated Americanism, *a Brit*, should never be used in writing.

broadcast
Use *broadcast* for both the past tense and past participle: *They broadcast his speech*; *his speech was broadcast.*

brothers
Both *the brothers Wright*, *the brothers Wesley* and *the Wright brothers*, *the Wesley brothers* are correct, though there is an increasing tendency to use the latter order. But we always speak of *the brothers Grimm* (perhaps to avoid possible misunderstanding). *Sisters* is always placed after the name: *the Brontë sisters.*

burnt/burned
1 For the adjective always use *burnt*: *burnt paper*, *burnt sienna*, *a burnt offering.*
2 For the past tense and past participle of the verb either *burned* or *burnt* may be used, but the latter is more common in the transitive sense:
□ He *burnt* his fingers
□ The acid has *burnt* a hole in my jacket,
and the former in the intransitive:
□ The fire *burned* for several days.
Burned is also preferred for the figurative use:
□ A desire for revenge *burned* within him.
(See also **past tense and participle**: **regular or irregular form?**)

bus

No apostrophe. *Omnibus* is now used only in official contexts, or to describe a book containing a large number of stories or plays, usually by the same author, or of the same kind.

business

Note the position of the *u* and *i* in the spelling.

but

1 Co-ordinating conjunction

a Similarities between but and and On the use or non-use of a comma before *but*, the use of *but* before a relative pronoun (*but who, but which, but that*), and *but* used at the beginning of a sentence, see **and**. The same rules apply to both.

b Not only . . . but also With the correlatives *not only . . . but also* it is perhaps rather pedantic to insist that the *also* must never be omitted. A sentence like the following may be regarded as quite acceptable English:

□ *Not only* beginners, *but* even experienced craftsmen, may learn much from this book.

c The redundant but Beware of falling into the corner of the redundant *but*, exemplified in the following sentences:

□ *But* that, however, is another story.

If *however* is used *but* is not needed: or alternatively omit *however*. (See **however/how ever 3**.)

□ He is not a native of this town, *but* he came here from London.

Here, again, the second statement does not contrast with the first: it bears it out and amplifies it. Omit *but* and use a colon instead of a comma, or alternatively retain the comma and omit the second *he*. *But*, however, is correctly used in the sentence:

□ I am not a native of this town, but I have lived here ever since I was a child of two.

d Not so much . . . as The following sentence shows a common misuse:

□ The story is concerned *not so much* with historical events and political doctrines, *but* with human motives, passions and behaviour.

Another unidiomatic use of *but*, probably through the influence of *not with . . . but with. Not so much* must be followed by *as*, not by *but*.

2 Subordinating conjunction In sentences like:

☐ It never rains *but* it pours
☐ We ne'er see our foes *but* we wish them to stay,
the word *but* is a subordinating conjunction introducing an adverb clause. A frequent mistake is to use *what* after it as in:
☐ We never arrange a game of cricket *but what* it rains.
Omit *what*. *But* in this use is formal.

3 Preposition When *but* means 'except' it is a preposition, and therefore should be followed by the objective case: *everyone but me, everybody but them, all the players but him*, etc. Usage, however, permits the subject case when it is immediately followed by a verb to which it appears to be (though actually it is not) the subject, so that an objective would sound strange:
☐ Everyone *but she* knew the answer
☐ The boy stood on the burning deck, whence all *but he* had fled.

by/bye

By-election, by-way, by-pass, by-product, by-street, bygone times, by and large, by and by (presently): but *by the bye, bye* (at cricket and in other games), *bye-bye* (colloquial for *goodbye*), *bye-byes* (childish for *sleep*). Either *by-law* or *bye-law* is correct.

C

can/may

Can (past tense *could*) means 'to know how to' or 'to have the ability to'. *May* (past tense *might*) means 'to have permission to'. *Can* and *could* are, however, often used to ask for permission or make a request:
☐ *Can* we go when we have finished our work?
☐ He asked if he *could* borrow the newspaper.
There is no objection to this, though in more formal written style *may* and *might* are preferred. (See also **may** and **could**.)

cancel/postpone

Cancel means 'to put off altogether'. *Postpone* means 'to put off until a later date'.

cannon/canon

A *cannon* is a large, old-fashioned gun and a *canon* a person who has humorously been described as 'a big shot in the church'. The real meaning is a particular type of priest with special responsibilities.

cannot

1 Can not American English permits *can not* (two words), but in British English it is spelt as one. Caution is, however, necessary. In the following quotation, *can not* is correctly printed as two words:

□ Family life *can not* only give security, but also provide children with values and standards with which to face the world.

Cannot would be incorrect, for it is the positive, not the negative verb that is used here; the *not* belongs to *not only*, which is correlated with *but also*.

2. Can't Where the contracted form *can't* is concerned, see that the apostrophe is placed in the right position (a frequent misspelling is *ca'nt*). (See also **abbreviations 3**.)

canon

See **cannon/canon**.

canvas/canvass

Canvas (noun) is a coarse material used for painting on or for sails. *Canvass* (verb) means 'to solicit votes':

□ The painting was valuable but the *canvas* was in bad condition

□ George will *canvass* for the Labour Party the week before the election.

capable

Capable of doing, not *capable to do*. The same applies to *incapable*. Both must be followed by an active, never by a passive construction. We cannot say *capable* (or *incapable*) *of being done*.

capacity

Full to capacity is acceptable. The adjectival use in expressions like *a capacity crowd*, *a capacity audience* is journalese which has spread into fairly general use.

capital letters

The general rule is, of course, that capital letters are used for all proper nouns and for adjectives derived from them; but the following points should be noted:

1 Races of people Though words denoting races of people require a capital, those differentiating people by the colour of the skin or other physical characteristics do not: *Jew*, *Jewish*, *Arab*, but *negro*, *albino*, *pigmy*. (See also **nationality**.)

2 Nouns derived from proper names Words which are proper nouns or adjectives by origin but have ceased to be thought of as such, or are no longer closely associated with the place or person in question, have no capitals: *indian ink, indiarubber, plaster of paris, brussels sprouts, french windows, venetian blinds.* Similarly, vehicles, garments, etc named after persons or places are written with small letters: *wellingtons, cardigans, hoover, biro.*

3 Verbs derived from proper nouns Verbs derived from proper nouns have a small letter: *americanise, anglicise, pasteurise, bowdlerise.*

4 Days, months, etc The names of the months, the days of the week, religious festivals, and special secular days or occasions (*Remembrance Day, New Year's Day, May Day*) have capitals, but the names of the seasons should be written with small letters.

5 Places Use small letters for the points of the compass when they merely indicate direction, but capitals when they are the recognised or substitute name for a particular geographical region or area:

□ The sun rises in the *east* and sets in the *west,*

but:

□ Many years of his life had been spent in the *East.*

Note also *we travel south for our holidays,* but *We travel to the South Coast for our holidays*; and *northern England,* but *Northern Ireland.* Also, of course, *East Anglia, South Kensington, West Midlands.*

6 Religions Capitals are needed for the names of religions, religious denominations or their adherents, and adjectives derived from them; but use a small *c* for *christian name.*

7 Political parties Names of political parties and their adherents have capitals: *the Labour party*; *a spokesman for the Conservatives.* But when the party-political sense is not intended, there is a small letter: *conservative opinions, liberal views.* Note also: *the Left, the Right,* but *right-wing, left-wing.* (See also **liberality/liberalism.**)

8 Particular common nouns Words like *channel, straits,* which are normally common nouns, are written with a capital when they mean a particular one and stands as a substitute for the full name: *the Channel* (the English Channel), *the Straits* (of Dover, Gibraltar, etc), *the Peninsula* (Spain and Portugal).

9 Professions Words like *bishop, doctor, professor, headmaster, chairman,* when used alone, usually take a small letter, but they must have a capital when they are part of a recognised title or

description or when referring to a particular person:
☐ Many *bishops* were present at the meeting,
but:
☐ The *Bishop* of London chaired the meeting:
and:
☐ X was a *professor* at Oxford University,
but:
☐ X was Aston *Professor* of English History.

10 Names of institutions, etc Where institutions or organisations are referred to in a general way, they have a small letter; when a particular institution is described it has a capital:
☐ Not every country has a democratically elected *government*,
but:
☐ The *Government* had a majority of twenty votes last night;
and:
☐ The *universities* are facing severe financial restraints,
but:
☐ I studied at York *University*.

11 Periods of history and events These normally have a capital letter: *the Middle Ages*, *World War II*. When the word is used in a more general sense, however, it has a small letter: *the Renaissance*, but *a renaissance in country dancing*.

12 Academic subjects The names of academic subjects other than languages (which must, of course, have capitals), are normally written with a small letter, but a capital may be used when the word is thought of as the name of a course in a curriculum or a subject in an examination:
☐ A good knowledge of *mathematics* is essential to an engineer
☐ She is very interested in *history*,
but:
☐ She passed in *History* but failed in *Mathematics*.

13 Roads In the names of roads the word *road* should be spelt with a capital if it is part of the actual name, but not otherwise: *Richmond Road*, *Queen's Road*, *Harrow Road*, but *the Richmond road*, *the Harrow road* (the roads that lead to Richmond and Harrow respectively). The use of a hyphen followed by a small letter (*Ebury-street*, *Brompton-road*) cannot be justified, though it is found in some newspapers.

14 God The use of capitals for pronouns referring to God or

Christ is best confined to theological contexts; elsewhere use small letters.

15 Registered trade names Use capitals for registered trade names of commercial products, materials, vehicles, etc: *Anadin tablets, Mini, Rover*, but small letters for general or non-trade names: *aspirin tablets, nylon, estate car.*

16 Prefixes with proper nouns When a prefix is hyphenated to a proper noun or adjective the noun or adjective retains its capital letter, but the prefix is not given a capital: *un-English, non-Catholics, non-Christian religions, anti-British feeling, pro-Russian elements. Nonconformists* (in its religious sense), however, is written as one word and has an initial capital letter.

In the titles of literary works, names of organisations, etc, both the prefix and the word to which it is attached must have a capital: *Anti-Vivisection League, Anti-Apartheid Organisation.*

17 In verse In verse the traditional method is to begin each line with a capital letter. Some modern poets, however, use capitals only if the punctuation requires it, as they would do in prose. In quoting such verse, the practice of the author must be respected.

capitalist

The word should be spelt with a small letter, whether used as a noun, or as an adjective: *capitalists, capitalist countries.* The contrasting term *Communist* is spelt with a capital, since there is a Communist party; but there is no capitalist party.

carcass/carcase

The dead body of an animal. The former spelling is to be preferred.

carefree/careless/careful

Carefree means 'without worry or care':

☐ School was over for the holidays and I felt happy and *carefree.*

Careless means 'without taking proper care':

☐ This exercise is full of *careless* mistakes.

Careful means the opposite of *careless*: 'taking proper care; taking trouble':

☐ He was praised for his neat and *careful* work.

case

1 The expression (*in*) *the case of* is over-used and can be easily avoided. The following are a few examples. The suggested amendments are given in brackets.

☐ *In many cases* candidates misunderstood the question. (*Many candidates misunderstood the question.*)
☐ The standard of living of the working class is higher than was *the case* thirty years ago. (. . . *than it was thirty years ago.*)
☐ If that is *the case.* (*If so.*)
2 The elliptical *in case* or *just in case* (*I'll take my umbrella, just in case*) is allowable colloquially, but in written English the clause should be completed (*in case it rains*).
(See also **inversion of verb and subject**.)

cause

Wrong use of preposition:
☐ We shall do our best to find out the *cause for* the delay.
For *for* substitute *of. Cause* is followed by *for* only when it means 'ground' or 'justification': *There is no cause for alarm*; *you have no cause for complaint.*

ceiling

Note the spelling. See **spelling 1**.

celebrate/celibate

We *celebrate* birthdays, anniversaries, successes and victories by throwing parties. A *celibate* person is someone who has taken a vow never to marry. Priests and nuns in the Catholic Church vow to lead a *celibate* life in order to devote themselves entirely to the service of God.

centre

1 (verb) *Centred on* or *upon*, not *around.*
2 (verb or noun) The American spelling is *center.*
3 centre/middle In everyday English we need not restrict *centre* to its strict mathematical use. A vase of flowers may be placed in the *centre* of a table, or a table in the *centre* of a stage, ie roughly equidistant from the four corners. There are also certain traditional combinations where *centre* must be recognised, eg *centre forward* (at football), *Centre Court* (at tennis), *centre aisle, centrepiece, the centre of the town, the city centre*, but generally the idea of 'mid-way between two other things, groups or extremities' should be expressed by *middle*: *the middle of the road, to part one's hair in the middle, the middle shelf, the middle class*, etc.

cereal/serial

Oats, barley and wheat are *cereals*:
☐ Cornflakes and Weetabix are breakfast cereals.

A *serial* is a story which appears in parts in a magazine, on television, etc:

☐ Many of Dickens's novels appeared first in *serial* form.

chairman

Used for both sexes. *Chairwoman* has not been fully recognised as correct English. A lady chairman has been addressed as 'Madam Chairman'. Following legislation on women's rights, an attempt has been made to make such words acceptable; the word *chairperson*, or even *chair*, is also sometimes found. Language and convention change slowly, however, and *chairman* is still the accepted form for both sexes. The change is more far-reaching in America. (See also **gender in nouns 3**.)

charge

Often used incorrectly as in:

☐ The baby was left *in charge of* a neighbour.

It was the neighbour who was *in charge of* the baby; the baby was left *in the charge of* the neighbour. *In charge of* means 'having care of, or authority over':

☐ Drunk while *in charge of* a car

☐ Superintendent Collins is *in charge of* the investigations.

The idea of 'subject to the care, control or authority of' is expressed by *in the charge of*.

check

1 Check up on No more than an alternative for check: *Check up on this information*; *check up on his story*. Use the simple verb whenever possible.

2 Check one's luggage An Americanism, meaning to deposit one's luggage at a left-luggage office and receive a ticket, or check, in return. In British English the above expression simply means to go through one's luggage to make sure nothing is missing.

3 Check out In the sense 'to investigate or prove to be in order or true after investigation': *The detectives checked out the statements*; *the stories all checked out* is an Americanism that is coming into informal British usage. It should be avoided in writing.

cheque

1 In British English the word denoting a draft on a bank is always spelt *cheque*. Americans often spell it *check*.

2 In restaurants in some parts of America a waitress gives her customers a *check* for their meal. The correct English term is *bill*.

chilblain

Note the spelling with only one *l*.

childish/childlike

Childish means 'suitable for a child; behaving like a child'. This word is often used with pejorative overtones to criticise a child or adult who is behaving younger than his years:

□ You don't want that book, Mark, it's too *childish* for you
□ Don't sulk – it's *childish*.

Childlike means 'having the pleasing qualities of a child'. This is a more positive word which shows approval:

□ The young girl followed her with *childlike* trust.

childish words

Words like *mum, dad, auntie, dolly* (for *doll*), *granny, grand-dad, pussy*, have their place in childish speech, but should not appear in written English, except, of course, in dialogue.

childlike

See **childish/childlike**.

choler/cholera

□ At first sight, the timing of today's broadcast of the new production of Dylan Thomas's *Under Milk Wood* is little short of disastrous. But when *cholera* has subsided, it will be seen to be an excellent arrangement. (*The Times*)

An unfortunate mistake. *Cholera* is the name of an extremely unpleasant disease which is often fatal. The writer has confused *cholera* with *choler*, an old and very poetical word for 'anger'.

choose

See **pick/choose**.

chord/cord

Chord means 'a combination of harmonising notes'. *Cord* means 'a thin rope'. Vocal *cords* not vocal *chords*.

christian name

The name given to a child at its baptism or christening. Today, when not all children are christened and the names chosen by the parents are not necessarily from the Bible, there is a tendency to use *forename* or *given name*, especially on official forms. The word for the family name is *surname* (see **surnames**). For the lower case initial letter, see **capital letters 6**.

cord

See **chord/cord**.

chronic

Frequently used incorrectly, as in *My rheumatism is chronic today*; *I've a chronic headache. Chronic* does not mean 'very bad' or 'very painful', but 'of long duration'.

church

Write the word with a small letter when describing the building, a service of worship or a particular local assembly of believers:

□ It was cool and quiet in the ancient *church*

□ Are you going to *church* tonight?

□ The *church* was learning to respond to the Word of God more.

Use a capital letter when referring to Christians universally, a particular denomination, the institution or the ordained ministry: *the Church militant, the Methodist Church, relations between Church and State, to go into the Church.*

On whether the expression is *go to church* or *go to the church*, see **the 7.**

city

1 Cities and cathedrals There is a very widely held, but erroneous, belief that in Britain a city must have a cathedral, and that any place with a cathedral is a city. This is not so. There are cities without cathedrals, and cathedral towns that are not cities. The right of a town to call itself a city is granted by the sovereign; a church is elevated to the status of a cathedral by the Archbishop of Canterbury. Quite frequently, when a town becomes a city, the Archbishop follows the sovereign's lead and raises the oldest, or the principal, parish church to the status of a cathedral; but not always. Cambridge was created a city by King George VI in 1951, but it has no cathedral. Southwell has a cathedral but is not a city.

2 A cathedral city (town) Not merely a city or town which has a cathedral, but one which has grown up around the cathedral, or which owes its fame to its cathedral as its principal public building, eg Canterbury, York, Lincoln, Ripon. Birmingham, Manchester, Liverpool and Sheffield all have cathedrals, but we should not call them *cathedral cities.*

3 The City (The banking and financial quarter of London.) Should be spelt with a capital *C. The City Editor* (of a newspaper): the person in charge of that part of the newspaper which deals with banking, the Stock Exchange and financial matters generally.

clad/clothed

Outside poetry, where it survives as an archaism, *clad* is obsolete as a participle, though it is found in certain traditional compounds like *ill-clad*, *well-clad*, *iron-clad*, and expressions like *clad in mail*, where the dress is scarcely thought of as clothing in the ordinary sense. In all other senses *clothed* is the normal word today.

claim (verb)

The use of *claim* in the sense of 'assert' or 'maintain' as in:

☐ He *claims* that he has broken the record for long-distance flying,

used to be condemned, but by now it can be regarded as established. *Claim* can be followed by an infinitive construction only when its subject is also the 'subject' of the infinitive, as in:

☐ He *claims* to have done it

☐ She *claimed* to be the daughter of a well-known business man.

The following sentences, in which the infinitive has its own subject, are all incorrect, however:

☐ He *claimed* it to be entirely his own work

☐ She *claimed* the invention to have been made by her late husband

☐ He *claimed* the voting to have been in his favour.

clergyman/minister

In America *clergyman* is used of any minister of religion, no matter to what Church or denomination he belongs. In Britain it is usually reserved for ordained ministers of the Church of England. Other Protestant denominations speak of their *ministers*.

Use a small letter for *minister* when it merely denotes the office or vocation, a capital when it is a substitute for the name of a particular person:

☐ He gave up the profession of surgeon to become a *minister*

☐ The Reverend J. S. Thompson, a retired Methodist *minister*

☐ Both services next Sunday will be conducted by the *Minister*.

clichés

These are fixed phrases and idioms which are used to excess. George Baker neatly defines a *cliché* as 'a coin so battered by use as to be defaced'. There are many categories of *clichés*:

☐ phrases: much of a muchness, to all intents and purposes

☐ metaphors that are now pointless: lock, stock and barrel

☐ formulas: far be it from me to . . .
☐ nicknames, sobriquets: the Iron Duke
☐ quotations: cups that cheer but not inebriate
☐ foreign phrases: longo intervallo, bête noire
☐ catch phrases which enjoy a vogue for a short period: elementary, my dear Watson!, the $64,000 question.

These examples and many others can be found in Eric Partridge's *Dictionary of Clichés* and *Dictionary of Catch Phrases*. (See also **jargon**.)

clothed

See **clad/clothed**.

cloths/clothes

An advertisement in the window of a local newsagent's read:

☐ Children's *cloths* for sale. Very reasonable prices. Phone 37092.

The writer of the advertisement has, of course, made a common spelling mistake. The card should have read *Children's clothes for sale*; a *cloth* is a piece of material used for a special purpose (floorcloth, dishcloth, tablecloth).

c/o

An abbreviation meaning 'care of'. It is used in an address on an envelope in front of the name of the hosts:

☐ Mr Alan Worthington
c/o Mr and Mrs Blake
7 Osborne Avenue
Weatherbury
Wessex

If the name of the hosts is unknown, *at* should be used instead of *c/o*:

☐ Mr Alan Worthington
at 7 Osborne Avenue

coarse/course

Coarse means 'rough'. *Course* means 'a series of lectures, lessons, etc', 'the ground over which a race is run'.

Cockney

Do not use *Cockney* as a synonym for *Londoner*. Not all Londoners are Cockneys. It is often said that a *Cockney* is 'one born within the sound of Bow bells', but today the word also connotes certain characteristics of speech, manner and social background.

coherence/cohesion

Coherence means the 'logical progression of thoughts', whether in speech or writing: *the coherence of his argument. Cohesion* means the literal sticking together of two objects or substances, or the metaphorical sticking-together of friends, social groups, nations, etc.

collaborate/corroborate

Collaborate means 'to work together with someone else'. It may have negative **connotations:**

☐ The traitors *collaborated* with the enemy,

or positive ones:

☐ The architects *collaborated* for three years in the designing of the new cathedral.

Corroborate means 'to support or confirm something by evidence':

☐ The new evidence *corroborated* his earlier statement to the police.

colleague

Should be used only of professional people and office workers, not of manual workers, shop assistants, drivers and conductors of public service vehicles, etc. See also **acquaintance**.

collect

Often (and wrongly) used nowadays for *fetch*:

☐ I called at his office to *collect* a parcel

☐ I will call and *collect* it on my way home.

Literally the word means 'to bring together or gather'.

Its uses, therefore, are: (a) 'to collect sets of things as a hobby': *collect stamps, collect china, collect dolls,* etc; (b) 'to cause to accumulate': *Curtains easily collect dust*; and (c) 'to get together something that is to be put with others of the kind': *to collect the rent, to collect the laundry.*

collective nouns

Ivan Sparkes, in his *Dictionary of Collective Nouns and Group Terms,* classifies collective nouns as follows:

1 Ancient phrases Ancient phrases such as *an exaltation of larks* or *an abomination of monks,* which also reflect some of the views of the medieval users. They are little found today, but retain a certain appeal through their quaintness.

2 Terms relating to one particular group Many of these refer to animals and are very restricted in use: *a charm of goldfish, a cete*

of badgers, a sedge of herons, etc. Others are more common: *a pride of lions, a picket of strikers, a pinch of salt or snuff, a phalanx of infantry*, etc.
3 General terms For example, *flock, pile, heap, herd*, or *shoal*, which can apply to a wide variety of persons, animals or objects.
4 Terms ending in -y or -age Words or names which are made collective by the addition of an ending such as *-y* or *-age*: *fruitery, assemblage, baggage.*
5 Witty punning terms For example, *a dilation of pupils.* A group of prostitutes has variously been called *a flourish of strumpets, a jam of tarts* and *an anthology of pros.* Somewhat similar is the use in humour. What is the answer to this riddle?
☐ What do you get when you give figs to a canary? – A chirrup of figs.
(See also **bevy**.)
There is also the difficult question of whether a particular collective noun takes a singular or plural verb. For this purpose, four main types may be distinguished:
a Words like *clothing, furniture, luggage, crockery*: what we may call 'class' collectives. These denote a number of different things that fall into the same general class (*crockery*, for instance, means cups, saucers, plates, dishes, etc taken collectively). These always take a singular verb and are referred to by a singular pronoun. There is no plural form of the noun, nor can it be preceded by the singular indefinite article: we cannot speak of *luggages* or of *a luggage.*
b Words like *people, folk, kindred*: distributive collectives. These always take a plural verb.
c Words like *the clergy, the police*: generalising collectives. These usually refer to professions or occupations. They usually take a plural verb and are referred to by a plural pronoun.
d Words like *committee, congregation, audience, staff, personnel, the public*: group collectives. Many of these have plural forms (*committees, audiences, congregations*), which of course take plural verbs and pronouns; but with most, the singular form can be treated as singular or plural according to circumstances. Generally the singular is to be preferred, but it is not always possible. While we can say:
☐ The audience has already expressed its approval,
we cannot say *The audience is requested to be in its seat by 7.25*;

we must use *are requested* and *their seats*. On the other hand, we should probably say *The committee* is (not *are*) *divided on the question*, since one thing is divided into two or more parts. But whether we choose to use a singular or a plural, the important thing is that we must be consistent, at least throughout the same sentence.

collocation

Collocation refers to a group of words found frequently together that tend to form a distinct unit: *to abandon hope, abandon ship*! (See also **meet 2**.)

colon

A punctuation mark (:).

1 It separates two co-ordinate clauses where the second clause explains the first:

☐ Martin had never felt so happy: Sheila loved him.

2 It separates two clauses where one is in contrast to the other:

☐ Speech is silvern: silence is golden.

3 It introduces a list or an example:

☐ The box contained a collection of articles: a few books, various papers, foreign coins, stamps and paperclips.

Where the list introduced starts on the following line, the colon may be followed by a dash:

☐ The following candidates passed with distinction:–
J C Andrews, W A Barsley, J Charlesworth, P G Dutton.

4 It introduces a fairly long passage of direct speech, as a comma would introduce a shorter passage:

☐ Introducing the speaker, the Chairman said: (Here follows a verbatim report of his speech, or the relevant parts of it, in inverted commas.)

5 It introduces a literary or documentary quotation within the body of the paragraph. In this case the quotation should not be more than one sentence long:

☐ If I may quote from the Managing Director's last report: 'Property revaluation shows a surplus of £21.7 million over book value.'

Where the quotation is lengthy it is written in a separate, indented paragraph. The following example is taken from a literary essay:

☐ This extract from *Adam Bede* describes one of the Dutch interiors:

(Here follows a lengthy descriptive passage in a new indented paragraph.)

(For further notes on quotations, see **quotation**.)

come

1 Sometimes misused for *become*, as in the sentence (from a documentary source):

☐ The matter will be further reviewed when the position *comes* vacant.

2 *Come*, when followed by an adjective as a complement, expresses the idea of progression from one state to another (usually to one that is desired; *go* is generally used for one that is not desired: *come clean, come right, come true*, but *go wrong, go bad, go rusty*). When there is no sense of progression, but merely a statement of the final state or situation that arises, *become* should be used: *become angry, become senile, become anxious.*

comic(al)

Comic describes the intention, *comical* the effect: a *comic* story, paper, costume, etc, but *a comical appearance, a comical situation.*

comma

A punctuation mark (,).

Of all the punctuation marks, the comma allows most opportunity for a writer to express his personal taste and preferences. In the light of the two-fold purpose of all punctuation to serve as an aid to reading by indicating natural pauses, inflections of the voice, etc and to make clear the meaning of what is written, we may distinguish the following uses of the comma:

1 As substitute for and It is a substitute for *and* in the enumeration of a series, but the final *and* is usually retained:

☐ Oats, corn, maize and barley

☐ He was tall, fair and rather stout

☐ He entered the room, locked the door, took out his papers and seated himself at the desk.

(See also **and**.)

2 Where adjectives qualify the same noun Compare these two sentences:

☐ She was a tall, slim girl

☐ She was a pretty little girl.

Commas are used in the first sentence because the adjectives have equal weight in qualifying the same noun. There are no commas in

the second sentence because *little girl* has the force of a compound.
3 To separate repeated words It is used to separate words which are repeated for the sake of emphasis:
□ He speaks very, very quickly.
4 To indicate a parenthesis It indicates a parenthesis or an interruption and separates it from the rest of the sentence. The parenthesis may consist of a single word or a group of words:
□ This, however, is certain
□ The story, such as it is, may be summarised as follows.
Since a parenthesis is an insertion into a sentence, *two commas* are needed to separate it from the sentence. If the parenthesis is removed, the remainder should form a complete and natural grammatical sentence in itself. The commas in the following sentence have been wrongly placed:
□ The immediate cause of, though not the reason, for the strike . . . .
Omit the words between the commas and we have *The immediate cause of for the strike* – obviously not grammatically correct. The second comma should have been placed after *for*.
Often the inclusion or omission of commas changes the meaning of a sentence. This is a clear case of the comma acting as a written indicator of the pauses and intonation patterns of normal speech. Compare the following pairs of sentences:
□ Did he do it then?
Did he do it, then?
□ There are, too, many people who give only part-time service
There are too many people who give only part-time service.
(See also **parenthesis**.)
5 To distinguish defining and non-defining expressions It is used to distinguish a non-defining expression from one which defines. This is a very important use and must be carefully observed. Compare these two sentences:
□ My brother who is an engineer has gone to Australia
□ My brother, who is an engineer, has gone to Australia.
The first sentence implies I have several brothers. The clause *who is an engineer* defines: it describes the brother I am talking about. Here there are no commas. The implication of the second sentence is that I have only one brother. The clause *who is an engineer* merely adds extra information about that brother. The information is like a parenthesis and is separated off by two commas.

Compare also:

□ In the country where I lived as a boy the people worked long hours (defining)

□ In the country, where I lived as a boy, the people worked long hours (non-defining).

6 To mark off a noun in direct address It is used to mark off a noun or pronoun in direct address:

□ Gentlemen, the time has come when . . .

□ Is that you, Mary?

If direct address is followed by words which qualify it, the whole combination should be marked off by a comma:

□ Fellow citizens of this great city, I stand before you today . . . .

Where the phrase occurs internally, two commas are needed:

□ And now, ladies and gentlemen, we come to the most interesting exhibit of all.

7 To separate participial phrases It is used to separate participial phrases from the rest of the sentence:

□ The horse, seeing how high the fence was, refused to jump.

8 To separate verbs like say from direct speech: It separates the verbs *say*, *shout*, *reply*, etc from direct speech:

□ 'Your dinner is on the table,' she shouted

□ 'All right,' he replied, 'I'm coming now.'

(See also **inverted commas 1b**.)

9 To separate co-ordinate clauses It may be used to separate two co-ordinate clauses joined by a conjunction, though there is a tendency in modern usage to leave the comma out:

□ I am going out now, but I hope to find everything ready when I get back.

If the subjects of the clauses are different, the comma is more likely to be kept:

□ I have to go now, but Mr Haverall will arrive shortly.

10 To separate a main and subordinate clause Where the main clause follows the subordinate clause, a comma may be used to separate the two:

□ Although it was raining heavily, the match continued.

A comma is never used when the main clause comes first. As a general rule, the longer the subordinate clause is, the more likely it is that a comma will be used. However short or long the clause, a comma should always be inserted if, without it, the reader would have difficulty in interpreting the construction of the sentence or would even be misled. Consider this example:

☐ While Sancho Panza hides the gold disappears – stolen by a simpleton.

A comma after *hides* would avoid an initial misreading.

11 On the use of commas in writing numbers, see **numbers: method of writing 2**.

commando

Strictly, a small body of soldiers operating independently, but since World War II also used of a single member of such a body. This latter use is now recognised. Compare *a Wren, a Waaf*, where a similar development has taken place.

commemorate

Note the spelling: first a double *m* then a single *m*.

commence

See **begin/commence/start**.

commercial jargon

There is no reason why a business letter should not be written in normal English. The following are some of the commoner pieces of commercial jargon to be avoided:

☐ inst, ult, prox (Write the name of the month.)

☐ same (Change to *it* or *them*.)

☐ enclosed please find (Change to *I enclose*.)

☐ your esteemed favour (Change to *your letter, order, enquiry*.)

☐ your good selves (and even worse) your goodselves

☐ further to your letter, to our conversation (Use *with reference to* or reword the sentence.)

☐ your communication to hand (Change to *we have received your letter*.)

☐ I beg to inform you, I beg to remain (see **beg**.)

(See also **-ese** and **jargon**.)

commission

This word is spelt with a double *m* and a double *s*.

commissionaire

Spelt with a double *m* and double *s* but only one *n*.

commit

In the past tense, past participle and present participle, the *t* is doubled: *committed, committing*. For the general rule, see **spelling 6**.

committee

Note the spelling; three pairs of double letters. On whether to use a singular or plural verb with *committee*, see **collective nouns d**.

commonsense

Does such a word exist? It should always be written as two separate words when used as a noun (*Use your common sense*), and as a hyphenated compound rather than as one word when used adjectivally: *common-sense precautions.*

comparatively

Should not be used in the sense of 'rather' or 'fairly'. *Comparatively easy* does not mean 'fairly easy', but 'easy in comparison with something else'. (See **relatively**.)

comparatives

1 The comparative degree is used when two things are compared:

□ This wine is *better* than that one,

the superlative for more than two:

□ This wine is *the best* of the three.

It is incorrect to say *Which is the better of the three methods?* Amend to *Which of the three methods is the best?* The superlative instead of the comparative, however, is allowable where in actual fact only two things are concerned but where more than two might have been:

□ I shall go by *the cheapest* route.

Similarly, *Which do you like best?*, for 'Which do you prefer?' has become a set phrase invariable in form, whether applied to two or to more than two things. We should never say *Which do you like better?* Note also *I like that one best*; *I will have the one that costs least*. The combinations *like best* and *cost least* express the general idea of preference and cheapness respectively, regardless of number. The fact that in a particular case only two things may be concerned is purely coincidental.

2 Wrong use:

□ This box is three times *heavier* than the other.

Amend to *three times as heavy as*. (See **times**.) Since the comparative indicates merely superiority, and is not in itself confined to any definite limit, there cannot be multiples of it. It can be modified only by adverbs of degree, like *much*, *little*, *rather*, *scarcely*, *barely*, *far*, or by a statement of a definite amount, as *five kilos heavier*, *50 pence dearer*.

3 Adjectives like *unique, dead, blind, dumb,* which express an absolute idea of which there cannot be degrees, obviously cannot have a comparative. One thing cannot be more unique than another or one person more dead or more dumb than another. But words like *full, perfect,* etc, which express completeness, may be used in the comparative to denote a nearer approach to the complete notion:

□ A *fuller* account will appear next month

□ We could not have had a *more perfect* day for the garden party.

Some words which normally belong to the first group fall into the second when they are used figuratively:

□ Nothing is *more dead* than the centre of a large city on Sunday morning.

(See also **more**.) On use of *the* with comparatives, see **the**.

compare to/compare with

Compare to means 'to state a resemblance between':

□ Shakespeare *compared* the world *to* a stage.

Compare with means 'to place side by side, noting the resemblances and the differences (usually with the stress on the differences)':

□ *Compare* this *with* that, and you will see which is the *better*

□ Most working people are well off *compared with* what they were in the 1950s (not *compared to*).

By comparison and *in comparison* are usually followed by *with.*

complacent/complaisant

Complacent means 'self-satisfied'; *complaisant* means 'ready to oblige':

□ Don't be so *complacent*, you haven't passed your exams yet

□ The new secretary is very *complaisant* and offered to take work home with her.

The second term can sometimes have pejorative associations; *a complaisant husband* could be one who overlooked his wife's infidelities too easily. The respective nouns are *complacency* and *complaisance.*

compound adjectives

An out-of-the-way place, a give-and-take policy, a take-it-or-leave-it attitude, a couldn't-care-less philosophy, an on-the-spot account, etc. Such long compounds sometimes sound inelegant and awkward. Perhaps the best advice is to avoid compounds of this kind wherever possible, especially in written English. (On the use of hyphens, see **hyphen**.)

comprise

An example of misuse:

□ The delegation was *comprised of* the following persons.

Is/was/will be comprised of is always incorrect. The alternatives are *was composed of the following persons*, and *comprised the following persons*.

compulsive/impulsive

A *compulsive* action arises from an obsession. A *compulsive* gambler is one who cannot refrain from gambling, a *compulsive* eater is one who cannot stop eating.

An *impulsive* action, however, is a spontaneous one.

conceit

Note that, in the spelling, the *e* comes before the *i*. For the rule, see **spelling 1**.

concerning

See **about/on**.

concur

Concur *with* someone *in* an opinion: *The Minister concurred with the questioner in condemning capital punishment*. The *r* doubles in the past participle, past tense and present participle: *concurred, concurring*. See **refer**.

confer

The *r* doubles in the past participle, past tense and present participle: *conferred, conferring*. See **refer**.

confide

Confide *in* a person; confide information, documents, a secret, etc *to* a person:

□ He was such a good listener that everyone *confided in* him

□ He was a terrible gossip, so it was no use *confiding* her secret *to* him.

confronted

When *confronted* is used adjectivally, to denote the situation that one is in, it is followed by the preposition *with*: *We are confronted with a difficult task* (compare *covered with, surrounded with*). When it is a participle forming part of a passive voice, *by* is used when the noun that follows denotes the person or the thing that actually confronts one:

□ As he entered the room he was *confronted by* a policeman/*by* a scene of disorder.

With is used when it represents the person or the thing that is placed or brought before one:

□ He was *confronted with* a bill for over twenty pounds/*with* a demand for his resignation.

congratulate

Congratulate someone *on* something. (Not *for* or *at*, both frequently, though wrongly, used before a gerund.)

connection/connexion

Either spelling, although the latter is found only occasionally. American usage also favours *connection.* Similarly, *inflection/inflexion.*

connotation

The *connotation* of a word represents the attributes commonly associated with it. It contrasts with *denotation*, which is the word's primary meaning. For example, *home* has the connotation of warmth, but its denotation is 'the place where one lives or comes from'.

conscience

Note *sc* in spelling. Also, *conscious* and *science.*

consent

See **assent**.

consequent on/subsequent to

Note the prepositions. *Subsequent to* merely means 'after'; *consequent on* means 'following from, as a result or consequence'.

consider

I consider it a good thing (not *as a good thing*). The infinitive *to be* is understood after *it*. Similarly, *You may consider the matter settled* (not *as* settled); but:

□ We will *consider* Hamlet *as* an example of a Shakespearian tragedy

□ The Board are *considering* a young man from London *as* a possible successor to Jones,

since here *consider* has a different meaning ('think about, give one's mind to') and the phrase introduced by *as* signifies the capacity in which the play or the person is to be considered.

consideration

Do not say that something is *under active consideration.* The adjective *active* is pointless (though it seems to have become firmly established in officialese), and in any case it is better to write or say *is being considered* than *is under consideration.*

considering

For use in such sentences as *Considering its lack of training, our team did very well*, see **-ing 3**.

consist of/consist in

Consist of means 'to be composed of or made up of':

□ The drink *consists* mainly *of* water, with a little flavouring added.

Consist in means 'to have as an essential element':

□ Courage *consists in* overcoming one's fears.

contagious/infectious

A disease which is spread by physical contact is *contagious*: one that is spread by bacteria in air or in water is *infectious*. When used metaphorically, there is no difference between the two words: *infectious/contagious laughter*.

contemporary

1 The meaning is 'living, existing or occurring at the same time as the person or event mentioned'. It is synonymous with *modern* or *present-day* only if no other time or person is mentioned, when it means contemporary with ourselves, as *contemporary fashions* or *an exhibition of contemporary paintings*. If, however, *contemporary* is used in conjunction with the name of a particular person or a particular period of time, it means contemporary with those. The following sentence is, therefore, incorrect:

□ St Paul, it is true, did not live in the *contemporary* world, but it is remarkable how applicable much of his teaching is to *contemporary* problems.

What world did St Paul live in, then? Clearly, he was a man born before his time! Tennyson and Browning were *contemporary* poets, but they are not modern poets. *Elizabethan plays presented in contemporary costume* means 'in Elizabethan (not modern) costume'; Matthew Arnold's reputation with *contemporary* critics means 'with critics of his own day', not with those of the present time.

2 One person is *contemporary with* another, or *the contemporary of* another. *Contemporaries of each other* gives redundant information: *contemporaries* alone is sufficient.

contemptible/contemptuous

Contemptible means 'deserving of contempt', *contemptuous* 'showing, or expressive of, contempt'. In August 1914 the Kaiser was alleged to have spoken of 'Britain's *contemptible* little army'. His remark was a *contemptuous* one.

The correct preposition to follow *contemptuous* is *of*, not *about*:

☐ The Kaiser was *contemptuous of* Britain's army.

continual/continuous

Continual means 'going on all the time (as if no end were in sight)', 'constant or frequent':

☐ I'm tired of her *continual* moaning.

Continuous means 'going on all the time without a break but having an end in sight':

☐ They made one *continuous* journey overland to the next town.

contracted forms

Couldn't (could not), *wouldn't* (would not), *hasn't* (has not), *it's* (it is), *he's* (he is), etc. An apostrophe should replace the missing letter, but it is often wrongly placed. The following headline comes from the *Western Mail*:

☐ Crash Victims Say Hospital Staff *Did'nt* Spot Injuries.

The word *Did'nt* should read *Didn't*.

(For detailed notes on placing the apostrophe in contracted forms, see **abbreviations 3**.)

Contracted forms should not be used in formal writing. They should be written out in full.

control

In the past tense, past participle and present participle, the *l* is doubled: *controlled*, *controlling*. For the rule, see **spelling 6**. Also *controllable*.

convalesce

Note the *sce* ending. Similarly, *convalescent*.

cord

See **chord/cord**.

core

See **corps/corpse/core**.

corporal/corporeal

Corporal means 'pertaining to the body': *corporal punishment*. *Corporeal* means 'bodily as opposed to spiritual; having bodily substance': *A ghost has no corporeal existence*.

corps/corpse/core

Corps means 'a body (of soldiers)'. *Corpse* means 'the dead body of a human being'. (Compare **carcass**.) *Core* means 'the centre of an apple, pear, etc'; 'the most important part; the centre; the heart'. *Core* is used in several idiomatic phrases: *to the core* (*English to the core* means 'completely English'); *rotten to the core* means 'thoroughly bad'; *the hard core* (*By 2 am, only the hard core was left at the party*). The *Evening Standard* provides a good illustration of how to confuse these words:

□ Greenwood clearly intends entrusting the job of winning the European Championship for the first time to the hard *corps* of players who have secured seven wins and two draws from ten matches.

The writer should have put either *to the corps of players* or *to the hard core of players.*

correlatives

The name given to pairs of conjunctions or conjunctive expressions which always go together, like *either . . . or, neither . . . nor, both . . . and, not only . . . but also.* The points to notice are:

1 Each initial correlative must have its correct complementary one. The following is a typical violation of this rule:

□ An illiterate person is one who can *neither* read *or* write.

Neither must be followed by *nor*, not by *or*.

2 *Not either* is followed by *or*, not *nor*, since *not* applies to both correlatives: *If it is not either useful* or *ornamental* . . . (not *nor ornamental*).

3 *Neither* is used for other purposes than that of correlation. The rule stated under **1** above applies only to the correlative use. *Neither* should not be followed by *nor* as a matter of course, or the effect will be contrary to the one intended. Here is an example where this has occurred:

□ He is *neither* hero *nor* saint. *Neither* is he sadist *nor* criminal. (*The Inquirer*)

The first sentence is correct, but in the second one *nor* should be *or*. It is not correlated with *neither*, which is merely used to link and contrast this statement with the preceding one. What the writer, in effect, is saying is *But he is not sadist or criminal, either. But . . . not . . . either* becomes the introductory *neither*. And besides, its position in the sentence stops it from correlating *sadist* with *criminal*, as the next section explains.

4 Care must be taken that the correlatives are correctly placed. Mistakes very frequently arise here. The rule is that all words that apply to both the correlated terms must precede the first of the correlatives. The following violation of this rule is quoted by Gowans Whyte (*An Anthology of Errors*):

□ She had noticed nothing *either* to cause her the least doubt *or* the faintest anxiety.

The two terms correlated are *the least doubt* and *the faintest anxiety*. The word group *to cause her* applies to both, and should therefore stand outside both, being placed before *either* (*. . . to cause her either the least doubt or the faintest anxiety*). Here are some further examples of wrong placing. The corrections are given in parentheses.

□ You will *either* carry out my instructions *or* I will give the work to someone else. (*Either you will carry out . . . .*)

□ We have *neither* had a visit from him *nor* has he written to us. (*We have not had . . . .*)

□ He was *not only* insolent, *but* he *also* threatened us. (*Not only was he insolent . . . .*)

□ His speech *neither* brought credit to him *nor* prestige to his party. (*Brought neither credit to him . . . .*)

(See also **either**, **neither**, **nor/or** and **not only . . . but also**.)

corroborate

See **verify/corroborate** and **collaborate/corroborate**.

could

1 Might or could?

□ We climbed up an electricity pylon. It was a foolish thing to do, for we *could* have been killed. (from a schoolboy's essay)

Substitute *might* for *could*. Possibility is better expressed by *might*.

2 Would or could? *Could you lend me 50 pence?* Acceptable as a more courteous way of making a request than *would you?* or *will you?* Similarly, *Could you close the window, please?* (See also **can/may** and **may**.)

council/counsel

Council means 'an assembly'; also used before a noun, as *a council house, a council estate, a council school* (where it means 'built by the local Council'). *Counsel* (verb) means 'to advise'; (noun) 'advice'; also 'one who gives advice' (usually a barrister), as *counsel for the defence, take the opinion of counsel*. *Queen's Counsel* has the same form for the plural as for the singular (*several eminent Queen's Counsel*), but the abbreviated form is *QCs*.

course

See **coarse/course.**

covered in/covered with

Both prepositions are permissible, though *in* is used only when *covered* has the force of an adjective used after a verb, rather than a participle:

☐ His boots were *covered in* mud.

The strict participial use must be followed by *with*:

☐ The table was *covered with* a white cloth

☐ The fruit should be put into a pan and *covered with* water.

When *covered* means 'hidden' or 'submerged', and the word following the preposition is thought of as the agent, then the correct preposition is *by*:

☐ The pathway was *covered by* the dense foliage

☐ The fish should be just *covered by* the white wine.

These are the passive forms corresponding to *The dense foliage covered the pathway* and *The white wine should just cover the fish.*

credible/creditable/credulous

Credible means 'believable' (*a credible story*); *creditable* means 'bringing credit or honour to one', 'deserving of credit': *a very creditable achievement. Credulous* means 'ready to believe anything': *a credulous person.* These three adjectives give the nouns *credibility*, *credit* and *credulity* respectively.

The words are often confused. Discussing the performance of a famous actor, a critic from the *Guardian* writes incorrectly:

☐ . . . he can glide through the part without either a sense of strain or any lack of *credulity.*

The word needed is *credibility.*

A journalist in the *Evening Standard* writes, also incorrectly:

☐ The thought of Ashton and Skinner humbly praying for anything stretches my *credibility* to breaking point.

Since it is the writer's readiness to believe that is *stretched to breaking point*, the word needed here is *credulity* not *credibility.*

crescendo

Wrong use: *The applause rose to a crescendo. Crescendo* is an Italian word meaning 'growing'. As used in music it denotes a gradual increase in volume, not the point at which the greatest volume is reached. *A crescendo of applause* is acceptable, but applause rises to a *climax.*

criteria

This is a plural noun and should take a plural verb. *A criteria* is wrong. The singular is *criterion.* (See also **phenomenon, bacteria, data.**)

critic/critique

Critic means 'a person who criticises'. *Critique* means 'a piece of criticism'. *Critique* is found as a verb in American English, but its use was condemned by 93% of the 136 members of the Usage Panel questioned by William and Mary Morris for the *Harper Dictionary of Contemporary Usage* (Harper & Row, 1975).

curb/kerb

Curb is always used as the verb, and also as the noun when it has to do with checking or restraining: *to place a curb on one's expenditure.* The metaphor comes from the strap that passes under the jaw of a horse. For the edge of the pavement or the raised edge round a hearth, British English usually uses the spelling *kerb*, though *curb* is not incorrect. It is, indeed, the older form, and is still used in America. Similarly, *kerbstone* or *curbstone.*

currant/current

Currant is a dried fruit. *Current* is the flow of water, electricity, air, etc.

d

dare

1 When *dare* means 'to challenge' it is followed by a personal object and the infinitive with *to*: I *dare* you to do it. The past tense and the past participle are *dared.* Third person singular, present tense: *he dares.*

2 When *dare* means 'to have the impudence' it is also followed by the infinitive with *to*, but has no personal object:

□ He *dares* to accuse me of dishonesty.

Past tense and past participle: *dared.* Third person singular, present tense: *he dares.*

3 When *dare* means 'to be bold enough' or 'to have the courage' it takes an infinitive without *to*. Third person singular, present tense: *dare*, not *dares*:

☐ He *dare* do all he says he will

☐ She *dare* not say what she thinks.

Past tense and past participle: *dared*, though the old-fashioned past tense *durst* is occasionally heard in dialects, especially with *not*.

4 dare say Should be written as two words (*I dare say he will come*), though it is sometimes printed as one when the stress is on *say*:

☐ A: He's a pleasant sort of fellow.

☐ B: I *daresay*, but I don't trust him.

Used only in the first person and the present tense.

dash

A punctuation mark (–). It is longer than a hyphen and separates parts of sentences, whereas a hyphen joins parts of words.

1 It separates a parenthesis from the main body of the sentence (see **parenthesis**). For this use two dashes are needed, one at each end:

☐ Those who knew Pop – and there were few in the town who did not know him – learnt to love him.

2 It attaches an afterthought or comment to the end of a sentence. The dash is used here only when the comment which follows is not a complete clause:

☐ Of the young men going into industry, many can scarcely write their name or read a simple sentence of English – a sad commentary on our educational system.

3 To attach a final summing-up to a sentence. Here the words that follow the dash may, and usually do, constitute a complete clause, or even several clauses:

☐ Friends, money, power, position – all these he had before he reached middle age.

4 To denote an abrupt change of subject, or a sudden abandonment of one construction and the substitution of another:

☐ You take the pin in the fingers so, and – but perhaps this doesn't interest you? (A A Milne, *The Boy Comes Home*)

5 To show that a sentence is unfinished or has been interrupted:

☐ A: I was about to say –

☐ B: I am not interested in what you were about to say.

6 To give warning that something startling or unexpected is about to follow:

☐ After I had resided at college seven years my father died and left me – his blessing. (Goldsmith)

7 To denote a pause between words or hesitancy in speaking:

☐ One – two – three – go!

☐ I – er – should like to say – er – how much we appreciate – er – this – er – generous offer.

Note: (a) A comma is never used together with a dash. When the dash is employed it supersedes any comma that would otherwise have been used. (b) On the use of a dash with a colon, see **colon 3**.

data

Really a Latin plural, meaning 'facts given' (the singular *datum* is rarely used), and a plural verb is therefore to be preferred (*What are the data?*), but in certain contexts it is permissible to treat the word as a collective denoting a single body of facts rather than a number of individual points (compare **agenda**) and to use a singular verb:

☐ *Is* that all the data we have?

☐ The data *is* rather meagre.

date

Colloquially, a social meeting or engagement, usually between a boy and a girl. Americans also use the word as a verb: *I told Alan that I wouldn't date him again.* It should not be used in serious writing.

dates

1 Use figures, not words. Thus *the year 1822*, not *the year eighteen twenty-two*, and *on May 25th*, not *on May the twenty-fifth*. When reading aloud, however, say 'eighteen twenty-two', 'May the twenty-fifth'.

2 When saying dates aloud, remember *the*:

☐ March 1st = 'March *the* first' (or '*the* first of March')

☐ 18th July = '*the* eighteenth of July' (or 'July *the* eighteenth').

3 In a letter, the date is written under the sender's address in the top right-hand corner. Dates may be written in any of the following ways: *17 July 1981*; *17 July, 1981*; *17th July 1981*; *July 17th, 1981*. Sometimes, the date is written in numbers only: *2/6/81*. This should be avoided, as confusion may arise – to an

Englishman *2/6/81* means *2 June 1981*; to an American it means *6 February 1981*.

4 Write *from 1753 to 1785*, or *1753–1785*, but not *from 1753 – 1785*.

5 For dates in historical essays, it may be necessary to write AD (anno Domini = in the year of our Lord) and BC (= before Christ). BC follows the number of the year and AD precedes it: *230* BC, AD *1030*.

6 An apostrophe may be used in the plural of dates, though modern usage tends to omit it: *the 1850's* or *the 1850s*. (The apostrophe is never used, of course, if the plural is spelt in words: *in the eighteen fifties*.) The same applies when the hundreds are omitted from the number of the year, and are assumed as understood: *The General Strike of '26, The General Strike of 26*.

7 In essays, always write *nineteenth century*, not *19th century*. When used before a noun, the name of a century usually has a hyphen: *nineteenth-century poetry*.

days of the week

The adverbial use without the preposition is normal when the name of the day is preceded by *last* or *next* (*I saw him last Friday*), but otherwise *on* must be used: *I will come on Friday in the afternoon. I will come Friday* is an Americanism which is sometimes found in spoken English.

dèbut

Note the accent.

deceptive/deceitful

Both words mean 'deceiving', but the difference between them is really a question of intent. Words or appearances that are *deceptive* may not be deliberately so but *deceitful* words or behaviour intentionally deceive.

decimate

To kill one in every ten, not to reduce to one-tenth.

defective/deficient

Defective means 'having a defect or fault'. *Deficient* means 'lacking'. Examples:

□ The car was *defective* when we bought it, even though it was new from the factory

□ He was *deficient* in many of the qualities needed to make him a good doctor.

defence
(noun) Spelt *-ce*. American spelling is *defense*. (Compare **licence/license**.)

defensible/defensive
Defensible means 'that may be defended'; *defensive* means 'intended, or serving, to defend.' Examples:
□ His action was not really *defensible*, although he tried very hard to justify it
□ The Italian team is famous for its *defensive* football.

defer
Defer means 'to put off or postpone'; past tense and past participle *deferred*, noun *deferment*:
□ The judge *deferred* sentencing until the following day.
Defer to means 'to give way to; show respect for'; noun *deference*, adjective *deferential*:
□ My advice to you, young man, is to *defer to* your elders.
The *r* is doubled in the past participle, past tense and present participle: *deferred, deferring*. For the general rule, see **spelling 6**.

deficient
See **defective/deficient**.

definite/definitive
A *definite* proposal is one made in clear and unmistakable terms; a *definitive* proposal is a final one that will not be modified, and therefore must be accepted or rejected as it stands.

delusion
See **allusion/delusion/illusion**.

demur
Followed by *to* or *at*. It means 'to object to something':
□ Several members *demurred at* the suggestion that he should join the club.
This is a formal word.
The *r* doubles in the past tense, past participle and present participle: *demurred, demurring*. See **refer**.

denotation
See **connotation**.

dénouement
A word borrowed from the French and sometimes found without an accent in English. The *dénouement* ('unknotting') of a story, plot

or play is the moment when everything becomes clear and the mystery is revealed.

depend (on)

The *on* is usually inserted if the subject is any other word than *it*:

☐ Are we going away for a whole month this year? – It *depends* whether we can afford it,

but:

☐ That *depends on* whether we can afford it.

It all depends (without any further specification of what it depends on) may be acceptable in speech but should not be used in writing.

dependant/dependent

Dependant is a noun for a person who depends on another for his home and food. *Dependent* (*on*) is an adjective meaning 'depending on'. An immigrant will want to bring all his *dependants* (his wife, children, etc) into his new country. His *dependants* are *dependent* on him for support.

deprecate/depreciate

A common mistake is to use *deprecate* when *depreciate* is required. *Deprecate* means 'to express disapproval of':

☐ He *deprecated* the use of such extravagant language.

Depreciate means 'to belittle, lessen':

☐ Those who were jealous of his success always *depreciated* his achievements.

desert/dessert

Desert has two meanings: as a noun: *the Sahara Desert* and as a verb meaning 'to abandon'. *Dessert* is the sweet course (fruit or cake) at the end of a meal.

desiccated

Note the spelling, a single *s* and a double *c*. The word means 'dried up' as in *desiccated coconut*.

despite

Followed by no preposition. *Despite of* is incorrect. The idiomatic expressions are *in spite of repeated warnings* and *despite repeated warnings*.

dessert

See **desert/dessert**.

detour

Has no acute accent.

develop

No *e* at the end. Similarly *development.* No doubling of *p* before a suffix: *developed, developing, developer.* (For the general rule, see **spelling 6.**)

device/devise

The noun is spelt with a *c*, the verb with an *s*. (See also **practice/practise.**)

dice See next entry.

die/dye

Die (verb) means 'to cease to live; expire'; *dies, dying, died.*
Dye (verb) means 'to colour'; *dyes, dyeing, dyed.*
Die (noun), the old singular of *dice*, is now used only in the expression *the die is cast.* In other contexts *dice* is used as both singular and plural. *Die* meaning 'a stamp for embossing paper, or making a coin or medal', has the plural *dies.*

differ

We differ *with* someone when we do not agree with him, but we would say that our views differ *from* his. The past tense form and past participle are both *differed.* (For the general rule, see **spelling 6.**)

different(ly)

1 Followed by *from* or *to* but not *than. Different to* is often heard in speech and sometimes seen in print, and is becoming more acceptable. Before a clause: *different* from *what it used to be* not *different than it used to be.*

2 *Different* has certain syntactic peculiarities. In the first place, when used after a verb it can be preceded by the adverb *no*, which can be added only to the comparatives of other adjectives and adverbs:

□ The position today is *no different* from what it was two years ago

□ I shall treat her *no differently* from anyone else.

Secondly, in negative statements and in questions, though *very* is not impossible, it usually follows the comparative degree of other adjectives and adverbs, and takes *much*:

□ The weather today is not *much different* from what it was yesterday

□ Is the position today *much different* from what it was six months ago?

3 *Think different*, when it means not think in a different way but have different thoughts, is certainly correct:
□ I used to hold that opinion, but now I *think different.*
(See also **adverb or adjective?**)

digraph
See **diphthong**.

diphtheria
Notice the *ph* in the spelling.

diphthong
1 Note the *ph* in the spelling.
2 Diphthong and digraph The *æ* as in *Julius Cæsar* is not a diphthong. It should be called a *digraph* (ie two letters written as one). In pronunciation it has the value of a simple vowel, like that in *me*, *tea*, etc. *Diphthong* is a phonetic term; that is to say, it refers not to written symbols, but to sounds, and is used to describe two vowel sounds which are pronounced so rapidly one after the other that they merge together. Thus the sound in *mouse* begins with a similar vowel sound to that in *far* or *master*, and finishes with that in *do*. The plural *mice*, again, begins with a similar vowel sound to that in *far* or *master* but finishes with that in *ease*. In spelling, a diphthong may be represented by two separate letters (as in *mouse*, *house*, *chair*), or by only one (as in *mice*, *fame*, *cake*).

diplomacy
The management of a country's interests overseas by its ambassadors and diplomats posted abroad. The word has the extended meaning of 'the art of dealing with people tactfully'. Similarly, a *diplomatic person* is a tactful one.

discomfiture
The writer of this letter to *The Daily Telegraph* incorrectly uses *discomfiture* as a synonym of *discomfort*:
□ . . . I 'ventilated' this topic in your columns over a year ago together with criticisms of the bus-like *discomfiture* of the seats in the new first-class air-conditioned stock.
Discomfiture means 'embarrassment, frustration of one's plans'.

discover/invent
We *discover* something which already exists but is not yet known:
□ Columbus *discovered* America.
We *invent* when we create something that never existed before:
□ Who *invented* the bicycle?

discreet/discrete

Discreet means 'tactful; careful':

☐ She's a very *discreet* person. Your secret is safe with her.

Discrete means 'separate; detached': *two discrete parts.*

discuss/discus

Discuss is a verb and is spelt with a double *s* at the end. A *discus* (one final *s*) is a round object thrown by athletes.

disgusted

We are disgusted *with* a person and disgusted *at* or *with* a sight, a fact or an occurrence. *Disgusted by* is principally used after the passive: *He was disgusted by their behaviour.*

disinterested/uninterested

Wrong use:

☐ When I was telling him about my holiday, he fell fast asleep so it was obvious that he was *disinterested.*

The word required is *uninterested. Disinterested* means 'having no personal advantage to gain'. *Uninterested* means 'unwilling to give attention to; bored'. A judge should be *disinterested* in a case he is trying: he should not be *uninterested.*

dispel

In the past tense, past participle and present participle, the *l* is doubled: *dispelled, dispelling.* For the rule, see **spelling 6**.

dispersal/dispersion

Dispersal means 'the act or process of dispersing'; *dispersion* is the resultant state or situation. We speak of the *dispersal* of a crowd by the police (ie 'the scattering' or 'breaking up'), but:

☐ It was difficult to trace all the members of the family, owing to their *dispersion* over the various parts of the country (ie the fact that they lived *dispersed*).

dissociate

Use *dissociate* rather than *disassociate* as the opposite of *associate.*

distinct/distinctive

Distinct means 'clearly perceivable'; *distinctive* means 'peculiar to, or characteristic of, one particular thing': *A distinct smell of petrol,* but *Petrol has a distinctive smell* (ie one which distinguishes it from anything else).

distinguish

1 Meaning 'tell apart' When *distinguish* means 'to tell apart' or 'to discern a difference' the construction is either *distinguish*

followed by a plural object, or *distinguish one from the other*:
□ The twins were so much alike that you could scarcely *distinguish them*,
or:
□ . . . that you could scarcely *distinguish one from the other*.
The second is to be preferred.
2 Meaning 'make a distinction' *Distinguish between* is used when the verb means 'to make a distinction':
□ Courts of law should not *distinguish between* persons on account of their race, colour or religion.
□ You must *distinguish between* those private schools which are run primarily for profit, and are therefore really business concerns, and those which are supported by religious bodies or philanthropic institutions.
3 Meaning 'make out' Another sense of *distinguish* is 'to make out or perceive': *It was so dark I could hardly distinguish the gatepost.*

distraught
Note the spelling with the unpronounced *gh*.

distrust
See **mistrust**.

do
1 As a 'substitute verb' As a 'substitute verb' (ie one standing in place of some other verb which has been used previously), *do* can be used only after an *active* voice, never after a passive. The following sentences are accordingly incorrect:
□ He was told that the money would have *to be paid back*, but he refused *to do so*
□ Many nineteenth-century novels were published in monthly numbers, as Dickens *did* in the case of *The Pickwick Papers*.
2 Refers back to an imagined verb Closely allied to this error is the use of *do* to refer back to a verb which the writer imagines he has used, but which actually he has not:
□ The landlord asked for the payment of a week's rent in advance, and the tenant agreed *to do so*.
By the time he gets to the end of his sentence the writer has forgotten the beginning. He is under the impression that he has used the verb *to pay*, but he has not; he has used the verbal noun *payment*.

3 Omission of do
☐ I prophesied he would fail, and he *did do.*
Omit *do.* Here *did* is not a substitute verb; it is the emphatic *did* (short for *and he did fail*). With compound tenses, if the non-finite part can be understood and carried over from the previous verb, the substitute *do* is often omitted: *Anyone who has lived in a large industrial town, as I have . . .* (not *as I have done*).
4 Never refers back to verb to be If it is necessary to use a full compound tense of the substitute *do,* it should be remembered that it can never refer back to the verb *to be*:
☐ Anyone who has been over twenty years in India, as I have done . . .
☐ Those who have been down a coal mine, as several of us here have done . . . .
In both these cases substitute *have been,* or merely *have.* The mistake is most frequent when *being* or *having been* somewhere is thought of as meaning 'going, living, staying, travelling, visiting', etc.
5 In inverted constructions Another illegitimate use of *do* is in inverted constructions of the type *If war comes, as come it may do.* Here *do* is redundant as it merely duplicates *come,* the clause *as come it may* being an inversion of *as it may come.* To use *do* as well as *come* is like saying *as come it may come.*
6 On *do have,* in such sentences as *Do you have any brothers or sisters?*; *He said he didn't have any money,* see **have 3**.

doctor/Dr
Use the abbreviation *Dr* only before a personal name, as *Dr Johnson.* Do not write *They sent for the Dr.* When the word is used as a substitute for the person's full name and not merely to denote his profession, spell it with a capital: *We must thank the Doctor for his interesting lecture* (ie *Dr So-and-so*).
If *Dr* is prefixed to a person's name the doctor's degree should not also be written after it. Write *E J White, MA, DSc,* or *Dr E J White, MA,* but not *Dr E J White, MA, DSc.*
(For the punctuation of *Dr,* see **abbreviations 2d**.)

documentary
(noun) A film which gives a factual account of a real-life situation or activity, eg *Life in the Scottish Highlands, The Drug Problem, Teenage Unemployment, Farming in Yorkshire.*

Doomsday/Domesday

Doomsday for the day of judgement, but *Domesday Book*, the record of ownership of land in England, made by William I in 1086.

double negative

Few will be guilty of perpetrating the more obvious type of double negative, like *I haven't never been there*; more are likely to be caught by the semi-negative adverbs *hardly, scarcely, barely* which, like the full negative, cannot be combined with another negative word:

☐ They have *not* been here for *hardly* an hour

☐ There was *no one, scarcely,* who could hear what he said.

Amend to *They have been here* and *There was scarcely anyone.*

Certain double negatives, however, have become recognised idioms:

☐ I shall *not* stay *unless* I can help it

☐ I should *not be surprised* if it *doesn't* rain before the day is out.

(See **surprise**.)

doubt

1 Verb *I doubt* whether (*or* if) *he is honest.* (Not *that*, nor *as to whether.*)

2 Noun

☐ There is no doubt *that* . . .

☐ I have no doubt *that* . . .

☐ I have my doubts *about* it/*about* his honesty

☐ I have my doubts *whether* he is honest. (Not *as to whether.*)

doubtful

☐ It is doubtful *whether* he can do it (or *if he can do it*).

☐ I am doubtful *about* doing it.

☐ I am doubtful *of* the outcome.

dowry

So spelt, not *dowery.*

downstair/downstairs

See **upstair/upstairs**.

Dr

See **doctor/Dr**.

draft/draught

Draft: *a draft* of money, of soldiers, etc; *make a rough draft*; *to draft* a bill, a document, etc.

Draught: *a draught of water* (or any other kind of drink); *the draught of a ship*; *beer sold on draught*; *to exclude the draught* (from a

room, etc); *play draughts*; *a draughtsman*.
Draft is the preferred spelling in American English for all meanings.

drama

A usually serious play for the theatre, radio or TV. Also correctly used to denote plays of all kinds (comedy, tragedy, tragicomedy, farce, etc) collectively, as in *A History of English Drama*; *a course of lectures on eighteenth-century drama*. Incorrectly (though popularly) used to describe a play characterised by sensation, thrills and strong emotional appeal. This last should be called a *melodrama*.

draught

See **draft/draught**.

dreamt/dreamed

See **past tense and participle: regular or irregular form?**

drunk

The past participle of the verb *to drink*, but not the past tense, which is *drank*. It is incorrect to say:
□ He *drunk* the lemonade.
The correct verb forms are *He has drunk* and *He drank*.
As an adjective *drunk* is used only after a verb:
□ They were *drunk*.
Drunken is the correct word in front of a noun:
□ A crowd of *drunken* teenagers smashed the shop windows.
As a noun *a drunk* ('a person who is drunk') is permissible colloquially and in informal writing. Use *drunkard* more formally.

due (to)

1 Due to or owing to? It is still incorrect, although quite frequent even in educated use, to use *due to* as a compound preposition to introduce an adverb phrase of reason, as is done in the following sentences:
□ *Due to* illness, he was unable to go on his holiday
□ Many trains were late, *due to* the fog
□ *Due to* the state of the ground, the match has been postponed.
Either *owing to* or *because of* should have been used. *Due* is an adjective; therefore *due to* can be used only:
a As a complement to a verb, usually some part of the verb *to be*:
□ His absence is *due to* illness
□ The accident was *due to* the driver's failing to give a signal.

b Following a noun, and introducing an adjectival construction which qualifies that noun:
□ Mistakes *due to* carelessness may have serious consequences
□ A power failure, *due to* a fault in the cable, brought all the machinery to a standstill.
These may be regarded as ellipses of *which are due to carelessness* and *which was due to a fault in the cable* (ie of adjective clauses) and are therefore really another form of the predicative use.
2 Due to or entitled to? A person is *entitled*, not *due*, to something to which he has a right: *You are* entitled *to one new share for every two that you already hold* (not *you are due to one new share*).
3 *Due for* is recognised as idiomatic in sentences of the type:
□ Our salary scales are *due for* revision in the New Year
□ I am *due for* promotion to a higher grade in September.

dumb

In the sense of 'stupid', an Americanism, not recognised in British English. Etymologically it has no connection with the normal English word *dumb*. It is the German *dumm*, meaning 'stupid', introduced into America in the speech of German immigrants in the latter part of the last century, and then spelt *dumb* by analogy, or confusion, with the word meaning 'unable to speak'.

dwelt/dwelled

See **past tense and participle: regular or irregular form?**

dye

See **die/dye**.

e

eg

See **ie/eg**.

each

1 As an adjective When used as an adjective, *each* is singular; the noun it qualifies must therefore be referred to by a singular pronoun or possessive adjective, and it takes a singular verb: *Each person has a special seat allocated to* him, hasn't he? (not *them, haven't they?*) In conversation, however, it is common to hear *each* used with the plural, even by educated people.

2 As a pronoun When it is a pronoun it is always singular if it has no antecedent (*Each has his own ideas on the subject*), but if it refers back to an antecedent it may be either singular or plural, according to circumstances:

a When the antecedent is plural, *each* is also plural:

☐ The children *each have* a special task allotted to them.

b When the antecedent consists of two or more singular nouns which *each* individualises, the verb is usually plural:

☐ My wife and I *each subscribe* £10 a year,

but a singular verb is not impossible if the intention is to differentiate:

☐ The rural south and the industrial north *each has* its attractions for the tourist.

c When the antecedent consists of two plural nouns, each of which is referred to separately and individually, then *each* is plural:

☐ The French and the Germans *each claim* the territory.

3 Each of us, etc When *each* is used in the form *each of us/you/them/the passengers*, etc special care must be taken. The singular is still necessary in the sentence proper:

☐ *Each* of the men *has* been given his instructions

☐ *Each* of the successful candidates *was* presented with a certificate

An appended 'tag' question may be either singular or plural: if *each* individualises, it is singular:

☐ *Each* of the successful candidates *was* presented with a certificate, *wasn't he*?

but if it is collective it takes a plural tag:

☐ *Each* of us put 50p in the collection, *didn't we*?

4 Following a pronoun When *each* follows the pronoun (*we each, you each, they each*), verbs, pronouns and possessive adjectives, in both main sentence and tag, agree with the plural pronoun:

☐ *We each have* our problems, *haven't we*?

5 On the incorrect *between each*, see **between 2**.

each other

1 Each other or one another? The one-time 'rule' that *each other* can refer only to two, and that for more than two *one another* must be used, is no longer strictly observed. *The three men distrusted each other* is now accepted as correct.

2 The possessive The possessive always has the apostrophe before the *s* (*each other's*). The noun that follows the possessive is singular if each of the persons in question has only one of the things concerned: *They stayed in each other's house, borrowed each other's car, took each other's photograph*, etc.

3 Usage *Each other* may be used as the object or the indirect object of a verb:

☐ They saw *each other*

☐ They gave *each other* a present,

or it may be governed by a preposition:

☐ They have a high regard *for each other*

☐ They write *to each other* every week,

but it cannot be used as the subject of a verb, so these sentences are incorrect:

☐ They had no idea that *each other* knew the secret

☐ We thought *each other* was joking.

Amend to *They each had no idea that the other knew the secret*; *we each thought the other was joking.*

Similarly it is quite idiomatic for *each other*, when used as the object of a verb or a preposition, to be followed by an infinitive with an adverbial function:

☐ They helped *each other to* mend their bicycles,

but it cannot be followed by an infinitive to which it is the subject:

☐ They waited for *each other to* go first.

Amend to *Each waited for the other to go first.*

easy/easily

The usual adverb is *easily*, as in *I can do that easily*; *we found the house quite easily. Easy*, however, is idiomatic in the expressions *go easy, take things easy* and *easy come, easy go.* It is the adjective that is found in compounds with a participle, like *an easy-going attitude.*

eatable/edible

Mushrooms are *edible*, toadstools are not; but even things which are edible may sometimes be uneatable because of their condition, eg mushrooms which have been burned in the cooking, meat which is tough, or bread which has become stale. *Eatable* refers to palatability, *edible* to what may, normally, be eaten.

economic/economical

Economical has to do with saving: *the most economical method. Economic* means 'connected with the science of economics: relating to trade, commerce, the production and distribution of wealth, etc': *economic problems, a period of economic expansion.*

edible

See **eatable/edible.**

edifice

A rather pretentious word. In all ordinary contexts use *building.* Permissible figuratively if the suggestion is slightly scornful or derogatory: *Hitler's elaborate edifice of the Third Reich.*

editorial

Not the front-page news in a newspaper, but the main article found on the inside pages which discusses news items in greater depth and gives the views of the editor. Alternatives are *leading article* or *leader*:

□ The leader in *The Times* today makes a persuasive case for raising interest rates and devaluing the pound.

educational/educative

Educational work: work in connection with education (it may be administrative, organising or actual teaching). *Educative* work: work which educates those who undertake it. An *educational* tour: one arranged for the purposes of educating. An *educative* tour: one that results in educating those who take part in it, though it may not have been arranged with that object in view. An *educational* (not *educative*) organisation, body, institution, system, etc; *educational* (not *educative*) reforms; an *educative* (not *educational*) experience.

education(al)ist Use either word.

e'er/ere

E'er is short for *ever*: *ere* means 'before'. Neither word has any place in modern writing, except as an archaism or for humorous effect.

effect

See **affect/effect.**

effective/efficient/efficacious

Effective means 'capable of effecting (ie bringing about) a desired result', as *an effective method of preventing smuggling.*

Efficient means 'giving satisfactory results' as *an efficient heating system.*

Efficacious is used mainly of remedies, medicines, medical and surgical treatment, etc: *efficacious in cases of fever.*

egoist/egotist

Egoist: a selfish person; one who puts his own interests first. *Egotist*: a self-centred person; one who is continually speaking of himself, or trying to attract attention to himself. The distinction between these two words is, however, a very fine one and they are often used interchangeably.

either

1 With singular verb *Either of them/us/you* can be used only of two, and it always takes a singular verb even if the two groups concerned are each plural:

☐ If *either* of you *cares* to call, I shall be in this evening

☐ Both the management and the workers have so far remained firm, but the Minister is always ready to help if *either* of them *requests* him to do so.

2 When requiring a different verb With *either . . . or* the verb is singular if the correlated terms are singular, plural if the correlated terms are plural. If each of the terms requires a different verb, either in number or person, then it is usual to use the form that will go with the second of them:

☐ *Either* he *or* I *am* to go.

3 Position On the correct position of *either . . . or*, see **correlatives**.

4 Either and both *Either* in the sense of 'one *and* the other' differs from *both* in that it thinks of each separately (and therefore, if used as a subject, takes a singular verb), whereas *both* thinks of them together. Its use is restricted to those things where the two are complementary, the existence of the one implying the existence of the other, as *either side*, *either end*, *either hand*. We cannot say *Either son distinguished himself.*

eke out

The correct meaning is 'to make something, of which there is an insufficient supply, go further by adding something else to it or by supplementing it with something else'. If there is insufficient butter we may *eke it out* with margarine. Further points to notice are:

1 Subject The subject of *eke* is always a personal one; it cannot be the name of the thing that is added. For example, the margarine does not *eke out* the butter.

2 Object The object must be the thing that is insufficient, and is added to or supplemented.

3 Wrong use *Eke out* does not mean 'to use frugally or stretch (something) with difficulty further than it will conveniently go'. If we have only enough milk for twelve cups of tea we do not *eke it out* amongst twenty by putting less in each.

elder/eldest

1 Of close family relations Used only of close family relations, eg sons, daughters, sisters, brothers. It cannot be followed by *than*, and if used after a verb must be preceded by *the*:

□ He was *the eldest* of the three sons

□ She is *the elder* of the two;

but not:

□ Of Jane and Susan, Susan is *elder*,

or:

□ Susan is *elder* than Jane.

2 When implying age or experience There are also the expressions *an elder statesman* (one respected on account of his long experience) and, in the plural, *one's elders*, implying a considerable difference in age (usually as between children and adults). The expression *one's elders and betters* implies that one's moral character improves as one becomes older:

□ Little children shouldn't be rude to their *elders and betters*.

3 As a noun alone The noun *elders*, denoting certain officers in some churches, has no connection with age, but rather with the exercise of predominantly spiritual responsibilities. An *elder* could be, say, 30 years old.

elevator

British English speaks of a *grain elevator*, but a *lift* for passengers. Americans use *elevator* for both.

elicit/illicit

These words are often confused, as in:

□ And the question: 'What do you call a man who's lucky in love?' *illicits* the inevitable reply: 'A bachelor.' (*Guardian*)

It is not the word *illicit* which is needed here, but *elicit*. *Elicit* (verb) means 'to draw out (an answer, a statement)'. *Illicit* (adjective) means 'not legal'. Examples:

□ All the detective's attempts to *elicit* the truth failed

□ The man still denied any knowledge of the *illicit* sale of drugs.

(See also **illegal/illegitimate/illicit**.)

eliminate

Eliminate, except in slang or humorously, does not mean 'to destroy or kill', or the various associated senses that have been given to it in recent times, as in:

☐ Stalin *eliminated* anyone who opposed his policy.

It means 'to thrust out', or 'to get rid of', but not by killing. Of the competitors who enter for a race, a certain number are *eliminated* in the preliminary heats, and we *eliminate* from a list those names or items which we no longer wish to consider. Consider also the expression *to arrive at the answer by a process of elimination.*

Eliminate is sometimes misused for *exclude. Exclude* means 'to shut out completely'. People who are deliberately left out of a football team from the first are *excluded*; those whose names are admitted to a preliminary list but then deleted are *eliminated.*

élite

Note the acute accent. Similarly, *élitist.*

else

1 Followed by than *Else* is followed by *than* not *but*: *nothing but* and *nothing else than* are the alternatives:

☐ I insist that you tell me *nothing but* the truth

☐ He wanted *nothing else than* to go to sleep but he had to finish his essay.

Nothing else but is incorrect.

2 Possessives The possessive forms are: *anyone else's, no one else's, someone else's, who else's, anyone else's,* etc, not *everyone's else, anyone's else,* etc: *Who else's house have you called at today?*

3 Objective For the direct object the tendency is to use *who* rather than *whom*:

☐ *Who else* did you see?

☐ *Who else* have you given the information to?

4 Incorrect use as conjunction *Else* is often used incorrectly, as in *We shall have to hurry, else we shall miss the train. Else* is an adverb, not a co-ordinating conjunction. In sentences of this type *or else* (or simply *or*) must be used.

elusive

Sometimes misused for *illusory* (for which, see **allusion/delusion/illusion**.) *Elusive* is the adjective which comes from the verb *to elude*, and means 'not easily caught' or 'constantly escaping one':

☐ The police had great difficulty recapturing the escaped prisoner. He was very *elusive.*

The word can also be used metaphorically, as in *an elusive idea, an elusive concept.*

embarrass

A commonly mis-spelt word. Note the double *r* and double *s*.

emend

See **amend/emend.**

eminent/imminent

Eminent means 'outstanding, distinguished': *an eminent surgeon, an eminent sculptor, an eminent lawyer, a man known for his eminent kindness. Eminence* (noun) is *won, reached* or *gained*: *He won eminence as a physicist.*

Imminent means 'about to happen, threatening'. A heavy black sky, rolling thunder and a strong breeze show that a storm is *imminent.*

emolument(s)

When the financial rewards of an office or position come from various sources and are of various kinds, they may be correctly referred to collectively as the *emoluments* of the office. It is a formal word. It should not be used merely as a substitute for *salary*, which is paid from one source, usually only in money.

empathise

Correctly, the meaning is 'to identify oneself, totally, often in meditation, with an object, idea or person'. It is widely used today, particularly in America, as a more emphatic form of *sympathise.* (See also **sympathy/sympathise.**)

enable

See **allow/enable.**

end up

End up should be used (if it is used at all) only when the reference is to the final stage of a progression or series:

□ He entered the army as a Private and *ended up* a Brigadier

□ He started as an office boy and *ended up* as a director of the firm

□ If you go on like that you'll *end up* in prison.

But *The story* ends (not *ends up*) *with the discovery of the lost heir, and his marriage to the heroine*; *the discussion* ended *in deadlock.*

endow/endue

Endow can be used of material and non-material things: *He was endowed with great wealth*; *he was endowed with wisdom. Endue* can only be used of non-material things: *The child was endued with good sense and patience*. Both words are formal, especially *endue*, and are generally used in the passive.

enervate

Enervate is often used incorrectly:

□ As a useful and energetic chief executive for the Isle of Anglesey, the late Peredur Lloyd brought to his job a distinctive style and verve which were refreshing and *enervating*. (*Liverpool Daily Post*)

The word required is not *enervate* but *invigorate* which means 'to fill with life and energy'.

Enervate means 'to weaken', 'to destroy strength': *The attack of malaria left him enervated*. Clearly Peredur Lloyd's style and verve could not be both refreshing and enervating. The word is formal.

enhance

When used in the active voice, *enhance* must have an abstract noun for its object, and when in the passive voice an abstract noun for its subject:

□ This discovery has *enhanced* his reputation

□ His reputation has been *enhanced* by this discovery.

The following are incorrect: *It has enhanced him in reputation*, and *He has been enhanced in reputation*.

enormity

This is a word which is often misused as a synonym for *greatness* or *great amount*. A journalist from *The Observer* falls into this trap:

□ According to the players, they were up-tight for an hour and sat there like survivors of a blitz, unaware of the *enormity* of their achievement.

Similarly, a journalist from *The Times*:

□ . . . others tempted to become large-scale manufacturers and traffickers might well consider the risk worth taking, bearing in mind the *enormity* of the awards which could accrue.

The true meaning of *enormity* is 'outrageousness, great wickedness', as in *the enormity of their crime*.

enquire/inquire

The verb is now usually spelt *enquire*. *Inquire* is more common in America. *Enquiry* (noun) is a request for information and is more often used in the plural, as:

□ All *enquiries* to be made at the office.

Inquiry (noun) is an investigation, as *a court of inquiry, an inquiry into the causes of an accident.*
The agent-noun is usually spelt *enquirer.*
Do not use *enquire* if *ask* will do.

ensure/insure
We *ensure* (ie make certain of) the success of an undertaking, and take measures to *ensure* that instructions or regulations are carried out. We *insure* our lives, property, etc, and *insure against* death, accident, fire, loss of income, etc. The increasingly favoured American spelling is *insure* for both meanings.

entertain
We *entertain* a person *to* a meal, but *at* a hotel or restaurant.

enthuse
This verb (a back-formation from *enthusiasm*) is usually used with *over.* It is colloquial and should never be used in formal English.

entrée
Do not omit the accent in writing.

envelope
(noun) The verb is *envelop* (no *e* at the end).

envious/enviable
Envious means 'feeling or showing envy'. *Enviable* means 'likely to arouse envy'. This journalist from the *Coventry Evening Telegraph* has confused the two:
□ Bob's *envious* lifestyle centres around two completely different worlds.
Obviously, *enviable* is the word needed here.

equable/equitable
Equable means 'steady, regular, with not much variation'. A person of *equable* temperament is calm and not easily ruffled or upset. An *equable* climate is agreeable and much the same throughout the year.
Equitable means 'reasonable; fair'. We often speak of *coming to an equitable arrangement*, which means 'a friendly arrangement, fair to both parties'.

equally
Two things are *as good as* each other, or they are *equally good*, but not *equally as good.* Note also:
□ The garment is *equally* useful for country *and* city wear (not *or*).
The slogan *some people are more equal than others* is logically

absurd, though widely used in political argument. There is, however, no objection to *a more equal distribution of wealth*, or:

☐ Wealth is now distributed *more equally* than it used to be.

Here *more equal*(*ly*) means 'approaching nearer to the idea conveyed by *equal*(*ly*)'. Compare *a fuller account* at **comparative 3**.

equitable

See **equable/equitable**.

erase/raze

Erase means 'to scrape or rub out':

☐ Do the accounts in pencil then any mistakes can be easily erased.

It can also be used figuratively:

☐ She tried to *erase* the painful thoughts from her memory.

The verb is not, however, sufficiently dramatic in meaning for this sentence from a newspaper:

☐ Yet another had been erased by bulldozers and rebuilt elsewhere in supposedly modern style . . . .

The verb needed here is *razed* which means 'to sweep away or destroy completely'. *Raze* is frequently found in literary passages in the phrase *raze to the ground*, as in:

☐ The invading army *razed* the once magnificient city to the ground.

Do not confuse *raze* with *raise*, which is pronounced the same. See **raise/rise**.

ere

See **e'er/ere**.

-ese

This suffix means 'the language of', as in *commercialese*, 'the language of commerce'. It is generally pejorative, suggesting that the type of language in question is full of jargon, written in a style of its own. *Officialese* is the language of bureaucrats and civil servants. Sir Ernest Gowers wrote *The Complete Plain Words* (revised by Sir Bruce Fraser) in an effort 'to improve official English'. Many of the entries in this book are concerned with *commercialese* and other *-eses*. See, for example, **beg, blueprint, consideration, event, inst, ult, occasion, operative, per, purge, rehabilitate, same**.

For more general information, see **journalese, jargon, clichés, abstract language, commercial jargon**.

Eskimo

This spelling (plural *-oes*) has now superseded the older *Esquimau*(*x*).

especially/specially

Specially means 'for this special purpose, or to this special end, and no other'; *especially* means 'particularly, to a degree beyond others'. Both the following sentences, therefore, are incorrect:

☐ I went there *especially* to see him

☐ There is a shortage of well-qualified teachers of most subjects, but *specially* of science and mathematics.

In the first sentence *specially* is needed, in the second *especially*.

Esquire/Esq

The abbreviation is becoming much less frequent in modern English. It is used in an address on an envelope, but remember:

1 *Mr* must not be used as well.

2 *Esq* must not be used unless the christian name or the initials precede the surname. If they are not known write *Mr Johnson*, not . . . *Johnson, Esq*.

3 Any letters denoting degrees, honours, etc follow the *Esq*: *J C Smith, Esq, MA*; *R A Mitchell, Esq, OBE*.

At one time *Esq* was very restricted in its application; then it became a courtesy mode of address for anyone (of the male sex, of course) above the social grade of a manual labourer. Fifty years ago a middle-class person might have felt affronted, or considered his correspondent guilty of a breach of etiquette, if he had received a letter addressed to *Mr* . . . . There is not the same feeling about it today. *Esq* is felt to be very formal and *Mr* . . . is much more widely used. (See also **letters**.)

euphemism/euphuism/euphony

Euphemism is the use of a more pleasant term for something that might be offensive or distressing if referred to by its real name. *Pass away* and *depart this life* are well-known euphemisms for *die*, *loo* is a modern euphemism for *toilet* and many of the milder oaths are euphemisms for swear words, or to avoid the profane use of the names of God and Christ. We are using a *euphemism* again when, instead of saying *Go to hell*, we say *Go to blazes* (hell fire). Today, people are no longer *fat* but *chubby*, *portly* or even *cuddly*. Morris, in the *Harper Dictionary of Contemporary Usage*, quotes this delightful letter:

☐ I used to think I was poor. Then they said it was self-defeating to think of myself as needy, that I was culturally deprived. Then they told me deprived was a bad image, that I was underprivileged. Then they told me that underprivileged wasn't used, that I was disadvantaged. I still don't have a dime – but I have a great vocabulary!

Euphuism is an affected and artificial style of writing like that adopted by John Lyly in his work *Euphues* (1579). It is characterised by alliteration, antithesis, and frequent allusion to natural history and mythology. It had something of a vogue in the late sixteenth and early seventeenth centuries.

Euphony, a term sometimes confused with one or the other of the above words, means 'pleasantness of sound'. We avoid combinations of words like *confirmation of this information* on grounds of *euphony*.

The adjectives are *euphemistic*, *euphuistic* and *euphonious/euphonic* respectively.

even

See **particularly 2** for the importance of its correct position in a sentence.

event

Wherever possible, use *if* instead of *in the event of*, which is usually just official jargon.

eventuate

A word to be avoided. Use *happen* or *occur*.

ever/-ever

1 Preceding or following a noun Until recently it was considered best to avoid such combinations as *the biggest ever*, *the best ever*, etc preceding or following a modified noun. Today, they are generally acceptable. Of course, it remains perfectly correct to rephrase a sentence such as:

☐ France is planning to stage shortly *the biggest ever* offensive against the rebels

in this way: . . . *the biggest offensive it has ever launched*.

2 As a compound adverb In informal expressions like *ever so much*, *ever so small*, etc the combination *ever so* (which must always be written as two words) has become a compound adverb modifying the adverb or adjective that follows it; it cannot be used by itself to modify a verb. *I enjoyed my holiday ever so* is incorrect, for there is nothing for *ever so* to modify. Say *ever so much*, or, better still, *very much*.

3 Words ending -ever *Whoever, whichever, whatever, whenever, wherever, however* are written as one word only when *-ever* is generalising:

□ *Whoever* wants it may have it
□ Take *whichever* you like
□ I know nothing *whatever* about it
□ It is going to be difficult *however* we do it.

(See also **however/how ever** and **whoever/who ever**.)

When *ever* is emphasising (ie when the expression means something like 'what on earth', 'how on earth', etc) two separate words must be used:

□ *Who ever* told you that?
□ *What ever* shall we do?
□ *Where ever* have you been?
□ *How ever* shall we do it?
□ *Why ever* did you say that?

every

Singular. Strictly, therefore, it takes a singular verb and must be referred to by a singular pronoun or possessive adjective: *Every person brought* his *lunch with* him (not *their . . . them*). It is, however, progressively more common to find this mistake today, even in educated people's written language.

every day/everyday

Use *everyday* (one word) only when adjectival, as *an everyday occurrence, everyday conversation.* In all other senses, use two words:

□ He comes here *every day*
□ I have seen him *every day* this week
□ *Every day* somebody dies.

everybody/everyone/everything

1 Singular words Like *every*, all these words are singular. They therefore take a singular verb and should be referred to by singular pronouns and singular possessive adjectives: *Everyone/everybody promised* he *would keep* his *word* (not *they . . . their*), although this 'rule' is regularly broken today.

2 In 'tag' questions In 'tag' questions, however, the plural is permissible for *everyone* and *everybody* when the statement that precedes it has a collective rather than a distributive sense:

□ *Everybody* can't be clever, can *they*?
□ *Everyone* present made a wild rush for the door, didn't *they*?
The tag for *everything* must always be singular:
□ *Everything* looked beautiful, didn't *it*?
□ *Everything* has gone wrong today, hasn't *it*?
3 Everyone/every one The compound *everyone* can be used only to refer to people. For things, two words are necessary:
□ She dusted the books and put *every one* back in its place
□ She bought a dozen eggs, and *every one* was bad
□ I've looked at six houses so far, and found something wrong with *every one* of them.
Even for people two words must be used when the sense is 'every single one':
□ *Every one* of these pupils has passed
□ He had five children, and *every one* of them has done well in the world.

evince

A formal verb which means 'to show that one possesses a certain quality' (eg intelligence, skill, knowledge, etc):
□ He is a student who *evinces* intelligence and the ability to think clearly.
Do not use the word simply as a synonym for *show*, as in *He evinced great pleasure in being asked to launch the ship.*

evocative/provocative

Evocative means 'raising memories or emotions'. *Provocative* means 'causing anger or interest':
□ The child's behaviour was deliberately *provocative* and his mother smacked him
□ Professor Green's lecture was deliberately *provocative* in order to stimulate a lively debate.
The writer from this sentence of the *Radio Times* has obviously confused the two:
□ Here is this famous song, so *provocative* of a long ago and lost England of fogs and gas-lit music halls . . . .
Evocative is the word needed here.

ex-

See **late/former/ex-**.

exceeding/excessive

Exceeding means 'very great' but *excessive* means 'too great'. The

adverbs *exceedingly* and *excessively* are very common:
☐ It was *exceedingly* good food and we all ate *excessively.*

except/excepting

1 With objective *Except* is a preposition, and is therefore followed by the objective case: *Everyone except* me *has been informed* (not *except I, he, she*, etc).

2 Meaning 'unless' *Except* in the sense of 'unless' is archaic. Do not say *I cannot do it except you help me.* Use *unless.*

3 Except for *Except* excludes a particular one, or particular ones, from a group or a more general category: *everyone except me, all the girls except Vera, soft fruits except cherries.* If we wish to modify a whole statement by making a reservation, then *except for* is used. It may be placed either before or after the statement:
☐ *Except for* a few small firms, the whole industry is participating in the scheme
☐ I am quite well now, *except for* a slight cold.
But:
☐ *Except for* your help we should have been in a difficult position
is incorrect. Here the word required is either *but for* or *without.*

4 Excepting *Excepting* is used as a preposition only when it is preceded by *not, always* or *without*: *not excepting the police, without excepting even the highest-placed officials, always excepting the officers.* In such a sentence as:
☐ We have won every match so far this season *excepting* that against Arsenal,
excepting is wrongly used for *except.*

excessive

See **exceeding/excessive.**

exclamation mark

(American *exclamation point.*) A punctuation mark (!).

1 After interjections It is used after interjections and certain onomatapoeic words which are meant to imitate a sudden, sharp sound:
☐ Ah! Oh! Bang! Crash! You stupid boy!

2 After how or what It is used after sentences which use *how* or *what* as exclamations to show surprise or indignation:
☐ *How* rude he is!
☐ *What* an awful mess!
An exclamatory intention on the part of the speaker or writer is

essential to justify the use of the exclamation mark. Merely having the grammatical form of an exclamation is not in itself enough. There seems no case for using an exclamation mark in this example:

□ What a pity you didn't let me know before.

3 After expression of strong feelings It is used after sentences where particularly strong feelings are expressed:

□ I don't ever want to visit that house again!

4 Use of more than one exclamation mark Be careful not to use exclamation marks too often or they lose their force. Two exclamation marks should never be used together (*!!*), nor should they be used with question marks, as in: *What do you think you're doing here?!!* This is usual only in very informal letters, comic strips, cartoons, etc.

exclude

See **eliminate**.

exhausting/exhaustive

Exhausting work exhausts (ie tires out) the person who does it; *exhaustive* work exhausts (ie says all there is to be said about) the subject. Thus if the sense to be expressed is 'very thorough', 'leaving no stone unturned', use *exhaustive*: *exhaustive inquiries*, *exhaustive research*, etc.

explicit/implicit

In an *explicit* statement, the meaning is clearly expressed and we are left in no doubt. *Implicit* means 'implied', 'not fully expressed' as *an implicit threat*.

extemporary

□ Some of the speech seems to have been delivered *extemporary*. (*The Observer*)

Is there such a word? Several dictionaries give it, as an adjective, with an adverbial equivalent *extemporarily*, and if either is to be used it is the adverb which is required here. But there is really no reason for either of them, since *extempore* can be used both adjectivally (*an extempore speech*) and adverbially (*he spoke extempore*). (See the next entry.)

extempore/impromptu

(See the preceding entry.) An *extempore* speech is one which the speaker has not prepared beforehand, but makes up as he goes along. An *impromptu* speech is one of which the speaker has received no previous notice, or which he has not contemplated making. An *impromptu* speech is necessarily *extempore*, but an *extempore* speech may not be *impromptu*.

extended/extensive

Extended means 'made longer, lengthened'. *Extensive* means 'wide-reaching, comprehensive'. Here are some examples:

☐ The meeting between the two politicians was *extended* by another day as they had nearly reached agreement

☐ The Minister consulted the *extensive* research which had been carried out, before he came to his decision.

extenuate

To make an offence seem less serious:

☐ Whatever he says now cannot *extenuate* his terrible crime.

Although the verb is not often used, the phrase *extenuating circumstances* (circumstances which partly excuse the offense) is commonly found:

☐ The prisoner's sentence was reduced as there were *extenuating circumstances*: at the time of the crime he had been taking drugs to combat depression.

exterminate

Means 'to destroy utterly', and can be applied only to the destruction of a whole race or species in a particular locality, not to the killing of one person or even of a few. We cannot say that a tyrant *exterminated* anyone whom he regarded as a rival, or that a considerable number of rabbits have been *exterminated*. The meaning can be extended to refer to the complete eradication of beliefs, ideas, disease, etc.

extra/extra-

When the word is an adjective meaning 'additional' write as a separate word: two *extra* copies. When it is an adverb, meaning 'beyond the normal', use a hyphen if it might be mistaken for the adjective, but not otherwise: *an extra-thick blanket*, which means something different from *an extra thick blanket*. But no hyphen is needed in:

☐ The blanket is *extra thick*

☐ He worked *extra hard*,

since no ambiguity results from its omission.

extreme

So spelt, not *extream*. Similarly *supreme*.

extrovert/introvert

Two psychological terms which have been adopted into standard usage. An *extrovert* is a lively, sociable person who is willing to participate in any event. An *introvert* is someone who is quiet, withdrawn and socially timid.

f

face up to

Face alone is generally sufficient (*face the facts*, *face a difficult task*), but *face up to* may occasionally suggest determination, and then it seems justifiable:

□ He is a person who will *face up to* the most difficult task.

fair

See **blond(e)**.

falsehood/falsity/falseness

Falsehood means 'untruth', in the abstract and general sense:

□ In the long run truth will conquer *falsehood*.

Falsity means 'the false nature of a particular thing': *to expose the falsity of a charge or accusation.*

Falseness means 'disloyalty, treachery': *the falseness of his supposed friend*, *falseness of heart*, etc.

familiar to/familiar with

Familiar to means 'known to (by)', as *His face is familiar to me*; *familiar with* means 'having a fairly good knowledge of', as I am *familiar with* the countryside. *He was familiar to me*: I recognised him as someone I had often seen. *He was familiar with me*: he treated me as though he knew me well; he was too friendly for the occasion. (Usually with a deprecatory sense.)

Note also: *He was familiar with me*: he assumed a greater degree of amorous or sexual intimacy than was proper:

□ Henry is getting far too *familiar with* George's wife.

far

Far better, but *better by far*, *by far the better*, *by far the best*.

Far and away the best/the better of the two is an accepted colloquialism. The plain comparative or superlative cannot be used; it must always be preceded by *the*.

On *few and far between*, see that heading.
As far as/so far as (a) To denote a destination or stage of progress:
□ They went with us *as far as* Bedford
□ I have considered having a car, but I haven't got *as far as* buying it yet.
(b) To denote the limits within which a statement holds good, or the degree to which it is to be understood:
□ You may do it *so far as* I am concerned
□ He will help you *as far as* he can.
In so far (as) is three words. Do not write *insofar as.*

farther/further

Always use *further* (a) when the sense is 'additional' (*further information, further evidence*), or 'in addition':
□ *Further*, the committee are of the opinion that the time is not right
□ Have you anything *further* to say?
and (b) when it is a verb meaning 'to advance or promote': *to further one's own interests.* As an adjective or adverb denoting distance, both are acceptable, but *further* is probably more common, though in the superlative *farthest* is commoner than *furthest*.

fatal/fateful

Fatal means 'leading to death or disaster'. *He struck the guard a fatal blow* (a blow which killed the guard); *a fatal decision* (one with disastrous consequences).
Fateful means 'controlled by fate for either good or bad ends':
□ That *fateful* day when I decided to join the army . . . .

favourite

Do not omit the *u*. The spelling *-or* is American.

feasible

It means 'possible' only in the restricted sense of 'able to be done':
□ Your suggestion is *feasible*, though it might be rather costly
□ Travel to Mars may become *feasible* by the end of this century.
It does not mean 'probable':
□ It seems *feasible* that travel to the moon will be commonplace by the end of this century.
This sentence is incorrect.

featuring

Wrong use:

☐ My favourite Shakespeare play is *The Merchant of Venice*, *featuring* Shylock, Antonio, Bassanio and Portia.
A term from film advertisements, and even there it is used of the actors, not the characters in the play. It is a piece of jargon which should be avoided in normal English.

February
It is a common spelling mistake to omit the first *r*.

fed up
A colloquialism which does not appear in formal or written English. In more informal contexts the idiom is *fed up with*, not *of*.

female/feminine
As a synonym for *woman*, *female* is incorrect. *Females under the age of twenty-five are eligible for the post*. Say *women*.
Female denotes the sex of the creature to which it is applied (*the female of the species*, *a female swan*) or some physical part of such a creature (*the female form*, *female organs*, etc) which has sexual characteristics.
Feminine means pertaining to, or such as one associates with, a woman: *feminine charms*, *a feminine style of writing*. (Charms and writing have no sex, so *female* cannot be used.) Say that a person is *of the female sex*, not *of the feminine gender*. Only words have gender.

feminine gender, feminine forms
See **gender in nouns**.

fetch/bring
Fetch means 'to go and get, and then bring back here', as in the sentence:
☐ Will you please *fetch* me my coat from the other room?
Bring means 'to cause to come with' or 'come with' (usually used when the person addressed is near the object to be brought):
☐ *Bring* me my glasses from the kitchen table (come with my glasses)
☐ *Bring* your dog in with you (cause your dog to come in with you).

fête
Do not omit the circumflex.

few
1 A few *A few* is positive in sense, and is opposed to *none*; *few* is negative, and is opposed to *many*. *A good few* is allowable

colloquially. The expression is of fairly recent origin, and has arisen by analogy with *a good many*. *Quite a few* is illogical, but is accepted as an understatement for 'a fair number'.

2 With relative clause Care is necessary when *one of the few* is followed by a relative clause. The verb of the relative clause should be plural, since it refers back to *few*, not to *one*:

☐ He is *one of the few* people in this country who *have* a knowledge of Japanese.

It must be admitted, however, that sometimes, despite grammar, the singular verb sounds more natural:

☐ He is *one of the few men alive* who *was* able to study the German official documents captured by the Allied armies.

In such cases, provided no ambiguity can result, it seems justifiable to disregard grammatical rules and use the singular.

few and far between

The meaning is 'few in number, and far between them'. It is correctly used in the sentences:

☐ This summer the fine days have been *few and far between*

☐ . . . huge tracts of wild moorland, where the villages are *few and far between*,

but when we get to statements like:

☐ Nowadays well qualified science teachers are *few and far between*,

or:

☐ There may still be some households where grace is said before each meal, but they are *few and far between*,

it is a meaningless cliché, *few* alone is all that is needed.

fewer

For the difference between *fewer* and *less*, see **less 1**.

fiancé/fiancée

The man a woman is to marry is her *fiancé* (masculine), the woman a man is to marry is his *fiancée* (feminine).

The words are not equivalent in meaning to *boyfriend/girlfriend*. They should be used only if the persons are actually engaged to be married.

finalise

An Americanism, though becoming more widely found in British English. *The project has now been finalised* is acceptable if the meaning is 'The project has now been finally agreed upon and can now be carried out'. It is wrong if the sense is 'The project has now been completed'.

firm/firmly

See **tight/tightly**.

first/firstly

Firstly should only be used in an enumeration of the points of an argument, a list of reasons, etc, to be followed by *secondly*, *thirdly*, etc; but even here *first* is to be preferred.

fish/fishes

(plural) *Fish* may always be used as the plural whether thought of individually or collectively. *Fishes* is a rarer plural and only used when thought of individually.

flammable

Means 'liable to catch fire'; has the synonym *inflammable* when used of the properties of materials. This use of *inflammable* is deprecated by the British Standards Institution. *Flammable* is to be preferred on warning labels as there is less likelihood of misunderstanding, as *inflammable* could be taken to mean 'not flammable'.

flaunt

A word often used incorrectly; a leading article in the *Evening News* spoke of *flaunting the law*, meaning 'openly defying the law'. But *flaunt* does not mean this. The word required is *flouting*. To *flaunt* means 'to display ostentatiously': *wealthy people flaunting their riches*. The mistake is a common one. Here is another example, this time from the *Guardian*:

□ The Government is under no obligation to place large contracts in the way of companies which . . . choose to *flaunt* guidelines . . . .

Again, *flout* is the word required.

flout See previous entry.

flu

An abbreviation of *influenza*. When the word is written, no apostrophe is needed to indicate the abbreviation.

focused

Spelt with a single *s*, not a double; also *focusing* not *focussing*. For general rule, see **spelling 6**.

folk

Do not use *folk* as a substitute for *people*: *A large number of folk were present*. Amend to *a large number of people*.

Folk is a collective noun, and there is no plural, though colloquially *the old folks* has come to be accepted when the reference is to one's own relatives: but a church or club arranges a treat for the old *folk* (not the old *folks*). For the possessive the apostrophe should go before the *s*: *an old folk's outing.*

foot

1 Plural Modern usage now accepts *foot* or *feet* as a term of measurement: *He is six foot four* or *He is six feet four.* Metrication is making the term less common.

2 Compound adjectives In compound adjectives the singular *foot* is always used: *a two-foot rule, a twelve-foot plank* (compare *a five-pound note, a ten-pence piece*).

3 As an adverb Used adverbially to modify an adjective, *feet* is the correct word if the adjective follows a verb. Before a noun, the adjective and adverbial qualification usually combine to make a double compound, and *foot* is used: *The path was eight feet wide, a house approached by a path eight feet wide,* but *an eight-foot-wide path.*

for

See **because, for or as?**

forbear/forebear

Forbear is a verb (past tense and participle *forbore, forborne* respectively), and means 'to hold back from doing something'. *Forebear* is a noun and means 'ancestor' (usually in the plural: *one's forebears*). Both words are rather old-fashioned and formal.

forbid

Past tense and participle *forbade, forbidden* respectively. Forbid a person *to do* something, not *from* doing it.

forbidding/foreboding

Sometimes confused as in this incorrect instance:

☐ With its heavy iron gates and high, grey stone walls, the house had a *foreboding* appearance.

Forbidding is the word required, since it is an appearance which seemed to *forbid* or discourage any approach or entry. *Foreboding* means 'indicating or suggesting (something unpleasant) in advance': *the heavy, black clouds, foreboding a storm*; *a hard face, foreboding cruelty of character.*

forego/forgo

Forego means 'to go before'. Only the participles are in common use: *the foregoing facts, a foregone conclusion. Forgo* means 'to do without something to which one is entitled': *to forgo one's holiday.* Be careful over the spelling of the participles and the compound tenses: there is no *e*: *I am forgoing my holiday this year*; *he has forgone his holiday.* The past tense is *forwent*, but it is rarely used.

former

See **late/former/ex-**.

friend

See **acquaintance**.

frightful/frightfully

See **awful/awfully**.

frolic

When adding suffixes, add a *k*: *frolicked, frolicking.*
Similarly *panic, traffic*, etc. For the rule, see **spelling 7**.

-ful

Words ending in *-ful*, like *cupful, spoonful, handful*, have the plural *cupfuls, spoonfuls, handfuls*, not *cupsful* or *cups-full*, etc. *Two cupfuls* of milk is a measure (probably only one cup is used, twice over); *two cups full* of milk means two separate cups, each one full.
The general sense will determine whether we write *-ful* or *full* (sing), *-fuls* or *-s full* (plural).

□ He dropped a *bottle full* of lemonade

– it was the bottle, which happened to be full of lemonade, which he dropped, but:

□ He drank a *bottleful* of lemonade

– he drank the contents of a full bottle.

full stop

(American *period*.) A punctuation mark (.).
It indicates the end of a sentence. Any sentence which follows begins with a capital letter:

□ He left the hotel. It was raining outside.

If a sentence ends with a question mark or exclamation mark, no full stop is added:

□ Do you want to come with us tomorrow?

On the place of the full stop in conjunction with inverted commas, see **inverted commas 1**.
On the use of the full stop in abbreviations, see **abbreviations 2**.

fulsome

Use this word with care. It has nothing to do with *full. Fulsome* means 'excessive; insincere', as in *fulsome praise*, *fulsome flattery*, etc.

furnish

This is sometimes used unidiomatically, as in:

□ We shall be pleased to *furnish* you any information you may require.

The verb *to furnish* does not take an indirect object. We *furnish* a person *with* something. But in any case *furnish* is the wrong verb here. Use *supply you with*, *send you* or *give you*.

further

See **farther/further**.

g

gambit/gamut

Strictly, a *gambit* is an opening move in chess, in which a pawn or a piece is sacrificed to gain advantage later in the game. The word is used figuratively to mean any initial move as in:

□ Her opening gambit was to attempt to bribe the official.

Gamut means 'the whole scale or scope of a thing'. The whole gamut of emotions ranges from elation to despair, for instance. A journalist from the *Guardian* has confused these two words:

□ We covered the whole gambit of banking from cashiering, customers, current accounts and deposits.

Gamut and not *gambit* is the word needed here.

gamble/gambol

People who like to bet money for pleasure *gamble*. Spring lambs jump and *gambol* in the fields.

gamut

See **gambit/gamut**.

gaol/jail

The second spelling is to be preferred. The past tense and past participle of the verb are spelt *jailed* (one *l*).

gap

This is often used incorrectly:

□ The *gap* between imports and exports was cut further last month

☐ The trade *gap* has again fallen.

Both of these sentences are taken from BBC news bulletins. Strictly speaking, a *gap* does not *fall*, and if we *cut* a *gap* we make it bigger, not smaller. In practice, however, words used metaphorically often become established as accepted idiom, and logical sense loses its force.

(See also **mixed metaphor**.)

gasoline

The American word for *petrol*. Usually shortened to *gas*.

gather

See **assemble**.

gender

Here is an example of incorrect use:

☐ Being myself of *the feminine gender*, I suppose I should be favourably disposed towards any proposal which would place women on an equal footing with men. (from a women's magazine)

Gender is a grammatical term: words have *gender*. Substitute *the* female *sex* (not *the feminine sex* – see **female/feminine**.) Of course, the simpler way would be to say *being myself a woman*.

gender in nouns

1 People One class of nouns indicates the relationship between masculine and feminine by a grammatical ending:

☐ headmaster	headmistress	☐ hero	heroine
☐ waiter	waitress	☐ usher	usherette
☐ emperor	empress	☐ widower	widow
☐ god	goddess	☐ bridegroom	bride
		☐ fiancé	fiancée
		☐ executor	executrix

Note the spelling of the feminine forms, especially *empress*. (See also **fiancé/fiancée**.)

Some feminine forms, particularly in the case of the professions, are now little used, eg *authoress* and *poetess*.

A second class has no obvious formal connection between masculine and feminine forms:

☐ king	queen	☐ brother	sister
☐ wizard	witch	☐ father	mother
☐ uncle	aunt	☐ nephew	niece
☐ man	woman	☐ lord	lady
		☐ gentleman	lady

2 Animals It is possible to distinguish by a separate word between masculine and feminine in many cases. However, people without a special interest in animals tend to use either the masculine form (eg *dog* instead of the more precise *bitch*) or a more general word (eg *horse* instead of either *stallion* or *mare*).

☐ ram	ewe	☐ tiger	tigress
☐ cock	hen	☐ he-goat	she-goat
☐ bull	cow	☐ billy-goat	nanny-goat
☐ fox	vixen	☐ peacock	peahen
☐ drake	duck	☐ cock-pheasant	hen-pheasant
☐ lion	lioness		

3 Dual gender This is a large class, which is on the increase:

☐ enemy	teacher	guest	artist
☐ writer	speaker	friend	person

The Women's Liberation movement is making a determined attempt to change the status of some of the dual gender words. The objection to *chairman*, for instance, lies in the *man* at the end of the word. At many conferences today, particularly in America, one is asked to refer to the *chairperson* or simply the *chair*. It remains to be seen if this innovation will be taken up more widely. (See **chairman**.) Words of dual gender may of course be made more specific by various means:

☐ boyfriend	girlfriend	☐ manservant	maidservant
☐ man student	woman student	☐ male guest	female guest

gent

(for *gentleman*) An uneducated use. Do not use this word.

gentleman

Sometimes *man* should be substituted, as in:

☐ A *gentleman* who looked like a commercial traveller got into the carriage.

Use the courtesy word *gentleman* only (a) for direct address, as *Ladies and gentlemen*; *Gentlemen, you may now smoke*, and (b) when referring to a person in his presence: *This gentleman wishes to see the manager.*

gerund

See **-ing**.

get

I should have liked to come, but I couldn't get. Dialectal, not Standard English. Say *I couldn't get there.*

gipsy
Use this spelling in preference to *gypsy*.

glance/glimpse
(nouns) Both words mean 'a quick look'. There is, however, a distinction between them. A *glance* is intentional and well-aimed:
□ The boy was tempted to cheat and shot a furtive *glance* at his neighbour's answer paper.
A *glimpse* is more by chance:
□ I caught a *glimpse* of the Queen through the crowd.
There is the same distinction between the verbs *to glance* and *to glimpse*.

glossary
A list of explanations of special or difficult words used in a book (obsolete words, technical terms, etc).

gnaw
The past participle is *gnawed*, not *gnawn*.

go places
An Americanism, only recently recognised as idiomatic in British English. Slightly informal. *There is no doubt that young man intends to go places* (ie advance rapidly in his career). It is better avoided in serious writing.

God/god
Use a capital when it means the one supreme *God* (Jehovah), a small letter when the reference is to a pagan *god* and when the word is prefixed to the name of such a god: *the god Neptune*. *Goddess* always has a small *g* except at the beginning of a sentence. Use a small letter for *godfather, godson, godparents*, etc. Also for *godfearing, godforsaken, godless, godliness, a godsend*.

gold (adjective)/golden
Gold when the meaning is 'made of gold' (*a gold watch, a gold ring, gold coins*). *Golden* was formerly used in this sense also, but it is now archaic, though it is preserved in a few traditional phrases, like *the goose that lays the golden eggs*.
In modern usage *golden* is restricted to (a) colour: *golden hair, the golden corn, the golden colours of autumn*, and (b) figurative use: *a golden opportunity, the golden age, golden opinions, a golden wedding*. The word *golden* has a rather poetic quality about it.

good
See **well/good**.

goodbye

Some dictionaries hyphenate the word, but it is commonly written as one, and this spelling is recommended.

gorilla/guerrilla

A *gorilla* is a large ape; a *guerrilla* is a fighter who does not belong to the regular army.

got

Have got (instead of just *have*) has its place in spoken English, and is often useful for purposes of emphasis. *We've got to do it* is more forceful than *We have to do it*, and *I've got a present for you* is more natural than *I have a present for you.*

(See **have.**)

gotten

Quite common in American English as the past participle of *get*, but in British usage confined to the one phrase *ill-gotten gains/ wealth.* Apart from this, use *got.*

government

On whether this should have a capital *G*, see **capital letters 10**. On whether a singular or plural verb follows, see **collective nouns d**.

graffiti

An Italian borrowing. The singular *graffito* is rarely found. Perhaps by analogy with *spaghetti*, it is quite common to find the Italian plural with a singular verb in English. The singular should perhaps be accepted where one example of *graffiti* is being referred to:

I don't think this graffito is obscene, do you? In a generalising sense, the plural is preferred.

Graffiti are witty, abusive or contemplative comments or drawings scratched or painted on walls, doors, etc in public places. An official notice attached to a wall in London read:

☐ Bill Stickers Will Be Prosecuted.

Below, some unknown person had written:

☐ Bill Stickers Is Innocent!

Enscribed in the toilets of a Cambridge pub were the words *You don't buy your beer here, you only rent it!*

Many *graffiti* are mindless or obscene without even the grace of wit. In the first category come the efforts of football supporters: *MUFC* (Manchester United Football Club), *Arsenal rules, OK?*, or that ubiquitous phrase *Kilroy was here.*

group term
See **collective nouns.**

guerrilla
See **gorilla/guerrilla.**

guess
I *guess*, in the sense of 'I should think', though used by Chaucer, is now recognised only in American English.

h

habitual
Though the *h* is sounded, *an* is usually used as the indefinite article: *an habitual action.* (See **a/an.**)

hale/hail
Hale means 'vigorous'. It is rarely found today except in the expression *hale and hearty*, meaning 'strong and healthy'.
Hail is icy rain.

half
1 Singular or plural verb? Use a singular verb for amount or quantity and a plural one for number:
□ *Half* of the land *is* cultivated
□ *Half* of the apples *are* bad.
Particularly in the second case, *of* is optional.
2 In compound words *Half* is often used with other nouns, adjectives and verbs to form compound words. Some examples are given below. (For the use of the hyphen in compounds, see **hyphen.**)
a *Half a dozen, half an hour, half a pound*, etc (no hyphens), but *a half-dozen, a half-hour, a half-pound* (hyphenated).
b *The bottle was half empty* (and similarly for other adjectives), but *a half-empty bottle.*
c I *half* expected this would happen
□ We *half* promised to go (no hyphen).
But if the two words form a compound expressing a single notion, then a hyphen must be used: *to half-cook the food, to half-run to school.*
d The centaur was *half man, half beast* (no hyphens).

e No hyphen in *halfway*, *half past* (*six*), but hyphens for *half-day*, *half-holiday*, *half-hearted*, *half-pay*, *half-price*, *half-term*, *half-time*, *half-truth*, *half-wit*, *half-witted*, *half-yearly*.

3 In half Cut *in half*. Logically it should be cut *in halves*, but *in half* is much more common.

hand

On the misuse of *on the other hand*, see **other 4**.

handicap

Past tense is *handicapped* in British English. See also **worship**, and **spelling 6**.

hang

When death by hanging is meant, the past tense and past participle are *hanged*; in all other senses *hung*.

happen

If it has a personal subject *happen* has the idea that the event was accidental. It must be followed either by an infinitive:

□ I *happened* to overhear what he said.

or by on + a noun, where the sense is 'to find, come across by accident':

□ I *happened* on the very thing I wanted.

The second construction is somewhat formal, especially when the alternative *upon* is used:

□ I *happened upon* a peaceful, secluded glade in the forest.

harass

A frequently mis-spelt word. Note the single *r* and double *s*.

hardly

As an adverb of degree, *hardly* takes *when*, not *than*: *He had hardly recovered from influenza*, when *he developed measles* (not *than he developed measles*). The alternatives are *no sooner . . . than* *hardly . . . when.*

Speak of *hard-earned money*, *hard-won rights*, etc, not *hardly-earned* and *hardly-won*. (See also **adverb or adjective? 3**.)

have

The verb *have* is very common, yet difficult to use. It appears as an auxiliary verb (as in the perfect tense *I have done it*) and as a full, lexical verb:

□ I *have* sugar in my tea.

The position may be summarised as follows:

1 Meaning 'possess' In the sense of possession, it is particularly

British English to say *I haven't any books.* It is also permissible to say *I don't have any books*, although this use of the auxiliary *do* still retains a slight American flavour. There is, of course, the further alternative of the word *no*: *I have no books.*

2 As an auxiliary In English speech, and commonly even in writing, there is a strong tendency to use *have got* in the sense of possession: *I haven't got any books. Have* here functions as an auxiliary. The construction is best avoided in most written contexts. (See **got**.)

3 With auxiliary do Where *have* means 'to take, experience, receive', etc, it is usual for *have* to take the auxiliary *do*:

□ He *doesn't have* cream in his tea

□ *Did* he *have* any problems with the Customs?

(See also **do**.)

4 In the passive Except when *have* means 'to obtain' (*It can be had for the asking*) and, colloquially, 'to deceive' (*You have been had over that bargain*), the passive voice is not generally used. *A good time was had by all* is so obviously un-English that it should not be used except for humorous effect.

he or she

It is standard practise to use *he* as common gender, unless it is necessary that both sexes should be specified:

□ If a child is absent from school for long periods, *he* should be given extra work.

However, it is common today to find *he or she* used. This is not incorrect, but may produce awkward sentences:

□ If a child is absent from school for long periods, *he or she* should be given extra work.

□ *He or she* should be encouraged to catch up with his or her work as soon as possible.

Attempts to shorten this unwieldy combination to *he/she* or even *s/he* produce equally awkward sentences. (See also **his or her** and **gender in nouns 3**.)

headmaster

Write as one word. For the feminine form, see **gender in nouns 1**.

hectic

□ The child was feverish and her cheeks had a *hectic* flush.

This sentence illustrates the correct meaning of the word, that is 'having a feverish colouring'. It is much more common to hear it used to mean 'very busy' or 'exciting':

□ What a *hectic* day I've had.

Until recently it was considered to be colloquial in this sense, and even today some writers avoid it.

help

1 *Help* followed by an infinitive without *to* (*I helped him mend his bicycle, help me lift this box*), once condemned as an Americanism, is now accepted in British English. Although it is possible to omit *to*, it is never wrong to insert it.

2 *I could not help but laugh at what he said.* A confusion of two constructions: *I could not but laugh* (now somewhat archaic), and *I could not help laughing*. Use the latter.

3 *I shan't stay longer than I can help.* Illogical, since it should be *than I can't help*, but no one ever says this. The illogical is accepted idiom and may therefore be considered correct. Similarly with *unless I can help it*, though here the illogicality can be avoided by using *if I can help it*.

hence/hither

Both words are formal in all their uses.

1 Hence An adverb which has two meanings in modern English.

a 'from now', as in *three weeks hence* (three weeks from now).

b 'for this reason' as in:

□ The book is out of print, *hence* the difficulty in obtaining a copy for you.

Hence used to have a third meaning 'from here' (*Get thee hence!*) but this is now archaic. *Henceforth* and *henceforward* are both still used formally and their meaning is 'from this time forward; in future'. (See also **thence/thither** and **whence/whither**.)

2 Hither *Hither* is the converse form of *hence* meaning 'to here'. It is now archaic to say *come hither*. The fixed expression *hither and thither* is still in limited use with verbs such as *run, scurry*, etc:

□ They ran *hither and thither* in their efforts to make all the preparations in time.

Hitherto is an adverb meaning 'up till now; up to the present'. It is still in use today:

□ These papers are *hitherto* unknown manuscripts of Charles Dickens.

hers No apostrophe.

hiccup/hiccough
The first spelling is preferred.

high
See **tall/high**.

high/highly
Where altitude or position is in question, the adverb is *high*:
☐ The eagle soared *high* into the sky
☐ By middle age he had risen *high* in his profession.
Highly means 'to a high degree'. Generally, adjectives take *highly* (*a highly desirable residence, a highly infectious disease, a highly controversial question*); so do participles when the sense is that of degree or extent: *a highly qualified person, a highly praised achievement, highly seasoned food*. Note also *highly placed officials, highly paid workers*, but *a high-born person, high-sounding words* (ie a person born to a *high* social position and words that sound *high* in the sense of 'pompous'), *a high-pitched voice, note* etc.
In compounds the prefixed word is *high*. Thus goods for which a high price is charged are *high-priced goods*, not *highly priced*, a chair with a high back is *a high-backed chair*, and shoes with high heels *high-heeled shoes*. *High-rated property* is property on which the rates are high: *highly rated property* is property which is rated (ie esteemed) beyond most of its kind. (See also **adverb or adjective? 3**.)

highbrow
Having superior or intellectual interests and tastes. The word is often used with pejorative overtones, and is sometimes mistaken for another word altogether, as when a journalist of the *Hereford Evening News* wrote that opera was not for *eyebrow or élitist tastes*. *Lowbrow*, the converse of *highbrow*, has not gained the same acceptance.

hire/rent
We *hire* tools, cars, taxis, buses, boats, bicycles, etc. We *rent* television sets, houses, rooms, etc. *Hire* is short-term; *rent* is long-term. We *hire* a hall for a reception but *rent* a flat.

his or her
It has been standard practice to use *his* as common gender unless there is any real necessity to make the distinction: *Each member has paid* his *subscription* – not *his or her*. However, probably as a result of pressure from feminists, it is now not uncommon to find

his or her. The results are sometimes awkward:

□ Everybody must pick up *his or her* tickets at the counter.

A different change in English usage which is now taking place may make the argument academic in a few years' time – many people today say:

□ Everybody must pick up *their* tickets at the counter.

Their, although incorrect, does have the advantage of referring to both male and female! (See also **he or she**, **each** and **everybody/everyone/everything**.)

historic/historical

Historical means 'concerned with history' (*a historical novel, a historical society, a historical account*) or having an actual existence in history:

□ Many people doubt whether Robin Hood was a *historical* character.

Historic means having a long history attached to it (*Historic cities such as York and Chester, a fund for the preservation of historic buildings*) or such as will go down in history: *a historic document, a historic occasion, a historic trial.*

hither

See **hence/hither**.

hoard/horde

An election address once prophesied *hoards of government inspectors* if a certain party were returned to power. It was, perhaps, a printer's error, but it serves to illustrate the difference of meaning between two words that are sometimes carelessly confused. A *hoard* is a secret store or pile: a *horde* is, strictly, a large migratory tribe of savages, but in everyday English the word is more often used (always in a derogatory sense) of large crowds or numbers of any kind of persons: *hordes* of inspectors, trippers, ramblers, football fans, etc. It should not be used of non-personal things, as *hordes of official forms* or *hordes of begging letters.*

holiday

See **vacation**.

home/at home

Stay home, keep a person home are not accepted in British English, although they are common in American English. In Britain, we *go home, come home, arrive home, get home*, and *take, send* or *bring someone* (or *something*) *home*; but we *stay at home, live at home*, *work at home*, and *keep a person, goods* or *money at home*. *Home* is an adverb denoting destination, *at home* is an adverbial phrase, in which the word *home* itself is a noun, and denotes locality. *He is not at home* means 'He is not in the house'. *He is not yet home* means 'He has not yet arrived back from work, an outing, his holiday, etc'. An *at-home* (noun) is a social gathering in a home.

homely

To a speaker of British English, this is a pleasant adjective. If he describes a house as *homely*, he will think of warmth, simple but comfortable furniture and a cosy atmosphere. If he describes a person as *homely* he will see in his mind's eye a warm, welcoming person with a pleasant face. Mention a *homely* person to an American, however, and he will imagine someone plain and unattractive. The Americans have a colloquial word *homey* which does not exist in British English but which has all the values the British attach to *homely*.

honorary/honourable

An *honorary secretary* (abbreviation *Hon Sec*) of a society or association is one who gives his services without payment. Politicians and members of the Royal Family are often given *honorary degrees*: degrees conferred as an honour but which they have not worked for. The Queen has several *honorary military ranks*: ranks bestowed as an honour but for which she has no qualification.

Honourable, however, means 'worthy of honour' (*our honourable friend*) or 'showing honour' (*honourable conduct*). *Honourable* (abbreviated to *Hon*) is also the title given to the children of peers below the rank of Marquis. Members of the Privy Council (prominent public figures who advise the Queen) are given the title *Right Honourable* (*Rt Hon*) and, in debates in the House of Commons, MPs address each other as *Honourable*:

☐ As my *Honourable* friend, the member for Slough, has said . . .

☐ As the *Honourable* member knows . . . .

In this use, a capital letter is usual. The American spelling is *honorable*. (See **Right Honourable**.)

hope

1 Hope + infinitive As a verb, *hope* may be followed by an infinitive, either active or passive, referring back to the subject:

☐ I *hope* to see him on Monday

□ She *hoped* to be given an opportunity of expressing her views.
It cannot, however, take an object followed by an infinitive construction: we cannot say *They hoped her to be selected for the post*, or *We all hope the scheme to succeed*. Amend to *They hoped that she would be selected*, or *We all hope that the scheme will succeed*.

2 Hope in passive *Hope for* can be used in either the active or the passive voice:

□ We *hope for* an improvement

□ An improvement is *hoped for*

□ The reforms have not achieved all that was *hoped for*,

but *hope* can be used in the passive only when the subject is the impersonal *it* with an infinitive or a *that*-clause:

□ It is *hoped that* members will pay their subscriptions promptly

□ It was *hoped that* the reconstruction of the premises would be completed before Christmas

□ It is *hoped* to have the full details ready in time for the next meeting.

The following, however, are incorrect: *The work is hoped to be finished this week*; *he is hoped to make a full recovery*. The sentences should read:

□ It is *hoped* to finish the work this week

and:

□ It is *hoped* he will make a full recovery.

3 Hope of As a noun, in the singular and plural, *hope* is followed by *of* plus a gerund: *my hope of winning the next race* rather than *my hope to win the next race*.

how

□ I shall never forget *how* she refused to dance with me

□ He told me *how* his father had once been a wealthy man

□ She reminded me *how* I had once said that one could be quite happy without money.

Sentences of this type are quite idiomatic English. Very often *that* would be equally acceptable from a purely grammatical point of view, but *how* expresses a stronger element of feeling. It must not, of course, be confused with *how* which expresses method or means. If there is any possibility that, in a particular sentence, it will be so confused, then it should be avoided. For instance, *He told me how he had made over a thousand pounds in a few days* might mean simply that he told me *that* he had made that amount, or it might mean that he told me *the way in which* he had made it.

however/how ever

1 One word or two? Use one word when *ever* generalises (*However we do it, it will be a difficult job*) or when it means 'nevertheless' or 'in spite of that': *That, however, is another story.* If *ever* emphasises, then two words should be written:

□ *How ever* we are going to do it I do not know

□ *How ever* did you get your clothes in that mess?

(See **ever/-ever 3**.)

2 However in contrasts When *however* is used to contrast one statement with another, it needs a comma to separate it from the rest of the sentence, and two if it occurs parenthetically within the sentence:

□ *However*, we need not discuss that now

□ We need not discuss that now, *however*

□ His friends, *however*, had other ideas.

3 However meaning 'but' or preceded by but Contrastive *however* means very much the same as *but*; the two, therefore, should not be used together, as they are in such a sentence as *But that, however, can be left till the next meeting*. Either *but* or *however* is redundant. (See **but**.)

However may be correctly preceded by *but* when it is a generalising adverb of manner or degree:

□ *But however* you do it, you will find it a difficult task

□ *But however* hard he tried, he could not succeed.

hygiene

Note the *i* in the spelling. Also *hygienic*.

hypercritical/hypocritical

Hypercritical: too critical, especially of small faults and errors. *Hypocritical*: trying to make oneself appear more virtuous than one really is, saying one thing while doing something else, usually something worse.

hyphen

If there is any doubt whether a particular combination should be written as two words, one word, or with a hyphen, consult a dictionary. If one word is possible, that is to be preferred (eg *teaspoon* rather than *tea spoon* or *tea-spoon*, *today* and *tomorrow* rather than *to-day* and *to-morrow*). If the choice lies between two words and a hyphen, then choose the two words provided it does not violate sense or lead to ambiguity. In other words, dispense with the hyphen whenever possible. There are, however, certain cases where it must be used, or where it is advisable to use it; there are others where it should not be used. The following is intended as a guide.

1 With prefixes It links prefixes to nouns to form new words: *ex-soldier, sub-let, non-intervention, pro-British, anti-aircraft*. In long-established compounds the two elements are now written as one word, but the hyphen continues to be used if its absence would lead to a duplication of letters: *co-operating, re-employ, mis-shapen.* Even here, duplication may sometimes be necessary to avoid other complications. This unfortunate example of hyphenation comes from the *Guardian*:

☐ . . . and so once again a World Cup began with scrappy, disco-ordinated football . . .

Two hyphens would be ugly (dis-co-ordinated), so the only alternative is to duplicate letters and write *dis-coordinated*.

Re- may be hyphenated even in compounds which are usually written as one word, if it is used to emphasise the idea of *again*: *to assure and re-assure a person, to write and re-write a letter.*

A hyphen is always necessary when a prefix is attached to a noun or adjective beginning with a capital letter: *pro-German, anti-Nazi, non-Christian, un-English.*

2 To prevent ambiguity The hyphen is used to prevent ambiguity where words are similar. Compare:

☐ I am going to *re-cover* that old cushion

☐ I *recovered* the cushion from the dustbin.

Also *reform, re-form*, and *react, re-act*, etc.

3 To group words The hyphen is used to group words so as to avoid ambiguity: *an Irish-linen manufacturer* (the linen is Irish, not the manufacturer). *An old factory-cleaner* (the cleaner is old, not the factory).

☐ Four Minute Raiders Grab £$\frac{3}{4}$ m . . .

– A hyphen in this *Daily Telegraph* headline in *Four-minute* would have made it clear that the raiders were very quick, not a gang of dwarfs!

4 With adjectives before a noun In phrases consisting of an adjective + noun or an adjectival phrase, a hyphen is used before a noun: *nineteenth-century poetry, our next-door neighbours.* But they are not hyphenated after a noun or verb: *poetry of the nineteenth century, our neighbours next door.*

5 With adjectives modified by adverbs Usually, no hyphen is necessary when an adverb modifies an adjective: *a tastefully furnished house, a badly behaved child, an incredibly foolish act.* But with combinations such as *well-known, well-designed, ill-behaved, wide-open, half-hearted* where the first element might not at once be recognised as an adverb, the hyphen is necessary before a following noun: *a well-known fact, a well-acted play, a wide-open window, a half-hearted attempt.* No hyphen is required when the combination follows the noun and verb: *The fact is well known; the play was well acted; the window was wide open, the attempt was half hearted.* (For further examples, see **half 2**.)

6 With adjective-participle combinations Adjective-participle combinations like *hard-boiled, new-born, fresh-ground* are hyphenated whether used before the noun or after the noun and verb:

□ Pack some *hard-boiled* eggs for the picnic

□ These eggs are *hard-boiled.*

An adjective or participle preceded by a noun (*blood-red, red-hot, ice-cold, poverty-stricken, stage-struck*) also has a hyphen whether used before or after the word it describes:

□ She took hold of the child's *ice-cold* hand

□ The child's hand was *ice-cold.*

7 With compounds ending in -ed Compound adjectives made from an adjective followed by a noun with *-ed* added take the hyphen: *a good-sized house, a flat-footed person, a four-wheeled vehicle*, a *back-handed compliment.* (See **compound adjectives**.)

8 With compound cardinal numbers Compound cardinal numbers like *twenty-one, fifty-three*, etc are hyphenated; so are the corresponding ordinals: *one's twenty-first birthday.* With multiples there is no hyphenation of the cardinals (*two hundred, five thousand, three score and ten*), but the ordinals have a hyphen: *the two-hundredth anniversary.* Fractions are hyphenated when they denote a single amount: *two-thirds of a mile, three-quarters of a pound*, but there is no hyphen when a specified number of separate parts is intended:

□ Three quarters of the circle were coloured and the other quarter was left white.

(See **numbers: method of writing**.)

9 At the end of a line As far as possible, avoid splitting words at the end of a line, but if splitting is necessary, then (a) place the hyphen at the end of the first line, not at the beginning of the second, and (b) see that the word is so split that the part of it on the first line is recognisable as a sense unit and does not mislead the reader: thus *wonder-ing*, not *won-dering* or *wond-ering*.
10 Unnatural hyphens Avoid the unsightly and unnatural hyphens in *schoolboys and -girls, Englishmen and -women, grandfathers and -mothers*. Write *schoolboys and schoolgirls*, etc.

hypocritical

See **hypercritical/hypocritical**.

i

I

On *it's me* or *it's I*, see **me**. On *older than me* or *older than I*, see **than**. On *I* or *me* following prepositions, see **prepositions**.

ie/eg

The two are sometimes confused, though a little thought would avoid the confusion; *ie* stands for the Latin, *id est*, meaning 'that is', and should be used only when what follows is an alternative rendering, by way of explanation, of what precedes. If only *examples*, and not a full explanation, are given, then *eg* (Latin, *exempli gratia*, 'for the sake of example; for instance') should be used.

The following is thus incorrect:

□ professional people, *ie* doctors and solicitors.

There are other professional people besides doctors and solicitors; these two are only examples; *eg* should therefore have been used.

The abbreviations should never be in capitals within a sentence; always avoid beginning a sentence with *ie* or *eg* where an initial capital might be expected.

Contemporary practice is to omit the full stops (*ie* not *i.e.*).

ill/sick

When the reference is to health, ill is used only after a verb: *She is/has been/feels/looks ill.* We cannot speak of *an ill person.*

There is one exception to the above rule, and that is the compound *ill-health.*

Apart from this, the use before a noun always suggests condemnation, usually of a moral character (*ill deeds, ill repute, ill manners*), and the idea of physical illness is conveyed by *sick*: *a sick man, sick leave, sick pay.* In America *sick* is also used after a verb in this sense, but apart from the expression *to fall/go sick* this is not the practice in British English, where it suggests nausea or vomiting. Contrast *I feel ill* (unwell) with *I feel sick* (nauseated).

illegal/illegitimate/illicit

Illegal means 'expressly forbidden by law'. *Illegitimate* means 'not recognised by the law', or 'not having the sanction of law', as *the illegitimate use* of force.

Illicit does not, in itself, refer to law at all; it means 'not allowed'. The implied prohibition may certainly be, and often is, prohibition by the law, as when we speak of *the illicit smoking of marihuana,* or *illicit diamond-buying* but it may also be prohibition by rules or regulations of one sort or another: *the illicit use of a dictionary in an examination.* There is no law against it, but the rules of the examining body forbid it. (See also **elicit/illicit**.)

illegitimate

See previous entry.

illicit

See penultimate entry and **elicit/illicit**.

illusion

See **allusion/delusion/illusion**.

imaginary/imaginative

Imaginary means 'existing only in the mind'. *Imaginative* means 'showing powers of creativity or imagination':

□ The little boy spent all afternoon talking to Gerry, his *imaginary* friend

□ Her essay was lively and *imaginative* and won first prize in the competition.

imbue/infuse

Both words are formal and mean 'to fill or inspire'. A gifted lecturer may *imbue* his students with enthusiasm for their subject, or he may *infuse* new enthusiasm into his students. The constructions are: *imbue* someone *with* something; *infuse* something *into* someone.

imminent
See **eminent/imminent**.

immoral
See **amoral/immoral**.

immune
Followed by *to*, *from* or *against*. There is no definite rule, and normally authoritative dictionaries do not agree with one another. As a general guide, where *immune* means 'not susceptible' or 'not able to be harmed or affected', it is followed by *to*: *immune to* disease or unpleasantness. When it means 'protected', it is used with *from* or *against*: *immune from/against* attack, criticism, interference. When it means 'exempt' or 'not liable', it is used with *from*: *immune from* punishment or taxes.

impel
In the past tense, past participle and present participles, the *l* is doubled: *impelled*, *impelling*. For the rule, see **spelling 6**.

imperial/imperious
Imperial means 'pertaining to an empire or an emperor': *the imperial crown, imperial aspirations*. *Imperious* means 'overbearing, domineering': an *imperious* manner.

impersonate/personate
Impersonate means 'to mimic, copy, pretend to be another person, usually for purposes of entertainment'. *Personate* means 'to claim to be another person with intent to deceive, for wrongful purposes'. The latter is now rarely found, and *impersonate* has taken over its meaning:

□ He *impersonated* his neighbour in order to get more money from the Social Security Office.

implicit
See **explicit/implicit**.

imply
See **infer/imply**.

impossible
See **possible**.

impracticable/impractical
The two are sometimes confused – or rather the second is sometimes used for the first. A scheme, plan, idea, etc which cannot possibly be carried out is *impracticable*:

□ At one time it was thought *impracticable* for man to fly.

Impractical means (a) not much given to practical things, as *He is a very impractical sort of person*, (though for this, in British English at least, *unpractical* is often used) and (b) which could be done, but would require far too much time or trouble, as *an impractical suggestion*. (See also **practicable/practical 1**.)

impromptu

See **extempore/impromptu**.

impulsive

See **compulsive**.

in/at

We usually speak of a person living *in* a country and *in* a large town (*in France, in Birmingham*), but *at* a village or small town (*at Sharpthorn*).

For houses and places of residence use *in* for the kind of residence (*in* a cottage, a mansion, a bungalow, a flat, a hotel, a caravan); use *at* for a specific one: *at The Hollies, at 53 Cambridge Terrace, at the Portland Hotel.*

For places of work use *in* for the kind of place: *in* a shop, an office, a bank, etc. For a specific building or commercial concern use *at*: *at the Public Library, at Selfridge's*. For particular departments of a business, use *in*: *in the Accounts Department of the Electricity Board*.

in-law

Plural: *mothers-in-law, sisters-in-law*, etc, but 'to live with one's *in-laws*'.

in order that

Never followed by *can/could* or *will/would*. The usual verb is *may/might*:

☐ They arrived early, *in order that* they *might* get a good seat

☐ We are sending our representative to see you, *in order that* you *may* discuss the position with him,

but *shall/should* is also possible, mainly in negative clauses which express something that it is desired to avoid:

☐ They left by a side door, *in order that* no one *should* see them.

The infinitive, of course, is also correct after *in order*:

☐ He decided to go himself, *in order to find out* the truth.

in so far

Three words, not one. *Insofar* is sometimes seen, but it is an American spelling.

in to/into
See **into/in to**.

inculcate
Inculcate is a formal word, meaning 'to instil, fix in the mind'. We *inculcate* something *in* (rarely *on*) a person:
□ The headmaster inculcated a spirit of solidarity in staff and students.
An alternative construction is *inculcate* somebody *with* something:
□ The headmaster inculcated the staff and students with a spirit of solidarity.

incur
In the past tense, past participle and present participle, the *r* is doubled: *incurred, incurring*. For the rule, see **spelling 6**.

index
Plural: *indices* (scientific and mathematical signs), *indexes* (to books, documents, etc).

indicative
A manner in which a verb is expressed. It expresses a fact or asks a question, for example the verbs in:
□ *He has gone* to town
□ *Has he gone* to town?
Compare **subjunctive**.

indict/indite
Indict is a legal term meaning 'to accuse someone of a crime'; *indite* is a formal word meaning 'to compose, write'.

indifferent
Normally followed by *to* (*indifferent to* fame, money, worldly success, etc), but *as to* seems permissible where processes, courses of action, developments, etc are concerned:
□ I am *indifferent as to* the result
□ She professed herself *indifferent as to* the outcome of the negotiations.
Indifferent in the sense of 'impartial', as in Sir Philip Sydney's line, 'The *indifferent* judge between the high and low', is now archaic. In modern English *an indifferent judge* would suggest 'a mediocre judge'. (Compare *goods of indifferent quality*, and the phrase *good, bad and indifferent*.)

indite
See **indict/indite**.

individual

(noun) The only correct use is to denote one member of a group as contrasted with the group as a whole, as in:

□ The interests of the *individual* must sometimes be subordinated to those of the community.

Used in the sense of 'a person', without any suggestion of his being one unit in a greater whole, it is often derogatory or humorous:

□ He was not the kind of *individual* to take criticism lightly

□ A cadaverous *individual* emerged from a dark corner. It was a museum attendant. 'Come and see the tombs, Sir,' he pleaded. 'Come and see the lovely tombs.'

Do not speak of *a number of individuals* if you merely mean *a number of persons*. Do not say *The committee consists of the following individuals*, but *of the following persons*, though it is, of course, quite correct to say:

□ Applications should be addressed to the committee, and not to *individuals*,

since here there is a contrast between the committee as a body, and the individual people of whom it is constituted.

indoor/indoors

Indoors is the adverb (*to go indoors, stay indoors*, etc), *indoor* the adjective (*indoor games*).

infamous/notorious

Notorious means 'well known for something discreditable', and in this sense is the opposite of *famous*: *a notorious pirate, a notorious liar, a district notorious for its fogs.*

Infamous means 'evil' or 'wicked', though not necessarily well known on that account. It merely expresses a moral judgement, and therefore is not really an antonym of *famous*: *an infamous scoundrel, an infamous deed, a tyrant whose name has become infamous in history.*

The corresponding nouns are *notoriety* and *infamy*.

infectious

See **contagious/infectious**.

infer/imply

These two words are often used incorrectly. Here are two examples of incorrect use:

□ His words seemed to *infer* that he thought I knew the secret

□ What do you *infer* by that remark?

In both cases the word required is *imply*. *Imply* means 'to suggest, without actually stating; hint at'. *Infer* means 'to read a meaning into; draw a conclusion; deduce':

□ What do you *imply* by that remark? ('What do you mean to suggest by it?')

□ What are we to *infer* from that remark? ('What conclusion are we to draw from it?')

In the past tense, past participle and present participle, the *r* on *infer* doubles: *inferred*, *inferring*. See **refer**.

inferior

See **superior**.

inflammable

See **flammable**.

inflection/inflexion

See **connection/connexion**.

inflict

See **afflict/inflict**.

infringe

A recent use of the word *infringe* with the preposition *on* (or *upon*), meaning 'to encroach', is shown in this example:

□ . . . the development of practices which would *infringe* on the managers' traditional prerogatives.

Strictly, *infringe* is a transitive verb: we *infringe* ('break' or 'violate') laws, rights, prerogatives, etc; we do not *infringe upon* them. The new use has perhaps arisen by confusion with *impinge upon*.

infuse

See **imbue/infuse**.

-ing

(verbal ending) The parts of the verb ending in *-ing* are the present participle and the gerund. Here they will be treated together. The following are the chief points to observe (see also **as 2**.):

1 The misrelated participial phrase Be careful to avoid the error of the unrelated (or more often the misrelated) participial phrase or 'dangling modifier':

□ Standing at the top of the cliff, the people below were scarcely visible.

A participle has the force of a compound adjective, and qualifies the first noun or pronoun that follows it, in this case *the people below*. But it obviously was not the people below who were

standing at the top of the cliff, though that is what the sentence says. Possible methods of correction are:
a Alter the first part so that it is no longer a participial phrase: *From the top of the cliff* or *As we stood at the top of the cliff.* Both these are adverbial, and modify *were visible.*
b Retain the participial phrase, but follow it up with the word to which it really refers:
□ Standing at the top of the cliff, we could scarcely see the people below.
The error is particularly liable to occur with the impersonal subjects *it* and *there*:
□ Having heard the evidence, it should now be possible to arrive at a decision.
It – which here stands for the infinitive construction *to arrive at a decision* – has not heard the evidence. Amend to *We should now be able to arrive* . . . .
□ Not being stamp collectors, there was nothing in the exhibition to interest us.
Correct to *As we were not stamp collectors* . . . (adverb clause), or *Not being stamp collectors, we found nothing* . . . .
2 The elliptical clause The same error may arise with an elliptical clause such as:
□ While picking raspberries a wasp stung him
or with a phrase introduced by a preposition and a gerund:
□ On opening the door a cloud of smoke poured out of the room.
The wasp was not picking raspberries, nor did the cloud of smoke open the door. Correct to *While he was picking raspberries* . . . (complete the clause) or *While picking raspberries, he was stung by a wasp,* and *On his opening the door* . . . or *On opening the door he was met by a cloud of smoke pouring out of the room.*
3 Idiomatic constructions Certain absolute constructions based upon a present participle (some of them elliptical in character) are however, recognised as idiomatic. They modify or depend upon no other word in the sentence:
□ Considering its lack of training, our team did very well
□ Speaking of novels, what was the title of the one you recommended to me the other day?
□ Seeing it is your birthday, you may stay up an hour later tonight.

Referring to, often used (or misused) at the opening of business letters, is not one of these. It is a participial phrase which may be misrelated, as in this example:

☐ *Referring to* your letter of 3 August, the goods have been dispatched today.

4 Use of the apostrophe Should one write:

☐ I object to *my son* being punished for so trivial an offence

or:

☐ I object to my *son's* being punished . . .

and:

☐ I disapprove of *schoolgirls* using cosmetics

or:

☐ I disapprove of *schoolgirls'* using cosmetics.

Theoretically the form with the apostrophe should be used, since it is not my son that I object to, but his being punished, and not schoolgirls that I disapprove of, but their using cosmetics. In practice, however, the apostrophe is often omitted. Here are some general guidelines:

a For personal pronouns, always use the possessive form:

☐ Please excuse *my* coming late (not *me*)

☐ I object to *his* being punished (not *him*)

☐ There is not much likelihood of *their* coming now (not *them*)

☐ Do you think there is any possibility of *its* raining? (not *it*).

b For the demonstrative pronouns there is no genitive or possessive form, so we must say:

☐ There is no likelihood of *that happening*.

Of that's happening would be impossible.

c For singular nouns use the possessive form if possible:

☐ Please excuse *John's* coming late (not *John* coming), particularly with people, but do not hesitate to discard it if it sounds better:

☐ We were discussing the possibility of *the house* being converted into flats.

– *the house's* would sound awkward and unnatural. Similarly, change the form in speech if the possessive might be mistaken for a plural and so lead to misunderstanding. Thus we may write either:

☐ He did not like the idea of his *daughter* going out to work

or:

☐ He did not like the idea of his *daughter's* going out to work, although the latter is to be preferred in writing. In speech, however, it might be advisable to say *daughter*, since *daughter's* might be confused with the plural *daughters*.

d When we come to plural nouns the problem is merely one of the written form, since in pronunciation there is no difference between *dogs* and *dogs'*, *boys* and *boys'*, etc. Generally speaking, the apostrophe may be omitted:

□ The possibility of *aeroplanes* colliding in the air is very remote.

ingenious/ingenuous

Ingenious means 'clever': *an ingenious invention, an ingenious mind. Ingenuous* means 'innocent, frank, natural': *an ingenuous young girl, a face with an ingenuous expression.*

ingratiate

This is often used incorrectly, as in this example:

□ That student *ingratiates* all his tutors.

Ingratiate is a reflexive verb meaning 'to seek favour'. The correct construction is 'to *ingratiate oneself with* someone'. Amend to *That student ingratiates himself with all his tutors.*

inimitable

'Too good to be imitated.' A formal word until recently, this adjective has been cheapened by show business announcers who describe anyone and everyone as *inimitable*, meaning 'the one we all know and love':

□ 'And now, ladies and gentlemen, the moment you've all been waiting for. And here she is, the *inimitable* Stella Lane.'

Inimitable has become an adjective to avoid.

innovation

See **tautology**.

inoculate

Note the spelling. All the letters are single.

inquire/inquiry

See **enquire/inquire**.

inside (of)

Of follows *inside* when it is a noun: *The inside of the house.* It may also be used when *inside* is a preposition denoting place, though it is better omitted:

□ He parked his car just *inside* (*of*) the gate.

It should always be omitted when the reference is to time: *I shall be back inside an hour.*

inst

(Short for *instant.*) Once a respectable legal term, now a piece of commercial jargon for 'the present month':

□ We beg to recognise the receipt of your letter of the 25th *inst.*

Use the name of the month instead.

instantaneous/simultaneous

Instantaneous means 'immediate, over in an instant': *instantaneous death, an instantaneous reaction. Simultaneous* means 'happening at the same time as': *simultaneous translation.*

instructional/instructive

Instructional means 'educational': *instructional* films, pamphlets, diagrams, etc. *Instructive* means 'informative': *It was an unusually open and instructive report.*

insure

See **assure/insure** and **ensure/insure**.

intense/intensive

Intense means 'extreme': *intense emotion, intense heat*, etc. *Intensive* means 'thorough': *an intensive search, intensive study, intensive questioning*, etc.

interrupt

Note the double *r* in the spelling.

into/in to

These are often confused. Here is an example of incorrect use:

□ Entries for the competition should be sent *into* the Editor by 30 June.

This, from a daily newspaper, is typical of a very frequent mistake. *Into* is a preposition introducing an adverb phrase. A person goes *into* a room, a house, a shop, etc, a child falls *into* a pond, someone who is annoyed flies *into* a temper, and a conjurer changes a handkerchief *into* a loaf of bread. In all these, and in many more constructions like them, the single word is correct.

But two words (*in to*) must be written

1 when *in* is an adverb attached to the verb and *to* is a preposition introducing the phrase:

□ Entries should be sent *in to* the Editor

□ We went *in to* dinner.

2 when *to* is part of an infinitive:

□ They went in *to look* at the exhibition.

Frequently *in* and *into* are both acceptable:

☐ He put the papers *in* his brief-case
or:
☐ He put the papers *into* his brief-case.
☐ She poured the water *in* the basin
or:
☐ She poured the water *into* the basin.
Into suggests the whole process of transferring the papers from one place to another or of pouring the water from one receptacle to another; *in* suggests merely the resultant position.

introvert

See **extrovert/introvert**.

inundate

In formal English, this verb means 'to flood; cover with water'. The verb is quite commonly found in a figurative sense, however, where it means 'to overwhelm' as in:
☐ Since Mrs Simpson wrote to the local paper about her difficulties in arranging transport for her handicapped child, she has been *inundated* with offers of help.
Clearly, one cannot be *inundated* with a single object, and the following sentence from the *Guardian*, therefore, makes strange reading:
☐ Since the closure of *The Times*, Lord Chalfont has not been *inundated* with a platform from which to explain the demise of the Shah of Iran . . . .

invariably

This example is, strictly, incorrect:
☐ The alarm-clock almost always failed to wake us, so *invariably* we were late for school.
Invariably means 'never changing; without variation'. Many careful writers do not use it to mean 'almost always'.

invent

See **discover/invent**.

inversion of verb and subject

Inversions like *said she*, *replied the captain* are quite normal when they follow direct speech, but, except in verse, where they have long been recognised, they are best not used to introduce it. Sentences like:
☐ *Said Mr Smith*, We are very proud of John's achievement
are common in popular journalism and should not be copied.

Inversion of the type *Came the war*, to denote the next occurrence in a series of events, or in a narrative, is an idiosyncrasy of certain authors' prose style and should be avoided. Use inversions of this kind only after adverbs like *there, then, next*: *Then came the war*.
(For singular or plural verbs with inverted constructions, see **as 5**, **case 1** and **than 3**.)

inverted commas
(Quotation marks.) Punctuation marks ('. . .' or ". . .").
They are used in direct speech or around quotations. Although some newspapers still use double inverted commas (". . ."), modern usage now favours single ones ('. . .').

1 For direct speech
a Inverted commas are only used around words actually spoken:
□ 'I really can't think why Martin's so late,' said Sheila. 'He must have been held up in the traffic.'
b Where the words inside the inverted commas form a complete sentence, the full stop also comes inside the inverted commas:
□ 'He must have been held up in the traffic.'
The exception to this is where the sentence is followed by words such as *she said*, in which case the full stop follows them:
□ 'I really can't think why Martin's so late,' said Sheila with a sigh.
When a sentence is interrupted by words such as *she said*, *he replied*, etc, then these words are marked off by commas:
□ 'Yes,' said the secretary, 'Mr Hopkins will see you at ten tomorrow.'
c Any punctuation of direct speech belongs inside the inverted commas:
□ 'You clumsy boy!' the fat lady exclaimed. 'Who told you to ride your bicycle on the pavement?'
d Where there is a quotation within a quotation, it is marked off by double inverted commas. You must be careful that any further punctuation, such as a question mark, is correctly placed:
□ 'Did he say "I refuse to do it"?' asked the magistrate.

2 For quotations For a detailed treatment, see **quotation**. The following points may be noticed here as the most important.
a Do not use inverted commas for brief quotations of a few words which have become part of the common stock of idioms: *hoist with*

his own petard, an itching palm, a man more sinned against than sinning.
b For a verse quotation, use no inverted commas if it is set out in metrical form, and stands on a line of its own: but, even for a complete line of verse, inverted commas are needed if it is included as a syntactic element in a sentence:
□ Who does not know Gray's famous *Elegy Written in a Country Churchyard*, with its opening line,
The curfew tolls the knell of parting day,
perhaps the best-known line of poetry in the English language?
□ 'The curfew tolls the knell of parting day' is the opening line of Gray's *Elegy*.
c If a quotation consists of more than one paragraph, the quotation marks are placed at the beginning of each paragraph, to show that we are still continuing the quotation, but only the last paragraph has them at the end also.

3 Other uses

a Titles of literary works, names of newspapers, magazines, etc may be placed in inverted commas or they may be underlined in handwritten or typewritten scripts (to represent italics in print): but both methods cannot be used together. (See also **titles**.)
b Inverted commas (or alternatively underlining) may be used for the names of ships, aeroplanes, railway engines, etc. The word *the*, when used, should be given a small letter, and not included in the inverted commas, except for *The Times* and *The Economist*:
□ The sinking of the 'Titanic' (not 'The Titanic').
□ The sinking of the *Titanic* (not *The Titanic*).
c For the names of houses, inns or hotels inverted commas should not be used: *The Laurels, 21 Belvedere Road* (not '*The Laurels*').
d Inverted commas may also denote that a word is used in irony or sarcasm, in a sense which is not its generally accepted one, or that it is a slang or a dialect term. For this last purpose, however, they should be employed only if it is felt necessary to apologise for the use of such words. Where the slang or dialect word is natural in its setting, no inverted commas should be used. Inverted commas are correctly used in this example of irony:
□ The tablecloth was a silent witness that 'gourmets' had just dined.

There is no need for inverted commas for dialect in this Yorkshire joke:

□ Wife: 'What's up, luv?'
Husband: 'I'm 'ome sick.'
Wife: 'But this is yer 'ome.'
Husband: 'Aye, an' I'm sick o'it.'

invigorate

See **enervate**.

invite

The only correct use of this word is as a verb. It should never be used as a noun to replace *invitation.*

-ise/-ize

This suffix can be added to nouns and adjectives to form verbs. The meaning is 'to make': *popularise* is 'to make popular'. With this causative sense, the suffix is now widely accepted. However, it is still considered an unwanted Americanism by some and should be used with care. This is particularly true where there is no causative meaning attached to the ending. (See **itemize**, where the simple word *list* is much better English.)

The spelling is *-ize* in America and usually *-ise* in England. Whichever form one chooses, it is best to use it consistently. A few words must always be spelt *-ise* however: *advise*, *advertise*, *arise*, *comprise*, *compromise*, *despise*, *exercise*, *improvise*, *prise* (open), *supervise*, *surprise*, *televise*. If uncertain, refer to a good dictionary. Similar advice applies to the ending for nouns: *-isation/-ization.*

issue with

Since it is so common in the armed services, the expression *to issue people with things* has now become accepted in everyday English:

□ All the students were *issued with* two notebooks each.

It is, however, better avoided. Notebooks are *issued to* students: students are *provided with* notebooks.

it

For possible misuse in such sentences as *Having heard the evidence, it should now be possible to arrive at a decision . . .*, see **-ing 1**.

italics

Strictly speaking, since the word is an adjective (short for *italic type*) we should say that a word is printed *in italic* (compare *roman*, *gothic*), but *italics* has become accepted.

In print *italics* are used for titles of literary and musical works, and for names of newspapers and periodicals (see **titles** for details); for the proper names of ships, aeroplanes, etc; for foreign words and expressions which have not been fully adopted into the English language; occasionally to emphasise a word or draw special attention to it (though this should be resorted to very rarely); and to denote a word as distinct from the thing the word stands for:

□ 'A book was lying on the table.'
In this sentence *book* and *table* are both nouns.

itemize

An ugly word which should be avoided. Use *list* instead. (See **-ise/-ize**.)

its/it's

There is no apostrophe in the possessive *its*. *It's* is short for *it is* or *it has*. Even publishing companies are guilty of confusing the two. A sentence from a Hodder and Stoughton advertisement in *The Times* reads *Now in it's second printing!* And just to show how common the error is, here are two more examples, both from the *Guardian*:

□ Even as I write, a letter drops on my desk, proclaiming *it's author's* outrage at the praise which I had 'lavished on . . .'.

□ Cradled in a grand amphitheatre of hills, *it's* setting is striking, although the harbour beach is disappointing.

-ize (verb ending)

See **-ise/-ize**.

j

jail

This is the preferred spelling for noun and verb. See **gaol/jail**.

jargon

Strictly speaking, *jargon* is the specialised vocabulary of a particular trade, professional, academic or other group which is introduced into everyday English, where it is out of place. It has come to be used also in the sense of the mechanical, unimaginative copying of clichés, circumlocutions, etc, in place of simpler and more direct language. Any writer who has a regard for style and sincerity of expression will avoid it.

The specialised vocabulary (the *jargon*) of linguistics, for example, includes *equi NP deletion*, *nominalization*, etc. Such words are appropriate in professional linguistic literature, but not anywhere else.

In the more general sense of *jargon*, there are endless examples in commerce, journalism, etc:

□ The Company takes a positive stance towards growth.

(See also **clichés**, **commercial jargon**, **-ese** and **journalese**.)

jewellery/jewelry

Both spellings are accepted, though *jewellery* is to be preferred.

journalese

Means 'the language of journalism'. One might indeed wonder why newspapers and magazines should use language in different ways from anyone else. There is no doubt, however, that the popular press in particular certainly does, and its influence is felt in many other areas.

Some features of journalese are understandable in the context; short words rather than long ones are naturally used in headlines: *investigation* becomes *probe*; *questioning* or *interrogation* become *quiz*; *examination* becomes *test*.

Not just words are shortened but also paragraphs and sentences. In many newspapers today it is uncommon to find paragraphs longer than one or two sentences. Sentences themselves are brief, with few subordinate clauses. Within a sentence, one often finds concise constructions of the type:

□ Sixty-seven year old, unflappable ex-Prime Minister James Callaghan said today that . . . .

Generally most of these stylistic devices are best avoided. The striving for effect and for distinctiveness of this nature is best left to the newspapermen who feel the need for it.

(See also **-ese** and **nouns as adjectives**.)

judgement/judgment

Both spellings are common; *judgement* seems to be winning the battle in England, *judgment* in America.

just

For its position in a sentence, see **particularly 1**.

k

kerb/curb

See **curb/kerb**.

kidnap

Past tense is spelt *kidnapped* in British English. See **worship** and **spelling 6**.

kind

1 Kind of The construction *those kind of people, these kind of chocolates*, where we have a plural demonstrative adjective qualifying a singular noun (*kind*) is often heard in speech, and we should perhaps be tolerant of it as a colloquialism. It has, after all, a long history – the first record of its use dates back to 1380, and Shakespeare used it in *King Lear*:

☐ These kind of knaves I know.

None the less, it is best excluded from written English. The alternatives are *that kind of person, this kind of chocolates*, and *people of that kind, chocolates of this kind*. Incidentally we may notice that *this kind of chocolates* may refer to the make or brand whereas *chocolates of this kind* refers to some characteristic of quality of them. The same observations apply to *sort*.

2 What kind of a Some people object to *what kind of a* + noun, contending that the article should not be used; but there is a difference. *What kind of worker is he?* enquires about his trade or occupation. *What kind of a worker is he?* inquires about his proficiency or capability. Similarly:

☐ *What kind of* doctor is he? (a doctor of medicine, science, philosophy?)

☐ *What kind of a* doctor is he? (what are his capabilities as a doctor?)

☐ *What kind of* holiday did you have? (camping, touring, by the seaside?)

☐ *What kind of a* holiday did you have? (how did you enjoy it?)

3 All kind of *All kind of things* is often heard in speech, but is not accepted idiom. Amend to *all kinds of things*.

4 Kind of *She kind of giggled*. Accepted colloquially especially in America, but not to be used in most types of written English.

kindly

1 Kind and kindly What is the difference between *kind* and *kindly* as adjectives? *Kind* means 'characterised by kindness in itself; helpful': *a kind thought, a kind deed, a very kind person*, ie one from whom others experience kindness.
Kindly means 'prompted by kindness, or indicative of kindness; friendly': *a kindly smile, a kindly thought, a woman of a kindly nature.*
2 As an adverb As an adverb, *kindly* corresponds to the adjective *kind*; one who does a *kind* action acts *kindly*. The adjective *kindly* has no adverbial counterpart. We must say *in a kindly manner* or *in a kindly way*, not *kindlily*.
3 As a courtesy This is often used incorrectly, as:
☐ You are *kindly* requested to close the door behind you.
The request is not kind, though compliance with it would be. Amend to *Kindly close the door behind you* or *Please close the door behind you.* Of these two possibilities, the second is the better: it is shorter, just as courteous, and more grammatical. Therefore do not use *kindly* in requests where *please* will do. Why is it that those who draw up notices of this kind think that a circumlocutory manner is more polite than a simple and direct one? If *No Smoking* is felt to be rather short, *Please do not smoke* is every bit as courteous as *Patrons are earnestly requested to refrain from smoking*, and only half the length.
4 After thank you Do not say *Thank you kindly* but *Thank you very much.*

knelt/kneeled

See **past tense and participle: regular or irregular form?**

knit

When the reference is to knitting garments, the past tense and the past participle are *knitted*:
☐ She *knitted* her husband's socks
☐ She has *knitted* herself a cardigan
☐ This garment is badly *knitted.*
In all other senses both past tense and past participle are usually *knit*:
☐ He *knit* his brows
☐ The ends of the rope were *knit* together
☐ A play with a *well-knit* plot.
(See also **past tense and participle: regular or irregular form?**)

knot

(the unit of speed) A *knot* is one nautical mile an hour. A ship therefore travels at so many *knots*, not so many *knots an hour*.

Koran

There are other spellings, but this is the one recommended in English. Do not use inverted commas or italics. It should be spelt with an initial capital letter.

l

lack/absence

Here *lack* is used incorrectly:

☐ The poem is the more affecting because of the *lack* of all false sentiment.

The word required is *absence*, not *lack*. *Lack* means shortage or insufficiency of something necessary or desirable, as *lack of time*, *lack of money*, *lack of food*. We may speak of a person's *lack* of manners, experience, intelligence, etc, but not of his *lack* of nervousness, affectation or self-consciousness. *Absence* suggests 'non-presence, non-existence':

☐ His absence from home worried his mother

☐ The absence of reliable data slowed down the research.

laden

See **loaded/laden**.

lady/woman

To indicate sex, use *woman*: *a woman teacher*, *a woman doctor*, *women students*, *women writers*. Apart from its use to denote character or social rank, *lady* is a courtesy term, and should be employed only (a) for direct address, and then only in the plural, as *Ladies and Gentlemen* (*lady* used for this purpose is not standard English: the singular is *madam*), and (b) in the presence of the person concerned, but not directly to her:

☐ Could you find this *lady* a seat, please?

☐ If any *lady* owns this watch, will she please come forward and claim it?

laid

See **lay/lie**.

last

Last night, last Tuesday, last week, last month, last year, used adverbially, are idiomatic English, but not *last century.* We usually say *in the last century* or *during the last century.* Nor is it possible to say *last evening, last afternoon* or *last morning.* We must say *yesterday evening, afternoon, morning,* but it is not possible to say *yesterday night.*

late/former/ex-

When used of a person who has relinquished an office or a position (*the late Headmaster, the late Archbishop of Canterbury*), *late* in the sense of 'former' is not incorrect. It is best avoided, however, because of the ambiguity caused by another sense of *late* ('dead'), as in:

□ Mrs Farmer's *late* husband was a dentist.

If this sentence was intended to mean that Mrs Farmer had been married more than once, it would be necessary to refer to her *former* husband. The prefix *ex-*, attached to human nouns, also means 'former' and suggests the person is still living:

□ The ex-Headmaster will present the awards at this year's Prize Day.

latter

1 The latter *The latter* should be used only for the last of two. If more than two things or persons are concerned, *the last*, or *the last mentioned* must be used, or the noun must be repeated. *The latter* should never be used in the sense of 'the thing, or the person, just referred to' when it is the only one mentioned:

□ About a kilometre further on stood a large, old-fashioned house. *The latter* appeared to be uninhabited.

Latter is contrasted with *former*, and if there is no *former* there can can be no *latter.*

Even where two things or persons are concerned there is no point in using *the latter* if the sentence would be clear without it:

□ We knocked at the door, which was opened by a rather aged butler. *The latter* asked us our business. (One would hardly expect the door to make the enquiry.)

□ Our attention was attracted by a small boy, accompanied by a woman who appeared to be his mother. *The latter* was about thirty years of age. (There is no likelihood of our supposing it was the boy who was thirty years of age; and in any case, *she* would have been sufficient indication.)

2 Latter meaning 'the last few' *Latter* in the sense of 'the last few', or 'the part towards the end' is accepted in such expressions as *the latter years of Queen Victoria's reign, in the latter part of his life* (in the last few years), *the latter days of summer* (in the last few days of summer). It is a survival of an older use.

3 Latterly *Latterly* sometimes occurs as an adverb, but there is really no need for it. It conveys no more than *lately* or *recently*.

laudable/laudatory

Laudable means 'deserving of praise': *a laudable effort. Laudatory* means 'bestowing praise': *a very laudatory review of a book.* Both words are rather formal.

lawful/legal

There is a considerable area of usage where the two words overlap. Indeed, both OED and COD explain *legal* as meaning 'lawful', and vice versa. But there are differences, and one cannot always be replaced by the other.

Legal is always used when the sense is 'concerned with the law' or 'pertaining to the law': *the legal profession, a legal point, a legal ruling, legal documents, legal proceedings.* Anything which has to do with the application or administration of the law, that is to say, is denoted by *legal.*

But *legal* refers only to the law of the land. Where the moral or ecclesiastical law is concerned, *lawful* is the word:

☐ It is *lawful* for a Christian to bear arms

☐ It is *unlawful* to take away a man's human rights.

Lawful may, however, also be used when the law of the land is in question. There are the fixed expressions *one's lawful wife, to be engaged in one's lawful business, on all lawful occasions,* where *lawful* means 'conforming with the law', or 'not violating or transgressing the law'.

lay/lie

The confusion of the two verbs is very common and has a long history – it is found as early as 1300. *Lay* is transitive, ie it must have an object: *lay a book on the table, lay a carpet. Lie* is intransitive, ie it has no object: *Lie down, you will soon feel better.*

The parts of the two verbs are as follows:

☐ *Present*	*Present Participle*	*Past*	*Past Participle*
lie	lying	lay	lain
lay	laying	laid	laid

Note the spelling of the past tense and past participle of *lay*. There is no such word as *layed*.

Care must be taken not to confuse the two participles. It is common to hear in spoken English the incorrect *He was laid on the couch* when what was intended was *He was lying on the couch. He was laid* is correct only when the meaning intended is that someone placed him there:

☐ After his wounds had been dressed, he was *laid* on the couch by the porters.

Here is an example from the *Daily Telegraph* of another common mistake, the confusion of the past tense forms:

☐ One man was arrested. As police tried to drive him away demonstrators *laid* down in the path of their vehicle.

In this headline from the *Daily Mail*, the imperative forms have been confused:

☐ Britons In Iran Warned: *Lay* Low.

(See also **participles 4**, **stood** and **sat**.)

The noun forms also present difficulty. Say:

☐ The *lie* of the land (not *the lay of the land*).

Several hens have not laid for the last few days is accepted idiom. The direct object *eggs* is understood.

The verb *lie* in the sense of 'to tell a falsehood' is quite a separate word from that which is treated above. It has the present participle *lying*, and the past tense and past participle *lied*. Its use is quite regular.

leading question

Not the main question nor a pointed one, but one which prompts or even forces the answer that is hoped for, as:

☐ But then you made every effort to remedy the situation, didn't you?

leant/leaned

See **past tense and participle; regular or irregular form?**

leapt/leaped

See **past tense and participle; regular or irregular form?**

learn/teach

The verb *learn*, surprisingly, is often used where *teach* is the word required. It is not uncommon to hear sentences like:

☐ He *learnt* me to read.

☐ That'll *learn* you. You won't do that again.

Learn means 'to study', *teach* means 'to instruct'. The incorrect sentences should, therefore, be amended to *He taught me . . .* and *That'll teach you . . . .*

On *learnt* or *learned*, see **past tense and participle: regular or irregular form?**

least

On the use of *the* before *least*, see **the 5**.

leave

On *leave alone* and *leave go*, see **let**.

left

In political contexts, *the Left* (with a capital), but *left-wing* (small *l*). (See **capital letters 7**.)

leg

To give a person a leg up is an accepted colloquialism. *Leg* in the sense of a stage of a journey, or a round of a sporting event, is now accepted in Standard English:

□ The journey to the USA was the first *leg* of his trip round the world. The next *leg* will be Australia and India.

It is frequently heard on sports programmes:

□ Liverpool is through to the next *leg* of the FA cup.

legal

See **lawful/legal**.

leisure

Note the *ei* in the spelling.

lend

See **borrow/lend**.

leopard

Note the unpronounced *o* in the spelling.

less

1 Less and fewer There is very considerable confusion about *less* and *fewer*. The first is the comparative of *little*, the second the comparative of *few*. A simple rule to remember is that *less* is used for quantity, amount, size: *less time*, *less money*, *less height*, *ten pounds less*. These are often 'mass nouns' (ie nouns which cannot take the indefinite article: *a time*, *a money* are impossible in this sense.) *Fewer* is used for number: *fewer apples*, *fewer opportunities*, *fewer cars on the road*. It is usually before 'count nouns' (ie nouns which allow the indefinite article: *an apple*, *an opportunity*).

This rule is not inflexible.

To avoid awkward phrases such as *a few fewer*, *many fewer*, *several fewer*, it is better to use *less*:

☐ We could do with a few more workers and a few *less* supervisors.

Also, in the context of a numeral, many would accept *less*:

☐ Five more candidates entered this year than last, but three *less* passed.

Indeed, *fewer* is losing ground to *less* not just as in these examples but in nearly all cases. (See **few**.)

2 Less, lower and smaller Do not speak of *a less price* or *a less number*. Say *a lower price* and *a smaller number*.

lesser

A double comparative form, used in the sense of 'the less important or the less serious of two things': *the lesser light*, *the lesser of two evils*, *the lesser novelists of the nineteenth century*. It may be used adverbially: *a lesser-known painter*.

lest

Followed by *should* (*They took their umbrellas lest it should rain*) or by a subjunctive (*Lest* we *forget*), but not by *will* or *would*. It is infrequent today. In fact, it is sufficiently infrequent for a journalist in the *Daily Telegraph* to confuse it with *unless*:

☐ It was a rather elderly, staid, condescending but solicitous aunt gathering her voluminous skirts about her trim ankles *unless* she should inadvertently shock us. Use *for fear that* instead.

let

1 Let plus objective case *Let* is followed by pronouns in the objective case:

☐ *Let you and me* always do our best. (Not you and *I*.)

☐ *Let them* (or *those*, but not *they*) who make wars fight them.

2 Let meaning 'allow' Where *let* means 'to allow, permit', it is a common error to include *to* before the following infinitive:

☐ John's father would not *let* him go hang-gliding,

not:

☐ John's father would not *let* him *to* go hang-gliding.

3 Let alone *Let alone*, as in:

☐ I can scarcely afford to live in my present house, *let alone* in a more expensive one,

is acceptable in speech but should be replaced by *much less* in writing.

4 Let/leave go *Let go* and *leave go* are both accepted: *Don't let go until I tell you,* or *Don't leave go until I tell you.* Both expressions may be followed by *of* plus a noun or pronoun: *Leave go of the rope.*

5 Let well alone/leave . . . alone Except for the traditional phrase *let well alone, leave* (in the sense of 'do not interfere with'), as in *leave those flowers alone,* is preferred to *let* in writing.

letters

1 Sender's address Recent trends towards a more informal style of punctuation mean that it is no longer necessary to punctuate addresses in business or private letters. The sender's address, but not his name, should be written in the top right-hand corner of the paper together with the date. The Post Office in Britain likes to have the post town written in capital letters, and the postcode as the last line of the address. The address may be blocked (especially in typewritten letters) or indented as shown:

□ 75 Gainsborough Avenue
GREENFIELDS
Rothshire RA2 6BN
15 July 19__
	75 Gainsborough Avenue
	  GREENFIELDS
	    Rothshire RA2 6BN
	      15 July 19__

If there is a telephone number, it should be written in the top left-hand corner.

2 Recipient's address In formal or business letters, the name and address of the *recipient* are written on the left of the page and should begin on the line below the date:

□ The Manager
Super Bolts Ltd
Mill Lane
BRICKSTOWN
Rothshire RA7 6NR

3 The salutation The salutation is written on the left-hand side of the paper on the line below the date or under the address of the recipient, if it is included. Capital letters are used and the salutation is always followed by a comma:

□ Dear Sally,
□ Dear Mr Cartwright,
□ Dear Sir,

In America, a colon replaces the comma:
□ Dear Sally:
The letter itself begins under the comma (or colon) and each new paragraph is indented by the same amount. Alternatively, and especially in typed letters, there is no indentation. Each new paragraph begins at the left-hand margin.
4 The subscription The ending of the letter (or subscription) must be in keeping with the salutation. Some informal subscriptions are: *Yours, Best Wishes, Your friend, Love.*
In formal letters use *Yours sincerely* if the recipient is addressed by name in the salutation (*Dear Mr Smith*) and *Yours faithfully* if the recipient is addressed as *Dear Sir* or *Dear Madam.* Always write *Yours* with a capital letter, and remember that it does not have an apostrophe. A comma should always follow the subscription:
□ Yours sincerely,
Best wishes,
Leave at least a line's spacing between the end of the letter and the subscription. The subscription may be written level with the left-hand margin or begun just under halfway along the line.
5 The signature The signature is written on the line beneath the subscription. In very informal and friendly letters, the christian name is enough but a person's full signature should appear on formal letters. *Mrs* or *Miss* may be written in brackets after a woman's full signature, but this is less common today.
In typewritten letters, it is usual to write the full name and title of the person writing the letter at least two lines below the subscription, thus leaving room for the handwritten signature. The position or office may be typed below this, as in this example:
□ Yours sincerely,

(signature)

Dr Peter Jones
Lecturer in Education
6 Envelope address It is important to address the envelope clearly so that it is easily read. The address should begin halfway down

and approximately a third of the way across the envelope so that no postmark is stamped through any part of it. Again, the address may be boxed or indented.

(See also **Esquire/Esq**, **Messrs**, **Ms** and **pp**.)

liable

Liable for means 'responsible in law': *The child is only ten years old: his parents are liable for his behaviour.*

Liable to do something means 'having a tendency to do something': *We are all liable to make mistakes, she is liable to fly into fits of temper.*

Liable to something means 'suffering from or being subject to something': *He is liable to bad headaches*; *if you drink and drive, you're liable to a heavy fine.*

Do not use *liable* for mere possibility or probability. *We are liable to get fogs in November* is correct, but *We are liable to get a storm before the day is out* is not. *May have, are likely to*, or *shall probably* is required.

libel

A written statement, in writing or print, that damages a person's reputation. It does not cover damage to reputation by the spoken word, which is *slander*.

liberality/liberalism

Liberality means 'generosity'. *Liberalism* is a liberal outlook or policy in politics, religion, etc, or a broad, tolerant attitude of mind in matters of belief. The word should be written with a capital letter only if it refers to the Liberal Party and its doctrines. Thus write:

☐ At the moment the future for *Liberalism* seems much brighter than it has done for many years (ie for the Liberal Party and the principles for which it stands),

but:

☐ He always stood for *liberalism* in religion

☐ In many countries a new spirit of *liberalism* is in the air.

licence/license

Like *practice* and *practise*, *prophecy* and *prophesy*, the spelling with the *c* is the noun, that with the *s* is the verb. (The key to them all is *advice* and *advise*, which no one confuses.)

Licensed is spelt with an *s*, not a *c*: *Licensed to sell tobacco, a licensed hotel, I have licensed my car.* The adjective *unlicensed* is made up from the participle *licensed* with the negative prefix added, so that too must be spelt with an *s*: *unlicensed premises*. American usage spells both the noun and the verb with *s*. (Compare **defence**. See also **practice/practise**.)

lie

In the sense of 'to tell untruths', it is quite regular: *lie, lying, lied, lied*. In the sense of 'to recline', its principal parts are: *lie, lying, lay, lain*. (See also **lay/lie**.)

light years

Often used incorrectly as here:

□ The two pieces of legislation in question . . . remain unchanged since Queen Victoria nodded her head to them *light years* ago. (*Irish Times*)

Light years is a measure of distance, not of time: *Stars in our galaxy lie within 60,000 light years of earth.*

lightening/lightning

The spelling without the *e* is the noun (*a flash of lightning, a lightning conductor*), that with the *e* is the present participle and gerund of the verb *to lighten*, in whatever sense it is used:

□ The driver was *lightening* the load on his lorry

□ A scheme for *lightening* the burden of taxation

□ It has been thundering and *lightening* for the last half-hour.

For the figurative use, when the sense is 'quick, rapid', the spelling is *lightning*, since the figure is taken from the rapidity of the *lightning* flash: *to run like lightning, a lightning decision, a lightning war*.

like

(pseudo-preposition)

1 With objective case *Like you and me*, not *like you and I*. Though actually an adjective or an adverb, according to the context (it can have degrees of comparison since we can say *more like you and me*), *like* is treated as a preposition, and pronouns that follow it must be in the objective case.

2 As a subordinating conjunction These are incorrect:

□ Do it *like* I told you

□ Please leave the room *like* you found it.

Like should not be used as a subordinating conjunction to introduce an adverb clause of manner or comparison. Use *as*. It is, however, found in the works of many writers. (See **as**.)

3 As an ellipsis *I want a dress like Mary wears* is correct, since it is an ellipsis of *like that which Mary wears.* The group of words introduced by *like* is not adverbial but adjectival.

4 Like plus clause indicating quality It is permissible to use *like* instead of *as* when the words that follow it are felt to be descriptive of some characteristic or quality rather than to constitute a comparison of ways or methods:

☐ I can't sing *like* I used to. (The reference is to the quality of the singing rather than the manner.)

☐ He writes just *like* his brother did when he was young. (Descriptive of the style and appearance of the writing rather than the manner.)

5 Like for as if *Like* for *as if* is substandard: *It looks like we are going to have a thunderstorm.*

6 The like(s) of *The likes of us* should always be replaced by *people like us. I have never seen* the like *of it* (but not *the likes*) is quite acceptable, though less common than *I have never seen anything like it*. The plural *likes* is, of course, perfectly good English in the expression *one's likes and dislikes.*

likely

The following examples are not accepted English, either in Britain or in America:

☐ It will *likely* rain tomorrow

☐ Her train has *likely* been delayed by fog.

Use *probably* or *possibly*. There is no objection to *very likely.*

liquefy

Note the spelling, with the medial *e*, not *i*.

literally

Literally is opposed to *figuratively*. It should never be used merely to give emphasis (He *literally* ran down the road), and above all it should not be attached to an expression which is obviously metaphorical. *It literally rained cats and dogs* means that cats and dogs actually fell from the sky. Other examples of misuse:

☐ His eyes were literally glued to the television screen

☐ The tennis player literally wiped the court with her opponent

☐ The comedian's jokes literally brought the house down.

And a description of a tennis match from *The Scotsman*:

☐ Miss Navratilova also played superbly, literally knocking 15-year-old Tracey Austin off the court.

It is correctly used when it is employed to tell us that an expression which is generally understood metaphorically is, in this particular context, to be taken at its face value, and not metaphorically:
□ I *literally* kicked the rude fellow out of the room.

livid

Like *hectic*, *livid* refers to a colour. *Livid* is the bluish-grey colour of lead and the word is often applied to a person or the way he looks: *a livid bruise, a body livid with cold, a face livid with rage, a livid corpse*, etc. The adjective is often misused to mean 'very angry':
□ She was *livid* when I told her I'd lost the money.
This use is acceptable colloquially.

loaded/laden

For the past tense and past participle of the verb, use *loaded*. *Laden* is an adjective meaning 'heavily burdened': *a ship laden with treasure, the smoke-laden atmosphere*. We may say that a tree is either *loaded* or *laden* with fruit. Fire-arms are *loaded*. *Laden* is more poetic in style.

loan

Loan is a noun; the verb is *lend*. Do not say *He has loaned me his typewriter, this book has been loaned to me by a friend*, although these are quite acceptable in American English. British English does allow *loan* as a verb in formal situations, where the loan is for a long period:
□ The Tate Gallery *loaned* some of its treasures to the Louvre.
(See also **borrow/lend 3**.)

loathe/loth

Loathe is the verb, *loth* is the adjective: *I loathe castor oil*; *I was loth to do it*. The adjective may also be spelt *loath*, but never with a final *e*.

local

The local (a public house) and *the locals* (the inhabitants of a small town or village) are colloquialisms.

locate

It should only be used in the sense of 'to place; situate':
□ It is important to *locate* new industries where labour will be easily available
□ The greater part of Britain's coalfields are *located* in South Yorkshire, Durham and South Wales.

The use of the word as though it meant 'find' or 'discover' is incorrect: *We have so far been unable to locate the fault.*

look(s)

1 Look(s) *You can't judge a person by his looks* (ie his features, or his facial appearance – compare *good looks*), but *the look on one's face, the look in one's eye*, etc.

2 By the look *We are going to get a storm, by the* look *of it.* (Not *by the looks of it.*) Similarly, *by the* look *of things*, not *by the looks of things.*

3 Compounds Compounds like *good-looking, ill-looking, evil-looking, ugly-looking* must be written with a hyphen.

loose

See **unloose** and on whether to use *loose* or *loosely*, see **tight/tightly**.

Lord Mayor/Lady Mayoress

1 Be careful to avoid the solecism *The Lord and Lady Mayoress.* Say *The Lord Mayor and Lady Mayoress.*

2 Plurals: *Lord Mayors, Lady Mayoresses.*

3 The Lady Mayoress is the Lord Mayor's wife (or sometimes, if he is a widower, his daughter or other female relative). If a woman occupies the position of first citizen she is known as the Lord Mayor, just as a man would be. Her husband has no official position.

4 The designation *The Right Honourable the Lord Mayor of . . .* is enjoyed by the Lord Mayors of London, York, Belfast and Dublin in the British Isles, and by those of Melbourne, Sydney, Adelaide, Brisbane, Hobart and Perth (Australia), but not by any others. In Scotland the Lord Provosts of Edinburgh and Glasgow are likewise entitled to the prefix *The Right Honourable*. In no case should it be placed before the personal name of the dignitary in question, as it pertains to the office, not to the person who for the time being holds it. The correct style is *The Right Honourable the Lord Mayor of X, Alderman A B Carter*, not *The Lord Mayor of X, The Rt Hon A B Carter*. (See also **Right Honorable**.)

lot(s)

A lot of and *lots of* are treated as adjectives, equivalent in meaning to *many* or *much*, as the case may be. Any verb to which they are the grammatical subject, therefore, agrees in number, not with *lot* or *lots*, but with the noun or pronoun that follows *of*:

□ *A lot of money* has been wasted
□ *A lot of people* have been ill
□ There is *lots of time* to spare
□ There are *lots of opportunities* for young men in industry.
(See also **much 2**.)

loth
See **loathe/loth**.

loud/loudly
See **adverb or adjective?**

lowbrow
See **highbrow**.

luxuriant/luxurious
Luxuriant means 'growing abundantly or in profusion'. The word is usually applied to vegetation, foliage or hair. *Luxurious* is suggestive of costliness, extravagance or over-indulgence: *luxurious furnishings, luxurious ways of living, a person with luxurious tastes.* Recently *luxury* has also come to be used as an adjective, and has begun to displace *luxurious* in some of its applications. If it is used at all it had best be kept as an epithet descriptive of those things which may be considered luxuries in themselves (*luxury articles, luxury foods, luxury goods*), or which advertisers and publicists wish us to think of as such: *a luxury liner, a luxury hotel, luxury travel, luxury flats.* It can easily become a 'glamour' word, and for that reason is best avoided.

m

mad
The *Harper Dictionary of Contemporary Usage* states that the use of *mad* for *annoyed, cross* or *angry* is informal American usage: but it is not confined to the United States. It has long been used in that sense colloquially in Britain, and can be found so used in Shakespeare's plays: eg *The Merchant of Venice*:

□ Now, in faith, Gratiano,
You give your wife too unkind a cause of grief:
An 'twere to me, I should be mad at it.

But the fact that Shakespeare used it does not make it acceptable as a literary term today.

madam/madame

As a polite term of address for a lady, spelt without the final *e*. The abbreviated form (used only in speech, usually by a servant to her mistress or a commoner to the Queen) is spelt *Ma'am*.

The French equivalent of the English *Mrs*, prefixed to a married lady's name, is spelt *Madame*, and is abbreviated to *Mme*. The plural is *Mesdames*, abbreviated to *Mmes*. The French term *Madame* is also sometimes adopted by ladies in England, whether married or not, for professional purposes, especially by teachers of dancing, singing, music, elocution and acting.

magnanimity/magnitude

Magnanimity means 'generosity'. *Magnitude* means 'size, importance' as in:

☐ Many people fail to recognise the *magnitude* of the problem.

The writer of the following sentence has confused the two words:

☐ Here was a man, he thought, who liked honesty . . . and would show *magnitude*, even compassion, to a worthy opponent. (James Dillon White, *Fair Wind to Malabar*)

Obviously *magnanimity* was the word the writer was looking for.

majority

1 Majority for number *Majority* may be used only for number with countable nouns, not for amount or quantity with mass nouns: *The majority of the eggs were bad* is correct; *The majority of the butter was bad* is not. Similarly, we cannot speak of *the majority of the land, the majority of the time, the majority of one's wealth*, We must use *most*, or *the greater part*.

2 Majority or most? There is no objection to the use of *majority* in the sense of 'most', or 'almost all'. It is used in this way in the first of the examples given above. But although the use has become accepted, it is as well to remember that *the majority* really means the greater as opposed to the smaller number. Fifty-one out of a hundred is a *majority*, but it is not *most*. When the word is given the more extended meaning it is to draw attention, by implication, to the minority to which the statement does not apply. If we are not concerned with the minority, *most* should be used: *Most children like sweets* is a statement about children in general. *The* *majority of children like sweets* reminds us that there may be some who do not.

3 Majority: singular or plural? When *majority* means the numerical difference between the greater and the smaller figure, it is singular:

☐ The candidate's *majority was* just over three thousand.

When it means the greater group thought of as a body, it is also singular:

☐ *The majority is* always able to impose its will on the minority.

When it individualises within the group it is plural:

☐ *The majority* of electors *have* already made up their minds which way they are going to vote.

(See also **minority**.)

mankind

Singular number. Referred to by *it* and *its*, not *they* and *their*.

manner

His manner of doing it and *The manner in which he did it* are both correct, but *The manner how he did it* and *The manner of how he did it* are not.

All manner of things (where *manner* means 'kind') and *by no manner of means* ('under no circumstances') are both accepted English.

Well-mannered, ill-mannered, good-mannered and *bad-mannered* are all acceptable. Of the four *ill-mannered* is the least common.

manuscript

The abbreviation is *MS* (capitals, and only one full stop in more traditional usage) for the singular, and *MSS* for the plural. In reading aloud, the full word *manuscript* should always be pronounced, even though the abbreviated form is written or printed. Consequently, write *a MS*, not *an MS* (see **a/an 4**).

many

See **much 2**.

mask/masque

A *mask* is a covering or disguise for the face; *masque* is the dramatic performance.

masterful/masterly

These are often confused as in:

☐ He has done the work in a *masterful* fashion.

Masterly was required. *Masterful* means 'assertive, strong-willed, determined to be master'. *Masterly* means 'skilful, in the manner of one who is a master of his craft'. Thus *a masterly piece of work*, *a masterly stroke, a masterly exposition of the subject*, but *a masterful child*.

mathematics

☐ Mathematics *is* an important subject
☐ Mathematics *was* never my strong point
☐ His mathematics *are* weak
☐ It comes to £58 if my mathematics *are* correct.

When the study or science of mathematics is in question, the verb is singular. (See also **acoustics**, **politics**.)

To modify a following noun, the simple noun is used without an apostrophe: *Mathematics master*, *Mathematics teacher*, *a mathematics lesson*, etc.

mattress

Note the double *t* and double *s*.

may

1 May as possibility

a Past tense might Beware of using *may* as a past tense as in:

☐ We took our mackintoshes with us, as we thought it *may* rain.

The past tense is *might*, in the sense of 'possibility'. (See also **could 1**.)

b With perfect infinitive Whether we use *may* or *might* with a perfect infinitive (which itself, of course, denotes something in the past) depends on whether we think of the possibility as being a present or a past one:

☐ He *may* have been injured (in the absence of any information to the contrary the possibility still exists).

☐ He *might* have been injured (the possibility existed in the past, but exists no longer).

c With present infinitive With a present infinitive, *might* shows a more remote possibility than *may*:

☐ I *may* be dead by this time next year (a serious contemplation of the possibility).

☐ I *might* be dead by this time next year (a possibility that cannot be ruled out, but is not very likely).

d In questions In questions, *may* is not used in the sense of possibility. Instead one finds *can* or *could*:

☐ *Can* they have found a cheap house to rent?

The answer, interestingly, to this question is:

☐ Yes, they *may* have.

Similarly, one finds *could* in the question and *might* in the answer. (See also **could 2**.)

2 May as permission

a To ask permission A few people still insist that *May I*? is the only correct form with which to ask permission. *Can I?* should also be accepted. Note that *May I?* is often used to be extra polite or deferential to someone. *Might I?* is more hesitant or restrained than *May I?*

b Past tense The usual past tense of *may* denoting permission is *could*:

□ This afternoon my father says we *may* spend two hours visiting you, but yesterday we *could* only spend half an hour.

3 The contracted negative *mayn't* is rarely used.

4 On *may* and *can*, see **can/may**.

maybe/may be

Written as one word, it is an adverb synonymous with *perhaps*: *Maybe I'll go, and maybe I won't.*

May be (two words), preceded by *it*, is followed by a *that*-clause:

It may be that our letter never reached him.

me

It's me is recognised as idiomatic English, though *I* is generally used when followed by a relative clause introduced by *who*:

□ Who's that? – It's me,

but:

□ It is *I* who am to blame.

Colloquially, however, we would say *It's me who is to blame.* (See also **they**.) On the use of *I* or *me* after *than*, and on *older than me*, *taller than me*, etc, see **than 1**. On the use of *me* after prepositions see **preposition 2** and **pronouns**.

mean

To most British people, to describe a person as *mean* implies that he is selfish or lacking in generosity. In the USA it may also be a way of saying that he is spiteful or vindictive.

The expressions *a mean trick* and *to take a mean advantage of someone* are both perfectly good British English, although the latter is less frequent.

means

His means (monetary resources) *are insufficient to keep him. This means* (method) *of transport is a very old one. Several means* (methods) *of transport are available to you.*

meantime/meanwhile

Both are used as adverbs, though *meanwhile* is to be preferred in British English. On the other hand, *in the meantime* is preferable to *in the meanwhile*, though the latter is not incorrect. For *Greenwich Mean Time* write the two words separately (not *Meantime*). The abbreviation is *GMT.* (Compare *BST* under **summer**.)

media

A plural noun in the sense of 'mass media', ie television, newspapers, etc. Consequently, it has a plural verb. Do not write *the media is having a greater importance in our society*, but *the media* are . . . .

medical adviser

Usually just a piece of pompous jargon for *doctor*. Use the simpler word. (See **jargon**.)

medieval

The spelling *medieval*, not *mediaeval*, is now more common.

Mediterranean

Note the double *r* in the spelling.

meet

1 Meet/meet with We *meet* a friend, we *meet* a deputation. *To meet* (*up*) *with* has the same sense but is somewhat American and colloquial.

To meet with is acceptable, as well as *meet* itself, where the meaning is 'encounter' or 'come across':

☐ He *met with* considerable opposition in his new job, as few people agreed with his views.

Particularly common phrases using *meet with* are: *meet with* an accident, misfortune, resistance, success, approval.

2 Meet meaning 'answer' *Meet* alone can be used with the sense of 'answer' or 'satisfy':

☐ He was very intelligent and articulate and *met* all the criticisms with logical arguments.

Common collocations are: *meet* one's obligations, duties, expenses, bills, needs, demands, requirements, standards.

3 Meet halfway To *meet someone halfway* means 'to compromise, come to a mutually satisfactory agreement'.

melted/molten
The past participle is always *melted*. *Molten* is used immediately before a noun, and then only of things which we normally think of as hard, solid substances: *molten metal, molten wax, molten candle grease*, but *melted snow, melted butter.*

menace
(noun) The real meaning is that of 'threat', 'danger'. The use of the word as a synonym for *nuisance* is accepted colloquially.

mental
Often used in an unacceptable way as in *He's mental* (meaning 'he's crazy'), which is substandard English. The only accepted meaning is 'pertaining to the mind': *mental arithmetic, mental disturbances, to make a mental note.*

merely
For its position in a sentence, see **particularly 1**.

Messrs
In addresses use *Messrs* before the names of firms if they are also personal names, as *Messrs J P Brown & Co, Messrs Freeman, Hardy & Willis, Ltd*, but not otherwise. Do not write *Messrs The Excelsior Book Co, Ltd*, or *Messrs Barclays Bank, Ltd.* A difficult point arises when a firm happens to have a woman's name, since *Messrs* is considered the plural of *Mr*: simply write *Susan Small & Co.* But it is progressively more common to miss out *Messrs* in all cases, whether the firm has a woman's name or not. (See also **letters** and **Mr/Mrs**.)

metal/metallic/metallurgy
Note the doubling of the *l* in *metallic* and *metallurgy.*

meter/metre
A *meter* is an instrument for measuring, as a *gas-meter* and in such combinations as *speedometer, hydrometer.* A *metre* is (a) the unit of linear measurement, and (b) the 'measure' of verse. The names of the various *metres*, according to the number of feet in a line of verse, are, however, spelt *-meter*: *hexameter, pentameter, tetrameter*, etc.

For the adjective, *metric* is used when the reference is to the *metre* as a unit of linear measurement (*the metric system*), *metrical* when it is to the *metre* of verse (*a metrical version of the Psalms*).

meticulous
Strictly, *meticulous* means 'over or unnecessarily careful':

□ He is *meticulous* in everything he does,
but popular usage has changed the meaning to 'careful, exact or precise'.

metre

See **meter/metre**.

metric/metrical

See **meter/metre**.

mews

(A place where stables were once situated.) Singular:
□ The *mews is* just off Park Lane.
When used as a common noun the word should, of course, be spelt with a small letter, but if it forms part of the name of a road or a street, as it often does in London, a capital must be used.

micro

See **mini/micro**.

middle

See **centre 3**.

Midsummer Day

Note the spelling: not *Midsummer's*. But there is also *mid-summer's* (with a small letter and hyphenated). *Midsummer Day* is 24 June. *A mid-summer's day* means a day in *mid-summer* (ie the middle of summer). Compare also *We do not expect to get snow in mid-summer*.

might

See **could 1** and **may**.

militate/mitigate

Militate (*against*) means 'to work against'; *mitigate* means 'to make something less serious'. *Mitigating circumstances* are circumstances which partly excuse a crime or error, thus making it seem less grave. The writer of the following sentence has used *mitigate against* instead of *militate against*:
□ There are other factors which *mitigate against* successful treatment. (*New Society*)

mini/micro

Mini is an abbreviation of the adjective *miniature*. It became a vogue word in the 1960s with *miniskirts*, *minicabs*, etc. A more precise word such as *short* or *small* would often have been much better. None the less it has now become firmly established in the language. In writing, its use should be restricted to accepted fixed

phrases (*minicomputer, minibus*), and a more exact word used in its place wherever possible. Modern practice is to write compound words formed with it without a hyphen.
To denote even smaller size, the prefix *micro* has been used. There are times when it serves a useful purpose – to distinguish a *minibus* of about 12 seats from a *microbus* with 6–8 seats, or to describe the specialist field of electronics called *microelectronics* and its products (*the microchip, a microprocessor*) – but again it is best to avoid its widespread use in writing.

miniature

Note spelling.

minimise

Strictly, the verb *minimise* means 'to reduce to the smallest amount or number' as in:
□ The teacher should attempt to *minimise* for his pupils the difficulties of learning French.
However, it is now also widely accepted to mean 'underestimate', as in:
□ The difficulties experienced by adults learning a foreign language should not be *minimised*.
It should not be used to mean 'belittle' as in *He always minimised the achievements of others, though he magnified his own.*
(For spelling, see **-ise/-ize**.)

minimum

Minimum is often used incorrectly as here:
□ A *minimum* of business was transacted on the Stock Exchange yesterday.
Presumably what the writer meant was 'little business', but that is not what he has said. It is generally used to mean 'the smallest possible amount', which in this case would be none at all. However small the amount of business was, it was not a *minimum* if there might have been less. There are two respects in which a certain amount of latitude is allowable, but neither of them applies here. They are:
1 *Minimum* may be used in the sense of 'the smallest amount possible in the particular circumstances':
□ We will get the business cleared up with the *minimum* of delay
□ The re-organisation has been so planned as to cause the *minimum* of dislocation in the factory.

2 It may also be used in the sense of 'the lowest permitted or agreed upon', as when we speak of *a minimum wage, a minimum of two weeks' holiday a year*, etc. The meaning here is that there may be more, but there must not be less.
The *minimum* temperature for a room is that below which the temperature should not be allowed to fall, but the *maximum* and *minimum* temperatures during the day, or over a period of time, as recorded by the thermometer, are the highest and the lowest that were actually reached.

minister
See **clergyman/minister**.

minority
Here is an example of incorrect use:
☐ In only a *minority* of cases dealt with has prosecution been found necessary. (from the report of a children's welfare organisation)
Do not use the word in this way. *Minority* does not mean 'few', or 'comparatively few' (ie few when compared with the total number of cases dealt with), but the smaller as contrasted with the larger number. Forty-nine out of a hundred is a *minority*. (See also **majority**.)

minus
Should be reserved for mathematical or statistical contexts. Except possibly in light-hearted writing or conversation, do not speak of *a hat minus the brim, a bicycle minus the front wheel.*

mistrust/distrust
Not 'trust wrongly or mistakenly', but 'regard with misgiving or suspicion': *I mistrusted his motives*. We usually *distrust* a person or his word (ie have no faith in them, or place no trust in them). *Mistrust* is rather more vague, suggesting an uneasy feeling that things are not what they appear, or what we should like them to be.

mitigate
See **militate/mitigate**.

mixed metaphor
To be avoided. The results are often ludicrous and amusing:
☐ He needs the victory to feed an aching, psychological hunger, but Nicklaus is a kettle of fish of a different colour. (*The Observer*)
☐ The dangerous hot-bed of war which has sprung up in Laos must be speedily extinguished. (A cabinet minister)

☐ . . . he burst into tears and, like a lanced boil, made a clean breast of things. (*The Financial Times*)
These more obvious examples are sometimes deliberate for humorous effect. A comedian once described a certain politician, who was uncertain what attitude to take, as 'sitting on the fence with both ears to the ground', and another as 'bending over backwards to maintain a low profile'!
It is much more common to slip from the metaphorical to the literal without realising it so that targets are passed, raised, lowered, beaten, reached and achieved, gaps are made narrower by being cut, and a free flow of goods is made possible by reducing bottlenecks. (See **target**, **gap** and **bottleneck**.)

molten

See **melted/molten**.

moment

At this moment in time. A favourite expression of public speakers, especially politicians. It means 'now', and that is the word that should replace it every time.

momentary/momentous

Momentary means 'occurring in the space of a moment', as *a momentary thought, a momentary suspicion. Momentous* means 'important on account of the consequences': *a momentous occasion, a momentous decision.*

monogram/monograph

A *monogram* is a device consisting of two or more letters written together or intertwined, usually the person's initials. Found on note-paper, handkerchiefs, etc. A *monograph* is a treatise written on one particular subject.

more

1 More than one *More than one*, followed by a singular noun as subject, takes a *singular* verb, despite the fact that *more than one* is notionally plural:
☐ *More than one* person *has* been concerned in this.
But *more* + plural noun + *than one* takes a *plural* verb:
☐ *More persons than one have* been involved.
That is to say, the number of the noun always determines the number of the verb. (See also **singular or plural verb? 7**.)

2 More as comparative Generally, the tendency to extend the use of *more* to adjectives which normally make their comparative in *-er* should be resisted (*more common* instead of *commoner, more silly* instead of *sillier*), but there may sometimes be justification for it if it emphasises the notion attaching to the positive degree:

□ A *more silly* remark I cannot imagine.

It is often to be preferred also for compounds: *a more common-looking person, a more badly-spoken person, a more healthy-looking child*, rather than *a commoner-looking person, a worse-spoken person, a healthier-looking child.*

3 Comparing two characteristics of the same thing The ordinary comparative, like *bigger, taller, longer*, is concerned with a comparison of the same quality or characteristic in two different things (the size of this compared with the size of that, etc), but it is also possible to compare two different characteristics or qualities in the same thing. For this, *more*, not *-er*, is always used:

□ He is *more lucky* than clever (not *luckier*).

□ I was *more sorry* than angry at what happened (not *sorrier*).

The same is true when the comparison is concerned with the applicability or otherwise of the notion expressed by the adjective. *He is no younger than I am* merely compares the ages of the two persons, without telling us whether either is really young or old. *He is no more young than I am* means that it would be no more appropriate to call him young than it is to call me young. For the same two purposes, *more* can also be used before a noun:

□ He is *more* a fool than a rogue

□ He is no *more* a company director than I am (said of someone who claims to be, or is generally thought to be, a company director but is not so).

(See also **comparative.**)

mortgage

Note spelling.

most

1 Most meaning 'almost' *Most everyone has heard of sake, the famous Japanese wine* (– from an airline's guide to Tokyo). An Americanism. Use *almost.*

2 Most meaning 'very' *He told a most amusing story*; *she was most rude to me*. This use of *most*, in the sense of 'very', is very frequently heard, and may be accepted not only in colloquial English but also in writing.

3 On the use of *the* before *most*, see **the 5**.

mostly

The normal adverb of degree is *most*:

□ Of all the competitors she was the one who *most* deserved to win.

Mostly means 'for the most part, though not entirely':

□ His stories were *mostly* about his travels in foreign parts

□ The audience consisted *mostly* of women.

Occasionally the two may get confused, as in the sentence *She is the person who is mostly to blame.* Since the sense is 'she more than any other', *most* is required.

mowed/mown

Mowed is the normal past tense and past participle (*I have mowed the lawn*); *mown* is used only immediately before a noun and usually in compounds, as *new-mown hay.*

Mr/Mrs

1 Punctuation Do not use a full stop. The shortened spelling is now regarded as the only one. There is now no full form.

2 Mr and Esq *Mr* must not be written before a name if *Esq* is placed at the end. (See also **Esquire/Esq.**)

3 Plural Plural: *Messrs Smith and Jones, the Messrs Smith, the two Mr Smiths* (but never *the Messrs Smiths*); *Mesdames Smith and Jones, the Mesdames Smith, the two Mrs Smiths.* In spoken English *the two Mr Smiths* and *the two Mrs Smiths* are the usual forms. (See also **Messrs.**)

MS

Plural: MSS; see **manuscript.**

Ms

The energetic efforts of Women's Lib reformers, especially in America, have caused some people to replace *Mrs* and *Miss* with *Ms*, which does not indicate marital status. It remains to be seen whether feminist aspirations will become accepted practice. *Ms* is beginning to appear as an option in official documents. A passport application form, for instance, requires one to state 'Mr, Mrs, Miss, Ms or title'. (See **Women's Lib** for further instances.)

much

1 Much or very? Generally participles are modified by *much* (*The privilege has been much abused*; *her dress was much admired*) and adjectives by *very* (*very good, very old, very clever*). Certain participles which have largely lost their verbal force and are felt to

be adjectival, however, take *very*:
□ I was *very* interested in his story
□ We are *very* worried about the position
□ I feel *very* concerned about him.
Conversely, participles used before a noun to make a compound adjective with a modifying adverb, take *much*: *a much abused privilege, a much travelled person, a much discussed question.* (See also **very/much**.)
2 Much, a lot of, many In a positive sentence, except in very formal style, it is necessary to substitute *a lot of* for *much*. *He has much money* becomes *He has a lot of money*. *Much*, however, in interrogative and negative sentences is quite acceptable:
□ I don't have *much* money
□ Does he have *much* money?
(See also **lot(s)**.)
Many follows this pattern to a lesser extent. *He has many friends* is more acceptable than *He has much money*, but in both cases *a lot of* sounds more natural.
American English is more tolerant of *much* and *many* in positive sentences.

much more/much less

Often confused as in:
□ She scarcely bothered to look at us, *much more* speak to us.
Not *much more*, but *much less* (ie *much less* did she bother). *Much more* is correct however, in *I would help even an enemy if he were in distress, much more a friend* (ie *much more* would I help).

Muslim

This spelling is preferred to *Moslem*.

mutual/reciprocal

1 Correct usage If you can possibly avoid it, do not speak of people having *mutual friends, mutual interests*, etc. They have friends or interests *in common*. *Mutual* means 'acting in both directions in the same way, and at the same time': *mutual attraction, mutual regard, mutual distrust* (the attraction, regard, distrust, etc which two people or two parties have for each other). Consequently (a) do not use the words *of each other* with *mutual* (*a mutual dislike of each other*), since they are redundant; and (b) do not speak of *a mutual agreement*, since there can be no agreement unless both parties accept it. But *an agreement for* *mutual assistance* is, of course, correct, since it is the assistance which is to be mutual. What has been said of *mutual* applies also the adverb *mutually*.

2 Extension of meaning Both adjective and adverb may be legitimately extended from their strict sense to cover cases where the idea of 'common' is combined with that of 'each other', as *a scheme should be to our mutual advantage* (ie A, by seeking an advantage for himself, also brings an advantage to B, and vice versa); but it cannot be used if this idea of the effect or action of two persons or things upon each other is absent, as it is used in the following sentence from Wilkie Collin's novel *The Moonstone*:

☐ Mr Franklin and I had both talked of foreign politics till we could talk no longer, and had then mutually fallen asleep in the heat of the sun.

3 Mutual/reciprocal *Reciprocal* takes two things separately; *mutual* takes them together. Consequently *reciprocal* may be used, as *mutual* cannot, of one only in its relation to the other. If two countries reach an agreement for a reciprocal reduction of tariffs, and A reduces her tariffs on goods imported from B, then B may be said to take reciprocal action when she follows suit by reducing her tariffs on goods from A.

mythical/mythological

Mythical means 'untrue, having no real existence'. *Mythological* means 'concerned with mythology'.

n

naïve

Though *naïve* is the French feminine form, in English it is used for both sexes. The form *naive*, without the diaeresis over the *i*, is quite acceptable.

named

1 Named as Here is an example of *named* used incorrectly:

☐ He was *named as* John by his parents, but all his friends called him Jack.

Write instead *He was named John.* John, or whatever name follows the verb, is a complement. But:

□ Cardinal Wojtyła has been *named as* the successor to Pope John Paul I

is correct.

2 Named after *He was named Edward for his father.* This is an Americanism. British English would use *after.* This particular sense of *after* (meaning 'in imitation of') is found also in such expressions as *after the style of, after the manner of*:

□ A poem in heroic couplets, *after the manner of* Pope.

We also say that a child *takes after* (resembles) his father.

names

For the plurals of proper names, see **plural forms**, and for the possessive, see **apostrophe 3**.

nationalise/naturalise

Britain has several *nationalised* industries (ie industries taken over by the State); they include telecommunications, steel and the railways. *Naturalise* means 'to make someone the citizen of a country'. Immigrants to Britain apply for *naturalisation* after they have been in the country for some time. (For the spelling, see **-ise/ize.**)

nationality

A capital letter should always be used with nouns and adjectives describing nationality or origin: *a Spaniard, a German girl, Danish bacon, Lancashire cheese, an American accent, Roman ruins,* etc. When a connection between a product and its country of origin is fading, a small letter is used: *french windows, gum arabic,* etc. (See also **capital letters.**)

naturalise

See **nationalise/naturalise.**

naught/nought

Use the spelling *nought* when the numerical cipher 0 is meant, and *naught* where the meaning is nothing. Thus *How many noughts are there at the end of this number?*, but *set at naught, come to naught,* etc. This is consistent with the spelling of the adjective *naughty,* which originally meant 'good for nothing', but has since been weakened to a mild term of rebuke.

near by/nearby

The adjectival use (*a nearby field, a nearby town*) has been gaining ground and is now accepted. It is possible to use two words when the meaning is adverbial (*a field near by*), but even here one word is to be preferred.

nearly

See **almost/nearly**.

necessaries/necessities

Necessities are things which are absolutely essential for a particular purpose. *Necessaries* are things we may consider necessary but which we could do without, if need be. The only *necessities* for a picnic are food and drink; the *necessaries* for a picnic, contained in a picnic basket, may include cups, plates, sandwich box, vacuum flask, spoons and cutlery. Of course, whether many of the things which we call *necessities* really are indispensable may be a matter of opinion, but in calling them *necessities* we imply that they are:

□ In the modern home a television set is a *necessity*

□ Things that are the luxuries of one generation become the *necessities* of the next.

née

From the French, *naître*, meaning 'to be born'. This past participle is used to indicate a married woman's maiden name (ie her surname before she married). It is placed after her married name and before her maiden name: *Mrs F Harper, née Dewhurst.* This headline from *Time Out* is, therefore, rather perplexing:

□ John Lydon (nèe Rotten) and his Public Image.

Apart from the wrong accent, *née* should only be used after a woman's name. Poor Mr Lydon!

need

1 Usage *He need not do it*; *no one* need *starve* (not *He needs not* and *no one needs*). The same form is used for the past tense, but it is followed by the perfect infinitive: *He* need *not have done it* (not *He needed not*).

2 If need be *If* need *be*, not *If needs be*. *Need* is here a noun, and the expression means 'if there be need'.

3 On the difference between *need* and *want*, see **want 1**.

neither

1 Neither or none? As an adjective or a pronoun, *neither* should be used only where two things or persons are concerned. Do not say *neither of the three brothers*, but *none of the three brothers*.

2 Verb agreement *Neither* takes each of the two separately, not together: consequently if each is singular it must take a singular verb:
□ Both Smith and Jones were invited, but *neither has* accepted (not *neither have* accepted).
If each of the terms is plural, a plural verb is possible:
□ Both the Conservatives and the Liberals are to contest the constituency, but *neither have* yet announced who their candidate is to be.
The same principle applies to *neither of them*; the verb agrees with *neither* (which may be either singular or plural, according to the context), not with *them*.
3 As an adverb used for emphasis As an adverb used for purposes of emphasis, *neither* goes with a *positive* verb, *either* with a *negative*: to the statement 'I don't believe his excuse', reply 'Neither do I' or 'I don't either', but not 'I don't, neither'.
4 Neither . . . nor On *neither . . . nor*, see **correlatives**; but note also the following points:
a The correlation need not be restricted to two terms. Shakespeare (*Julius Caesar*) has:
□ I have *neither* wit, *nor* words, *nor* worth.
This is in accord with modern usage also. (See also **nor/or**.)
b When one of the correlated terms consist of alternatives, great care is needed not to confuse *or* and *nor*:
□ He said he had *neither* father *nor* mother, *nor* any brothers *nor* sisters.
The third *nor* is incorrect; it should be *or*: the correlated terms are *father, mother, brothers or sisters.*
c In the same way confusion between the introductory adverb *neither* and the correlative *neither* may lead to the incorrect use of *nor*:
□ I could not speak the language, *neither* had I friends *nor* acquaintances in the town.
Neither links the second statement to the first; it is not the first of a pair of correlatives. *Nor* should be amended to *or*.

never

Never means 'not ever; on no occasion'. It is common to hear sentences such as *I never saw you at the party*. It is, however, incorrect to use *never* when referring to one occasion. *Never* can

only be used in continuous context:
□ Bob: 'I didn't see you at the party, Jim.'
□ Jim: 'I've *never* been to any of Sue's parties.'

nevertheless
Written as one word. Compare **none the less** (which is three words).

next door
He lives next door, the people next door (two words), but *next-door neighbours* (hyphenated).
(See also **hyphen 4**.)

nice
A word which is much over-used in colloquial English to mean 'agreeable' or 'pleasant'. The weather, a dress, a house, a person and a dog can all be described as *nice*. It should never be used in formal style; a much more exact word should be used in preference.
Colloquially, *nice* is often found with *and* + adjective to emphasise the pleasant quality of the adjective: *nice and warm, nice and cool, nice and clean, nice and tidy*, etc.
The earlier meaning of *nice* ('precise, exact, scrupulous') is formal and rarely used. Examples: *Her manners are very nice* (meaning 'precise, delicate'). *He is not very nice about his salesmanship* (meaning 'scrupulous').

no one
Write *no one*, not *no-one*. (See **nobody**.)
The possessive of *no one else* is *no one else's*, not *no one's else*. (See **else 2**.)

no sooner
Followed by *than*, not by *but* or *when*. *We had no sooner set out than a thunderstorm broke.*

nobody
1 Nobody + singular verb *Nobody* is singular; it takes a singular verb (*nobody is/was*) and is referred to by the singular personal pronoun and possessive adjective (he, his):
□ *Nobody* likes *his* friends to take advantage of *him* (not *their* friends . . . of *them*).
This rule is widely broken.
2 Tag questions With tag questions referring back to *nobody*, the tag follows the usual rule, and is singular, when *nobody*

individualises within a specified or understood group, as *Nobody likes to lose money, does he?* (here the group is the entire human race), but plural when it denotes mere absence of anybody, as:

□ We kept ringing the bell, but *nobody* answered, did they?

□ *Nobody* has called while I have been out, have they?

These observations apply also to *no one*.

noisome

In this example, *noisome* is used incorrectly:

□ [The loud crack] happened two or three times again and by then it was accepted as a harmless *noisome* interference. (*The Observer*)

The adjective *noisome* has nothing to do with 'noise'; it means 'offensive' or 'disgusting'. Indeed, it is our sense of smell, not hearing, which would be offended, since *noisome* is almost always used to describe something which has a disgusting smell.

nom de plume

The expression is unknown in French and is no longer common in English. Use *pen name* or *pseudonym*. The French expression is *nom de guerre*.

non-

On the difference between *non-* and *un-*, see **un-**.

none

When it is a case of number, the verb can be either singular or plural according to the emphasis required. *None* with a singular verb individualises, giving the sense of 'not even a single one':

□ He's a university professor, but of his three sons, *none has* any great ability.

The sense here is that neither the first son, nor the second, nor the third, considered as individuals, has any great ability. *None* with a plural verb sees the subject collectively:

□ *None* of the letters *have* been opened yet.

The implication here is that all the letters in the pile are unopened.

none the less

Nevertheless is one word, but *none the less* must be written as three. It is one word in Standard American – a practice which might be encouraged in England so as to standardise the spelling of these two near-synonyms. Standard English, however, still insists on *none the less*.

nor/or

Nor is sometimes used after a negative statement with the meaning 'and . . . not':

☐ I cannot agree to your request now, *nor* make any promise for the future

☐ We did not think that he would come this month, *nor* indeed before Christmas.

Or, however, would be equally acceptable. In the second example, if we use *or*, it links *before Christmas* to *this month*, both adverbial expressions modifying *would come*: if we use *nor*, it 'picks up' the first part of the sentence *and we did not, indeed, think*, etc. (See also **neither 4** and **correlatives**.)

nostalgia

The sense 'a looking back with longing to one's past life or to past times' is accepted:

☐ Every time I see a picture of palm trees, I get a feeling of *nostalgia* for those beautiful beaches in Brazil I once knew.

The literal meaning of the word is 'home-sickness'.

not

For sentences like *I haven't never been there*, see **double negative**.

not only . . . but also

Also may be omitted if no misunderstanding can result and each clause has its own subject:

☐ He *not only* promised to fulfil the conditions, *but* he signed an undertaking to that effect

☐ *Not only* were the brakes defective, *but* the engine needed repair.

(For other points, see **correlatives**.)

nothing but

Be careful when using *nothing but*, followed by a plural, as a subject. Remember that the actual subject is *nothing*, and that *nothing* is singular. It must therefore take a singular verb: *Nothing but trees* was *to be seen* (not *were* to be seen).

notorious

See **infamous/notorious**.

nought

See **naught/nought**.

nouns as adjectives

There is often a useful distinction to be made by using a noun rather than an adjective to qualify another noun. The BBC quite

properly refers to its *Paris correspondent* (one of its correspondents who is stationed in Paris) rather than its *Parisian correspondent* (a correspondent who is a Parisian). We drink *China*, not *Chinese* tea. A *machine tool* is something different from a *mechanical tool.* We speak of a *wooden* box but we must say a *wood* fire.
However, it is a very common tendency today to use one noun before another rather than the perfectly adequate adjective or possessive of a noun. For example, the headline in the *Daily Telegraph*: *France requests navy frigates* instead of *naval frigates*; *barber shop* for *barber's shop*, and *teacher organisation* for *teachers' organisation.* Such forms as these are found in the writings of good authors so it is likely they will be fully accepted in time.
The use of nouns before proper names in such expressions as *headmaster John Summers, Prime Minister Winston Churchill, accountant William Matthews*, is typical of popular journalism and is best avoided. (See also **journalese**.)

nouns as verbs

The practice of using a noun as a verb is not a new one. For years people have *papered* rooms, *bottled* fruit, *bandaged* up a wound, and *oiled* a machine. There are many such verbs which have long been an accepted part of the English language, and we could not easily express ourselves without them. Others, like *to can* vegetables, *to censor* letters, *to buttonhole* a person, *to concrete* a yard and *to initial* a document (the last two really examples of words which, starting as adjectives, have first become nouns and then verbs) have been introduced more recently. To these, too, there can be no objection. Generally speaking, the use of a noun as a verb may be justified if it expresses a meaning for which there is no existing word. *To service* (a car or a piece of machinery) is not the same as *to serve*, and *to power* (provide with a source of power) has a different meaning from *to empower*, while *to site* (in its correct sense of 'to provide a site for') expresses a different idea from *to situate.* All these serve a useful purpose. But there is no justification for using a noun as a verb when a well-established verb, or a brief formula, already exists. There may be a restricted use for *to package*, *to condition* and *to contact*, but there is no excuse for *to bill* (charge to one's account), *to loan* (lend), *to message* (send a message to), *to signature* (sign), and *to suspicion* (suspect). (See also **loan**.)

Yet others are widely found in America but are not accepted in England: *to host* a dinner (act as host), *to author* a book (write), *to position* a building (place, site or situate), *to pressure* a politician (exert pressure on), etc.

number

1 A number of *A number of* (meaning 'many') is plural in sense and takes a plural verb:

□ *A number of* people *were* left behind.

The sample applies to *a large number of, a small number of.*

2 The number of *The number of* (meaning 'a mathematical or numerical figure') is singular:

□ *The number of people* who own colour televisions *is* increasing every year.

3 Numbers The plural *numbers* (meaning 'the total number of individuals that make up the membership of a group, body or institution') is a well-established idiom, but it is used only in relation to persons or animals, not to things. It, of course, takes a plural verb:

□ Our *numbers have* increased considerably since the minimum age for membership was reduced to eighteen.

(See also **singular or plural verb?**)

numbers: method of writing

1 In mathematics In mathematics, statistical matter or reports, numbers should be written as figures.

2 In formal essays In formal essays, numbers should be written as words if they consist of only one or two words; otherwise figures should be used: *twenty-five pounds, two hundred pupils, eight million people*, but *25,346 votes, 576 members.*

If following this rule means that both figures and words would be used in the same sentence, use figures each time:

□ There were *255* people in the hall and *80* more in the adjoining room.

An alternative convention that is gaining acceptance is to write low numbers in words and higher numbers in numerals. Whether this applies to numbers below and above ten or one hundred varies according to style.

Note that numbers of three digits or more expressing an imprecise or vague quantity should be expressed in words, especially when they are conventional names: *the Hundred Years War*; *thousands*

and thousands of people turned out to cheer the Queen.
In numbers expressing quantities, groups of three digits are separated by a comma, or, in technical writing, by a space: *36,579 units* or *36 579 units*. But this does not apply to numbers with only four digits: *6678 units*.
3 Dates and house numbers Figures should be used for dates: *16 April 1981* (see also **dates**) and for the numbers of houses (*65 Princes Street*).
4 Fractions Write fractions as words (*two-thirds* of the amount). On the use or non-use of a hyphen in fractions and numbers involving more than one word, see **hyphen 8**. Decimal fractions should be written as figures: ·25, 3·295.
5 Times of the clock For times of the clock, *half past two*, *twenty past five*, *seven o'clock*, or *2.30*, *5.20*, *7.00* or *7 pm*, not *two-thirty*, *twenty past 5* or *7 o'clock pm*.
6 Monarchs For kings and queens, *Henry VIII*, *George III* are to be preferred to *Henry the Eighth*, *George the Third*: but never *Henry VIIIth*, *George IIIrd* or *Henry 8th* or *George 3rd*.
7 Psalm and century *The twenty-third Psalm*, or *Psalm XXIII* or *Psalm 23*. *The eighteenth century*, not *the XVIII century*, and certainly not *the XVIIIth century* or *C18*. (There is, of course, no objection to writing the last in notes intended merely for one's own use.)

O

o/oh

1 O *O* is rarely used today. It is a mainly poetical device used before a vocative case in direct address (*O Mary, go and call the cattle home*; *O God of love*; *O King of peace*) and occasionally before a verb in the imperative, when the subject is understood but not written: *O talk not to me of that name*. It is never followed by a comma or any other punctuation mark.
2 Oh *Oh* is normally followed by a comma:
□ *Oh*, it's you, John
□ *Oh*, what a lovely house.

Another common phrase, *Oh dear*, has a comma at the end, not in the middle: *Oh dear, who can that be?* Use no comma at all when *oh* expresses a wish or longing and is followed by *for* or an *infinitive*:

□ *Oh* for some peace and quiet

□ *Oh to have* some time to myself.

An exclamation mark should be used only when the word is intended to express a sharp cry of pain or surprise.

oblivious

Followed by *of*, not *to*. Strictly, 'forgetful of, no longer conscious of':

□ She began to daydream and became *oblivious of* the noise and activity round her.

Modern usage has extended the meaning to 'not knowing, unaware':

□ Billy called his mother, *oblivious* of the fact that she had already left.

observance/observation

Observation of the landscape, the building, the parade, etc (ie the act of watching or noticing): *observance* of rules, regulations, religious rites, etc (ie paying due regard or attention to).

occasion

The use of *occasion* as a verb has recently become a piece of official jargon:

□ We do not wish to *occasion* you any inconvenience.

There is no need for it. It can usually be replaced by *cause* or some other simple verb.

occupant/occupier

Occupant(*s*) of a railway carriage, a seat, a room, etc (ie those who at the moment happen to occupy it). The *occupier* of a house or other premises (ie the person who lives or carries on business there permanently).

occupation

When an official form asks for 'Occupation' the answer expected is *bank clerk*, *teacher*, *stockbroker*, *bricklayer*, etc. On a form, this will do, but not elsewhere, for none of these is an occupation, but a person. Do not write *one of the most dangerous occupations is a miner*, but *that of a miner*.

occupier

See **occupant/occupier**.

oculist/optician

An *oculist* is a specialist in the treatment of diseases of the eye. An *optician* is someone who makes or sells optical instruments, especially lenses and spectacles. A synonym for *oculist* is *ophthalmologist*. Beware of the spelling.

œ

Words like *œcumenical*, with the initial **digraph**, are now often spelt with a simple *e*. But the digraph must be retained in French words, like *coup d'œil, hors-d'œuvre.*

of

1 Usage Normally, when constructions like *a crowd of people, a flock of sheep, a row of chairs, a bunch of grapes* are used as subjects, since the real subject word is the one that precedes *of*, it is with this that the verb must agree, not with the one that follows:

☐ A crowd of spectators *was* rapidly gathering

☐ A bunch of delicious-looking grapes *was* hanging over the wall.

This is not, however, an invariable rule; we must be guided by the sense, and sometimes by the consideration that too strict adherence to what is formally correct may give rise to difficulties later in the sentence. In some cases the notion of the verb is felt to be applicable to the second rather than to the first noun, and in such cases it should agree with the second:

☐ A gang of youths *were* singing at the top of their voices.

A gang of youths was *singing*, though correct from a formal point of view, would hardly sound right; and it would be quite impossible to go on with the singular – *at the top of* its *voice.* (See **agreement of verb and subject**.)

2 Of suggesting frequency *Of a Saturday morning*, *of an evening*, etc is old-fashioned usage, still retained in several dialects, to express frequency, repetition or regularity: *I always go to church of a Sunday evening*. Avoid it.

(See also **about/on**.)

off

Off of is uneducated usage. Do not use it.

official/officious

Official means 'done with proper authority'. *Officious* means 'quick to become involved, offer advice or use authority'. Example:

☐ The Government will issue an *official* statement this afternoon

☐ Nobody liked him because he was much too *officious*. He was always telling people what to do.
The latter word is pejorative.

often

For the comparative, *more often* is preferred to *oftener*: *more often than not, more often drunk than sober.*

oh

See **o/oh**.

Old English

Should be applied only to the English of the Anglo-Saxon period (before about 1100). It is incorrect to call the English of Chaucer and his contemporaries *Old English*. It is known as *Middle English*.

olden

Used only in *olden days* and *olden times*, and these expressions are best avoided in serious writing, since they are clichés. (See **clichés**.)

omnibus

See **bus**.

on

See **about/on**, and on whether to write *on to* or *onto*, see **onto**.

once/twice/thrice

It is British English to say *once* and *twice*, never *one time* and *two times*; these last expressions are American. Where Americans would say *one more time*, the British would say *once again*. *Thrice* was formerly the term for 'three times' but is now no longer used. After *twice*, the British join the Americans in saying *three times*, *four times*, and so on.

one

(generalising personal pronoun)

1 Possessive of one Here is an example of American usage:
☐ One should always be sure of *his* facts.
For British usage amend to *one's facts*. Where *one* is not carefully used, confusion may result as in this genuine example:
☐ *One* often does something *he* wishes *we* hadn't done, don't *you*?

2 You meaning 'one' Widespread in speech and to some extent in writing, *you* is replacing *one* as a generalising pronoun:
☐ *You* take a coin, put it into the slot and wait a second. Then *you* will find the machine works without difficulty.
As *you* is a pronoun of direct address, ambiguities can arise as to which function is uppermost – direct or generalising. For this

reason, especially in more formal contexts, it is better to use *one*.

3 One meaning 'I' The use of *one* where *I* is meant (*One can speak with some authority on this subject*) is generally not to be recommended, though it is frequent in upper-class speech.

4 On the use *one another* or *each other*, see **another 3**.

5 On the use of *one or other* or *one or the other*, see **other 1**.

6 In expressions such as *one of* + plural noun, the verb is singular, but difficulty may be experienced in a following relative clause. See **singular or plural verb? 11, 12**.

one word or two?

Many are entries in this book: see **already/all ready**, **into/in to**, **onto**, and for *a while* or *awhile*, see **whilst 4**. For compounds like *table spoon*, (or *tablespoon*?), *door mat* (or *doormat*?), consult a dictionary. Recently, there has been a growing tendency for people to write as one word expressions that should be two. The following are some examples: *alot* (of), *forever*, *incase*, *inbetween*, *infact*, *infront* (of), *inspite* (of), *innertube*. All these should be written as two words.

oneself

Note the spelling – not *one's self* or *onesself*, though *one's self* does exist, as a rather specialised term in psychology. The reflexive pronoun must be *oneself*.

only

Logically, *only* should be placed next to the word that it modifies; but we need not be too strict about this, provided no ambiguity or misunderstanding is likely to result. The following sentences may therefore pass as good English:

□ We *only* need another five pounds
□ He *only* arrived this morning
□ They have *only* been here a few weeks.

But the following might be misinterpreted, and should therefore be rewritten:

□ Such abuses can only be checked by the force of public opinion.

Only too pleased is acceptable in conversation, but *very pleased* is preferable in writing.

onto

Nowadays this appears so frequently as one word that it has been accepted as Standard English. *On to* is correct but old-fashioned. However, two separate words must be written in the following

instances: (a) when *on* has an independent meaning as an adverb and *to* as a preposition following it:
☐ Keep right *on to* the end of the road
☐ We decided to go *on to* Brighton
(b) when *to* is part of an infinitive:
☐ He went *on to give* an account of his experiences.

operative

1 Operatives or workers? Do not use *operatives* if it is possible to use *workers* (*building operatives* meaning 'building workers') or if a single noun would suffice (*printing operatives* meaning 'printers'). Occasionally there may be some justification for the word, if it denotes those who actually operate a particular service (*transport operatives*) as distinguished from other workers who are employed on maintenance, etc, but usually it is just a piece of meaningless and high-sounding jargon.

2 Operative as adjective Do not speak of the *operative* word in a sentence, or the *operative* clause in an Act or a document, if you merely mean the most important or the most significant. The real meaning is 'operating' or 'having effect':
☐ The new legislation concerning pension rights becomes *operative* at the beginning of the year.

opposite

☐ She sat *opposite* the window
☐ The bus stop is almost *opposite* the Town Hall (preposition)
☐ It had just the *opposite* effect to that which was expected
☐ 'Left' is *opposite* to 'right' (adjective)
☐ 'Left' is the *opposite* of 'right' (noun).

optician

See **oculist/optician**.

optimism/optimistic

☐ The Government are *optimistic* that a settlement will be reached in the dockers' strike.

A very common use of the word which is, strictly speaking, incorrect. Careful writers do not use *optimistic* to mean 'hopeful' but 'confident that good will come from every situation'. An *optimistic* person is one who always looks on the bright side of things. *Optimism* is the view that good will prevail, and an *optimist* is someone who has this outlook on life.

The opposites are *pessimism/pessimistic*. These words are also often

incorrectly used. *Pessimistic* does not mean 'unhopeful', as in:
□ The Government are *pessimistic* that a settlement will be reached,
but 'taking the gloomy view of life':
□ He has suffered so much that it's understandable why he has such a *pessimistic* outlook on life.
Pessimism is the tendency to see the dark side of life and a *pessimist* is someone who has this overall outlook.

or

See **nor/or**, **correlatives** and **agreement of verb and subject 2**. On the repetition of the article as in *Do you prefer the blue or the green dress?*, see **the 2**.

oral

See **aural/oral**.

orangutan

So spelt, not *orangutang*.

ostensible/ostentatious

Ostensible means 'apparent; not genuine; plausible'. It is usually restricted to use before a few words such as *reason* or *purpose*:
□ He bought the books – the *ostensible* reason for his visit – in the first few minutes, and spent the rest of his time looking at new cars in the showroom.
Ostentatious means 'over elaborate, exaggerated, showy':
□ Her *ostentatious* hat matched her outrageous behaviour. She simply had to be the centre of attention.

other

1 One or other *One or other* (if more than two are concerned), *one or the other* (if only two). Also: *someone or other*, *some person or other*, *somewhere or other*.

2 Other than Wrong use:
□ We could do no *other but* agree to the proposal.
Other is followed by *than*, not by *but*, when it excludes any alternative. *But*, however, may be used if the intention is not to exclude but to limit:
□ I have no *other* income [ie other than that already stated] *but* a few pounds which I receive as interest on my deposit account.
But even here *except* would be better.

3 Any other
□ York attracts more tourists *than any* cathedral town in Britain.

This implies that York is not a cathedral town in Britain. Insert *other* after *any*. The contrast is between York and the other cathedral towns.

4 On the other hand *On the other hand* is sometimes misused for *on the contrary*:

□ We do not regard the matter as a trivial one; *on the other hand* we are well aware of its gravity.

When the second statement contradicts or cancels out the suggestion contained in the first one, *on the contrary* is needed. *On the other hand* introduces a second statement in contrast to the first, but not irreconcilable with it:

□ Food here is cheaper than in Britain: clothing, *on the other hand*, is dearer.

otherwise

1 Otherwise meaning 'or else' When *otherwise* means 'or else', it is not preceded by *or*. The alternatives are:

□ We shall have to hurry, *or else* we shall miss the train

□ We shall have to hurry, *otherwise* we shall miss the train,

but not *or otherwise.*

2 Otherwise as adjective or noun Some people object to the use of *otherwise* as an adjective (*meals, cooked or otherwise*) and as a noun (*the success or otherwise of the scheme*). In such sentences, *otherwise* can often be replaced by one word which is opposite in meaning to the one with which it is co-ordinated: *cooked or uncooked, success or failure.* Sometimes it is merely tautological and should be omitted: *to report on the suitability or otherwise of the candidates.* However, it can convey a meaning rather more comprehensive than a mere opposite would do: *all forms of government, Communist or otherwise. Otherwise* suggests a variety of forms which the single word *non-Communist* would not.

ought

1 The negative The negative is *ought not* (abbreviated in speech to *oughtn't*). *Didn't ought, hadn't ought* and *shouldn't ought* are incorrect. So is *did ought* as an emphatic form: *You did ought to be more careful.*

2 Past form There is no separate past form. When the reference is to an obligation in the past, *ought* is followed by the perfect infinitive (*You ought to have done it*), though in subordinate clauses it may be followed by the ordinary (present) infinitive if the

reference is to an obligation felt at the time to which the clause refers:
☐ He knew that he *ought to visit* his brother, but he could not bring himself to do it.
3 Ought to + infinitive Combinations like *I ought, but cannot go* should be avoided. Whereas *can* and *cannot* are followed by an infinitive without *to*, *ought* is followed by one with *to*. Amend to *I ought to go, but cannot*.
4 Ought to or should? What is the difference between *ought to* and *should* when the latter is used to express obligation or duty? Quite frequently they appear to be interchangeable, but there are some cases where they obviously are not. We could not use *ought to* in place of *should* in fixed phrases such as the Victorian saying *Children should be seen not heard*. Similarly, it would seem strange to use it in the proverb: *People who live in glass houses shouldn't throw stones*. On the other hand, *He ought to be ashamed of himself* could scarcely be changed to *He should be ashamed of himself*. *Ought to* is stronger and more imperative than *should*, and the reason for this is probably that *should* merely expresses the speaker's view of the fact or situation, and therefore represents a personal opinion, whereas *ought to* relates the obligation to what is thought of as some kind of law (moral, social or physical) which has its force and validity irrespective of any particular person's view or opinion. If someone complains of tiredness in the morning, we might say to him *You shouldn't stay up so late* (that is merely our own view of the matter), but if we feel that late hours are likely to undermine his health, we should then tell him *You oughtn't to stay up so late*.
To sum up, then: we generally use *ought to* when a person has done wrong, or we think he is likely to, and we are reprimanding or warning him:
☐ You *oughtn't to* speak to your aunt in that way
☐ You *oughtn't to* leave it too late before you start.
We use *should* for general advice, where there is no suggestion of actual or possible wrongdoing. We may, however, also use *should* as a 'toned down' substitute for *ought to*, in order to spare a person's feelings. (See also **will and shall/would and should 4**.)

over

See **above/over**.

overall

The basic adjectival use of this word describes a measurement between two extremities, as in *the overall length of a ship*. It is now widely used as a synonym of *total*, *complete*, *supreme*, etc, as in the following expressions: *to give an overall picture*, *the overall profits of the company*, *in overall command*.

overflow

To overflow has the past participle *overflowed*, not *overflown*. Here is an example of the wrong past participle being used:

□ The River Medway has *overflown* its banks near Tonbridge. (a BBC news bulletin)

This would imply that the infinitive was *overfly*. There is, in fact, a verb *to overfly*, principally used in the jargon of flying:

□ The Red Arrows Display Team *overflew* the Biggin Hill airfield.

In ordinary English, the simpler *fly over* is to be preferred.

owing

On the use of *owing to* or *due to*, see **due (to) 1**.

p

pp

(Or *per pro*: *pro procurationem*) Strictly, it means 'by delegation to'. So it is the substitute's name that should appear after the *pp*:

□ Yours sincerely,
pp Helen Turner
Peter John Smith
Managing Director

However, the abbreviation is commonly understood to mean 'on behalf of' or 'representing' and so is placed immediately before the name of the person who is being signed for, in this way:

□ Yours sincerely,
Helen Turner
pp Peter John Smith
Managing Director

This is now a widespread commercial practice.
(See also **letters**.)

palate/palette/pallet

The *palate* is the roof of the mouth.
A *pallette* is the special board an artist uses to mix his colours.
A *pallet* is a mattress filled with straw. A *pallet* is also a metal or wooden plate used with a forklift to lift heavy goods.

pamper

Here is an example of incorrect use:
□ And it is publishers who are the most vulgar of the breed, *pampering* to the American money market. (*Evening Standard*)
Pamper means 'to indulge' or 'spoil'. We *pamper* much loved pets, favourite children, and often ourselves. The word the writer meant was *pander* which means 'to give gratification to (usually something distasteful or morally frowned upon). *Pander* must be followed by the preposition *to*. Certain newspapers in Britain's popular press *pander* to the public's taste for news of sin, sex and sensation.

panacea

Not 'an infallible cure', but a cure for all ills. Do not speak of *a panacea for indigestion* (or for any other particular complaint). The word is nowadays most frequently used in a figurative sense, with reference to social, political or economic ills.

pander (to)

See **pamper**.

parenthesis

(plural: *parentheses*)
1 Definition A word or group of words that interrupt a grammatically complete sentence. Care should be taken to avoid too frequent or over-long parentheses which make it difficult for the reader to connect the parts of the main sentence.
2 Usage Parentheses may be separated from the sentence in which they occur by commas, brackets or dashes. (See **brackets** and **dash**.) If commas are employed care must be taken to see that two are used, one at each end of the parenthetic words. A common fault of hasty or careless writers is to omit the second. In no circumstances must a dash be used at the beginning of a parenthesis and a comma at the end, or vice versa.
3 Commas and brackets Generally, if the parenthesis enters into

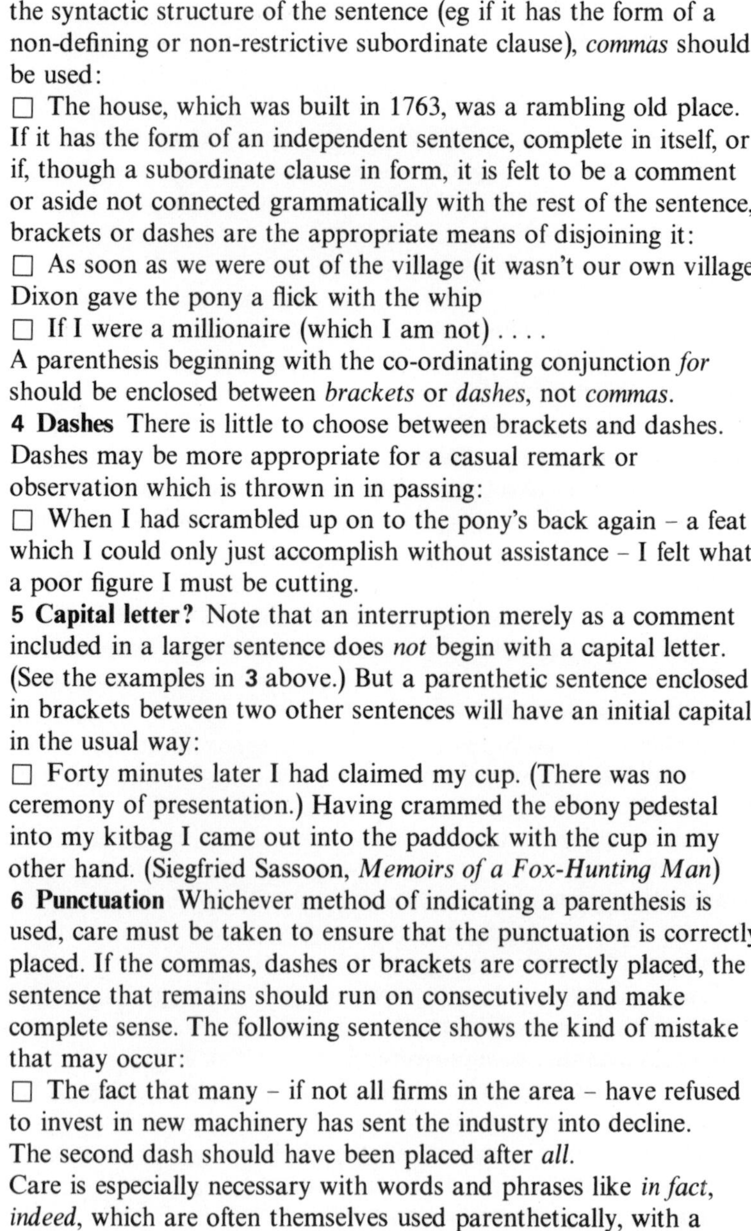

the syntactic structure of the sentence (eg if it has the form of a non-defining or non-restrictive subordinate clause), *commas* should be used:

□ The house, which was built in 1763, was a rambling old place.

If it has the form of an independent sentence, complete in itself, or if, though a subordinate clause in form, it is felt to be a comment or aside not connected grammatically with the rest of the sentence, brackets or dashes are the appropriate means of disjoining it:

□ As soon as we were out of the village (it wasn't our own village) Dixon gave the pony a flick with the whip

□ If I were a millionaire (which I am not) . . . .

A parenthesis beginning with the co-ordinating conjunction *for* should be enclosed between *brackets* or *dashes*, not *commas*.

4 Dashes There is little to choose between brackets and dashes. Dashes may be more appropriate for a casual remark or observation which is thrown in in passing:

□ When I had scrambled up on to the pony's back again – a feat which I could only just accomplish without assistance – I felt what a poor figure I must be cutting.

5 Capital letter? Note that an interruption merely as a comment included in a larger sentence does *not* begin with a capital letter. (See the examples in **3** above.) But a parenthetic sentence enclosed in brackets between two other sentences will have an initial capital in the usual way:

□ Forty minutes later I had claimed my cup. (There was no ceremony of presentation.) Having crammed the ebony pedestal into my kitbag I came out into the paddock with the cup in my other hand. (Siegfried Sassoon, *Memoirs of a Fox-Hunting Man*)

6 Punctuation Whichever method of indicating a parenthesis is used, care must be taken to ensure that the punctuation is correctly placed. If the commas, dashes or brackets are correctly placed, the sentence that remains should run on consecutively and make complete sense. The following sentence shows the kind of mistake that may occur:

□ The fact that many – if not all firms in the area – have refused to invest in new machinery has sent the industry into decline.

The second dash should have been placed after *all*.

Care is especially necessary with words and phrases like *in fact*, *indeed*, which are often themselves used parenthetically, with a comma at each end, but in a particular sentence may only serve to introduce a parenthesis. The second comma is apt to get misplaced. The following example is taken from the report of a well-known company:

☐ Tax uncertainties make forward planning extremely difficult, in fact, impossible for manufacturers and traders alike.

The second comma should have been placed after *impossible.* (See also **brackets**, **comma 4**, **dash 1**.)

parliament

Note the *i* in the spelling. Similarly, *parliamentarian*, meaning 'a person skilled in the rules and procedures of parliamentary debate'. Use a capital letter if a specific parliament is referred to: *the British Parliament.*

partake

Often used incorrectly, as here:

☐ Over fifty schoolchildren will *partake* in the operetta.

Partake of a meal; *take part in* a dramatic performance, a concert, etc.

partially

Wrong use:

☐ The letter was written *partially* in French and *partially* in English.

The word required is *partly. Partially* is an adverb of degree, and is opposed to *fully*: *The meat was only partially cooked. Partly* means 'as regards one part'.

participles

1 Usage The participles may be used in any of the following ways:

a adjectivally, in an attributive capacity immediately before a noun: *a crying child, a broken window.*

b predicatively, after a verb, as in the sentences:

☐ The money is still *owing*

☐ They found the tramp *sleeping* by the roadside

☐ We noticed that his coat was *torn.*

This use is much commoner with the past participle than with the present.

c to make the compound tenses of verbs:

☐ It is *raining*

☐ The sun is *shining*

□ Many houses were *damaged* in the gale
□ The cat has *eaten* the fish.
2 Old usage An older usage permits the verb *to be* before the past participle of certain intransitive verbs (*go, come, arrive, fall, rise*): *He is gone to London*; *the sun is risen*; *how are the mighty fallen!* The emphasis is on the resultant state rather than on activity or occurrence. This usage is today only found in formal contexts.
3 Before verb to be The type of sentence with an introductory participial construction followed by a tense of the verb *to be* (a kind of inversion of the continuous tense forms) is, of course, quite normal:
□ *Standing* in the doorway *was* a stout, dark-haired woman
□ *Tied* round the box *was* a piece of blue ribbon.
4 Regional usage *He was sat on the seat*; *she was stood by the window* (with an active meaning) are regional usage. In Standard English they could only mean that the person in question was placed there by someone else. Amend to *was sitting*, *was standing*.
(See also **lay/lie**.)
5 Misrelated participle On the misrelated participle, exemplified in the sentence *Looking from the upper window the scene was very impressive*, see **-ing**.

particularly

Like other adverbs such as *only, merely, simply, even,* the position in the sentence can be very important and drastically affect the meaning:
□ I *particularly* don't want to go to the party (meaning 'I refuse to go').
□ I don't *particularly* want to go to the party (meaning 'but I don't really mind').
A summary of the position is this:
1 Just, merely, purely, simply *Just*, *merely*, *purely* and *simply* usually precede the part of the sentence they modify:
□ He was arrested by the policeman *just/merely/purely/simply* because he had no means of identification with him.
2 Even *Even* normally precedes the part of the sentence it modifies:
□ *Even* the President knelt at the memorial to the dead (meaning

'to everyone's surprise, it was the President himself, as well as everyone else, who knelt').

□ The President *even* knelt at the memorial to the dead (meaning 'to show his respect for the dead, the President went so far as to kneel at the memorial').

3 Alone, too, as well *Alone*, *too* and *as well* follow the part they modify:

□ Willingness *alone* won't get the job done. You need skill *too*/*as well*.

(See also **too**.)

partly

See **partially**.

passed/past

Use *passed* when the word is a verb:

□ She *passed* her examination

□ Nearly five years have *passed* since then

□ Having *passed* the age of sixty-five, he decided to retire.

When it is any other part of speech, use *past*.

Notice the difference between *With all his examinations passed, he could enjoy a care-free holiday* (ie now that he had *passed* them all), and *With all his examinations past*, etc (now that they were all behind him, though possibly not all *passed*).

passive voice

Avoid the use of a double passive, as in:

□ Adjustments that are proposed to be made

□ The measures that were attempted to be taken

□ Alterations that were suggested to be made.

Amend to *Adjustments that it is proposed to make*, or *Adjustments that are proposed*; *the measures that were attempted*; *alterations that it was suggested should be made*.

(On passive verbs followed by the substitute verb *do*, see **do 1**.)

past

See **passed/past**.

past tense and participle: regular or irregular form?

There is some variation in the pronunciation and spelling of the simple past tense and the past participle of a set of common verbs. It is typically British English to spell and pronounce them with a final *t*; the regular *-ed* spelling and pronunciation is more usually found in American English. The verbs are:

☐ **Infinitive**	**Past tense and past participles**	
	Irregular	*Regular*
☐ burn	burnt	burned
☐ dream	dreamt	dreamed
☐ dwell	dwelt	dwelled
☐ kneel	knelt	kneeled
☐ knit	knit	knitted
☐ lean	leant	leaned
☐ leap	leapt	leaped
☐ learn	learnt	learned
☐ smell	smelt	smelled
☐ spell	spelt	spelled
☐ spill	spilt	spilled
☐ spoil	spoilt	spoiled
☐ sweat	sweat	sweated
☐ wed	wed	wedded
☐ wet	wet	wetted

peninsula/peninsular

Peninsula is the noun (*the Iberian peninsula*), *peninsular* the adjective (*the Peninsular War*).

people

A collective noun which needs a plural verb:

☐ All those *people are* going to the concert.

The singular is *person*:

☐ Jane is a very practical *person*.

Be careful not to confuse *people* with the more formal *persons*. A recipe in a cookery book will tell us that the dish is enough for four *persons*, and a notice in a bus will announce that only six *persons* are allowed to stand when all the seats are full. In normal English we should say *people*.

People can have a plural when it means 'tribe' or 'race', as in:

☐ The *peoples* of South America remained a mystery for centuries to European explorers.

per

1 Per meaning 'by'

☐ We are sending the goods *per* parcel post.

A piece of commercial jargon. Use *by*.

2 Per meaning 'a' or 'an' Expressions like *two pounds per hour*, *twenty-six pence per person, sixty pence per 100 grams, forty miles per hour* should be left to business and commercial usage, where they have their place. In normal English use *a* or *an*: *thirty pence a pound, six times a week, a hundred miles an hour.*

3 Usage Even in commercial English do not write *per year*, but *per annum. Per month* and *per day* are accepted commercialese, though strictly they should be *per mensem* and *per diem*. On *per capita*, see below.

per capita

A phrase that is often misunderstood, and consequently misused. It does not mean 'per head' (which would be *per caput*), but 'according to heads'. The Latin for 'head' is *caput*; *capita* is the plural. *A per capita payment* or *a payment per capita* is correct (ie a payment according to the number of people, a stipulated amount being allowed for each person). But *a payment of forty pence per capita, an allowance of 400 grams of butter per capita* are wrong, and should be amended to *forty pence a head, 400 grams of butter for each person* (or, in official English, *per head* and *per person*).

per cent/percentage

1 Usage *Per cent* requires no full stop. It should never be written as one word, but *percentage* is always one word. Use *per cent* after a number (*sixty-five per cent*) and *percentage* when there is no number: *a high percentage.*

2 Fractions It may be convenient to express an awkward fraction as a *percentage*:

☐ *17%* of the cars exported go to the United States,

and for statistical purposes it is often necessary to express all proportions as percentages – *33⅓%, 50%, 100%* – but in any ordinary context speak of *a third, a half, all*, etc;

☐ *A third* of the candidates failed (not *33⅓%*)

☐ *Half* of the food was wasted (not *fifty per cent* of the food)

☐ *All* the members signed the petition (not *a hundred per cent* of the members)

☐ There was *a full* attendance (not *a hundred per cent* attendance).

3 Percentage meaning 'a few' Do not say *a percentage* when you mean *a few, a small number*, or *a small quantity*:

☐ At every election there is a *percentage* of spoiled ballot papers

☐ Only a *percentage* of workers obeyed the call to strike

☐ We must always allow for a *percentage* of waste.

We might ask, 'What *percentage*?' Ninety-nine out of every hundred is a *percentage*, just as much as one out of every hundred.

perceive

Note spelling. See **spelling 1**.

perceptibly/perceptively

Wrong use:

☐ The audience was *perceptively* thinner after the interval on the first night. (*Daily Telegraph*)

Perceptively is the adverb from *perceptive* which means 'able to perceive, sensitive'. The word intended here was *perceptibly* (meaning 'noticeably').

perfect

(adjective) *Perfect*, being an absolute term, cannot normally be modified by *more* or *most* (compare **unique**). We cannot say that one thing is *more perfect* than another, or that it is the *most perfect* of its kind. But:

☐ We could not have had a *more perfect* day for the garden party is allowable. Here the comparative denotes a nearer approach to the idea expressed by the absolute (compare *a fuller account of the incident, a more direct route*).

A perfect genius, a perfect fool, a perfect nuisance are accepted colloquialisms, but should not appear in literary English. The same applies to *perfectly* in such expressions as *perfectly absurd, perfectly ridiculous*.

perfect tense

1 Usage The *perfect tense*, or *present perfect*, represents a past activity, occurrence or situation as being in some way connected with the present:

☐ We *have lived* here eight years (and we are still living here)

☐ There *have been* many strikes since the agreement was signed (from the signing up to the present time)

☐ I *have misplaced* my pen (the present position).

It must not be accompanied by any adverb or adverbial expression which denotes past time. We cannot say *I have seen him last Wednesday; we have been there several years ago*. With such adverbial qualifications a *past tense*, not a *perfect*, must be used: *I saw him last Wednesday; we were there several years ago*.

2 The double perfect Take care to avoid the error of the double perfect. This may occur in two forms:

a The duplication of auxiliaries to make a non-existent tense form, as in the constructions:

☐ If I had have known

☐ Had I have known

☐ I wish you had have seen him

or more often in the conversational form:

☐ If I'd have known

☐ I wish you'd have seen him.

These should be corrected to:

☐ If I had known (or *If I'd known*)

☐ Had I known

☐ I wish you had seen him (or *I wish you'd seen him*).

The perfect tense has the auxiliary *have* (I *have known*, you *have seen*), and the *pluperfect*, or *past perfect*, *had* (I *had known*, you *had seen*), but there is no tense form with the combined auxiliaries *had have*. The error is more frequent in negative sentences than in positive, possibly because the interposed *not* makes it less obvious:

☐ I should never have believed it if I *hadn't have seen* it with my own eyes

☐ He would have walked straight into the trap if you *hadn't have* warned him of it in time.

b A perfect tense form, followed by a perfect infinitive:

☐ I *should have liked to have stayed* another week.

Only one of the verbs should be in the perfect: either *I should have liked to stay* or *I should like to have stayed*.

3 Past tense with perfect infinitive Similar to the mistaken use of a double perfect is the combination of a past tense with a perfect infinitive: *I intended to have called on you yesterday*. Amend to *I intended to call on you yesterday*.

period

American term for full stop. See **full stop**.

permeate

This verb does not need a preposition, but it may be found with *through* or *among*:

☐ Water *permeates* the soil

☐ The smell of gas *permeated through* the house.

permissible/permissive

Permissible means 'permitted', or 'not prohibited':

☐ It is *permissible* to end a sentence with a preposition if it sounds more natural to do so.

Permissive means 'permitting, but not compelling'. A *permissive* clause in an Act of Parliament is a clause which permits people or organisations to do certain things if they wish, but does not make it obligatory for them to do so. The most common use of the word today in British English is in the phrase *permissive society.* The sense here is that society permits many activities such as abortion and homosexuality and attitudes previously considered unacceptable.

perquisite/prerequisite

If you apply for a job as a sales representative and are offered a salary with the usual *perquisites*, then you might expect the use of the firm's car for private motoring, a discount on any of the firm's products, etc. A *perquisite* is an agreed allowance to supplement one's income. In colloquial English, the word *perk* is used instead.

A *prerequisite* is a requirement necessary to achieve certain ends. Two 'A' levels, a smart appearance and an easy manner might be *prerequisites* for the job as sales representative.

persecute/prosecute

The early Christians were persecuted by the Roman emperors for their religious beliefs (meaning 'were treated cruelly because of what they believed').

Trespassers will be prosecuted (meaning 'legal proceedings will be started against anyone caught trespassing').

person/personage/personality

Person means merely a man or woman; it suggests no particular characteristics.

A *personage* is an important person. Do not speak of 'that *personage* with the red nose and the very loud voice'.

A *personality* is someone of a distinctive character, or someone who is well known:

☐ He is quite a *personality* in the district

☐ A number of television and film *personalities* were present at the reception.

(For notes on the difference between *persons* and *people*, see **people**.)

persona grata

The meaning of the expression is 'an acceptable person', or 'a person who is regarded favourably':

□ He is *persona grata* in that quarter (not *a* persona grata).

The opposite notion is expressed by *persona non grata*, and is more commonly found than the positive. Today, both are mainly restricted to diplomatic circles:

□ He was *persona non grata* to the country's government as a result of his spying activities, and so was obliged to leave the country immediately.

personage

See **person/personage/personality**.

personal(ly)

Both words are sometimes used pointlessly, but there are also certain common uses that should be accepted, at least in conversational English. In *a personal friend of mine* the word is pointless, and should be omitted, but *my personal opinion* seems allowable if it means that the opinion is not given in an official capacity, or that it does not commit any body or organisation with which one is connected.

□ *Personally* I should advise you to do so and so

implies that as an official of some kind, I might give different advice, in accordance with the policy of my committee.

If the words are not used to make a distinction of this kind they are a mere cliché.

Again:

□ The manager is dealing with the matter *personally*

is justifiable, since he might have delegated it to a subordinate; so are:

□ I have a *personal* interest in the matter

□ He has no *personal* ends to serve.

In such sentences as:

□ *Personally* I don't care for marmalade

□ *Personally* I prefer a country holiday to one by the sea,

personally is not strictly necessary, but is often used to emphasise *I* as opposed to anyone else.

personality

See **person/personage/personality**.

personate

See **impersonate/personate**.

perspicuous/perspicacious
Perspicuous means 'clear, easily understood'. Noun: *perspicuity*. *Perspicacious* means 'having the ability to see or understand clearly'. Noun: *perspicacity*. A person is *perspicacious*; his manner of expressing himself in speech or writing is *perspicuous*.

peruse
Wrong use:
☐ He rapidly *perused* the book and decided it was not worth buying.
Peruse does not mean 'to glance quickly through', but 'to read with care'. It is formal in style.

pessimism/pessimistic
See **optimism/optimistic**.

phenomenon
'An unusual thing or occurrence.' The plural is *phenomena*. It is common to hear the plural form used when the context demands the singular. This headline from the *Guardian* makes this mistake:
☐ A teasing *Phenomena*.
(Compare **bacteria**, **criteria**.)

phone
No apostrophe is needed now before the *p* to indicate it is an abbreviation of *telephone*.

physiognomy
Note the *gn* in the spelling.

pick/choose
There is a growing tendency for *pick* to take the place of *choose*. There is, however, a useful distinction worth maintaining. *Choose* suggests careful thought and deliberation, and the weighing of one thing against another; *pick* suggests merely selection, sometimes in a rather casual manner. We *pick* a winner and *pick* a cricket team, but *choose* the material for a dress or a suit, *choose* a birthday or a wedding present, *choose* a name for a child, *choose* a holiday resort, and *choose* one of several things that are offered us.

pigeon/pidgin
A *pigeon* is a bird.
Pidgin is a simplified form of language used for commercial purposes in a multilingual situation.

pitiable/pitiful
Pitiable suggests degradation or wretchedness: *a pitiable plight*, *a*

pitiable attempt. Pitiful means 'expressing or evoking pity': *a pitiful cry, a pitiful story.*

plaintiff/plaintive

Wrong use:

☐ 'Mr President, I really don't understand what's going on,' was the Ottawa delegate's *plaintiff* appeal. (*The Scotsman*)

The word needed here is *plaintive* (ie 'sounding sad'). A *plaintiff* is a person who starts legal proceedings against someone.

plumb

(verb) See next entry.

plunder

Sometimes confused with *plumb*, as here:

☐ The depths of Burke's thesis and programme-style are *plundered* in this last programme. (*Time Out*)

Depths are never *plundered*, they are *plumbed*. The figurative expression *plumb the depths* means 'to get to the bottom of something'. *Plunder* means 'to rob during a riot or war':

☐ The mob *plundered* the cathedral of its paintings and silver.

plural forms

A list of the plurals of words about which there may be some doubt is given in the Appendix. The following points, however, may be noted here:

1 Words ending in -y If the *-y* is preceded by a consonant the *-y* is changed to an *i* and *-es* is added: *lorry, lorries*; *Tory, Tories*; *penny, pennies.* But if the *y* is preceded by a vowel symbol an *-s* is added to the singular form: *monkey, monkeys.*

2 Nouns which end in -f or -fe These usually change the *f* to *v* and add *-es*: *thief, thieves*; *life, lives*; *half, halves.* There are, however, exceptions. The words in this list keep the *f* and add *-s*: *belief, cliff, dwarf, grief, gulf, handkerchief, hoof* (*hoofs* or *hooves*), *proof, relief, reef, roof, safe, strife, wharf* (*wharfs* or *wharves*).

3 Words ending in -o There is no consistent rule, but generally words in common use add *-es*, those in less common use merely *-s*: *potatoes, tomatoes, negroes*, but *contraltos, solos, ratios.* All abbreviated words ending in *-o* merely add *-s*; *photos, pianos, stereos.*

4 Compound nouns In compounds consisting of a noun and qualifying words, it is the noun proper that takes the plural inflection: *courts martial, prime ministers, mothers-in-law.*

Compounds in which none of the words is a noun add the plural termination to the whole group: *go-betweens, try-outs, fly-pasts.* Compounds where the basic noun, even in the singular form, is already a plural (eg *a lazy-bones*) do not add a further plural inflection: *all those lazy-bones.*

5 Proper names These do not follow the rules for common nouns. If they are English names they add *-s* or *-es* to the singular: *the Joneses, the Davises, the Merrys, the two Germanys, the Churchmans.* If they are foreign names, in English they also generally add *-s* or *-es* in accordance with the normal rules, irrespective of what would be the plural form in their own language: *the two Brutuses, the Borgias, the Lavals, the Hauptmanns.* But notice the special cases of *the Gracchi* (where the Latin plural is used), and of French names ending in an *-s* which is not pronounced, eg *Dumas.* The written form is the same for the plural as for the singular: *the two Dumas.*

6 For plurals of initials and abbreviations, see **abbreviations 4**.

7 For plural verbs following nouns, see **singular or plural verb?**

plus

Best confined to its mathematical use or to two things which are to be taken together to make a single amount or combination: *the accusative plus the infinitive, the weight of the contents plus that of the container.* The word should not be used simply as a substitute for *and, with* or *together with*:

□ We are sending you the machine *plus* a book of instructions

□ An elderly lady *plus* two dogs and a servant arrived

□ On one evening each week a new supply of books, *plus* a librarian, is sent.

But to give the price of an article as *£15 plus VAT* is correct.

poetess

See **authoress** and **gender in nouns 1**.

point of view

Often wrongly used for *view* or *views.*

□ A history of the Reformation from the Roman Catholic *point of view*

is correct.

□ Mr Johnson will now give us his *point of view* on the matter

is not. Mr Johnson gives his *view* or *views.* A *point of view* is the spot (metaphorically) on which one stands to look at something: what one sees from that point is a *view.* (See **viewpoint**.)

politics

When *politics* is thought of as a science, or as a field of activity, it is singular:

☐ *Politics is* the art of government

☐ *Politics has* no attraction for me as a career.

When it means political beliefs or doctrines, or political developments, it is plural:

☐ A person's *politics are* his own affair

☐ American *politics are* not easily understood by the average Englishman.

(See also **acoustics, mathematics.**)

pore/pour

To *pore* over a book or document, to *pour* out the tea. *Pore over* means 'to study closely' and is somewhat formal. *Pour* is commonly followed by one of several adverbs: *pour out, pour in, pour away.*

Portuguese

Note the *u* after the *g*.

possess/possession

The normal way to express possession is to use the verb *possess* with an object:

☐ He *possesses* intelligence/great wealth.

A more formal, less frequent way is to use *to be possessed of*:

☐ He *is possessed of* intelligence/great wealth.

The sense 'dominated by' (*possessed of the devil*) is archaic, though there is a survival of it, without the preposition, in the phrase *like one possessed* (ie 'out of his mind'), and in such sentences as *What on earth possessed you to do that?* The passive sense is now usually expressed by *by*:

☐ He was suddenly *possessed by* a desire to rush from the room.

In possession of is active (meaning 'possess'):

☐ My solicitor is now *in possession of* the documents.

In the possession of is passive (ie 'possessed by'):

☐ The documents are *in the possession of* my solicitor.

But not *My solicitor is now in the possession of the documents*, which would mean that the documents possess the solicitor, not vice versa.

possessive

See **apostrophe 3**.

possible

To be possible (or *impossible*) can be followed by an infinitive, either active or passive, only when the subject of the sentence is *it*:

□ It is *possible to be drowned* in a few centimetres of water

□ It was *impossible to hear* what he said.

With any other subject, the infinitive is not permissible. We cannot say *They are possible to be late*; *his speech was impossible to be heard*. Amend to:

□ It is *possible* that they will be late

□ It was *impossible* to hear his speech.

Usage, however, does permit *a result not possible to foresee*, *a question impossible to answer*, as ellipses of *which it was not possible to foresee*, *which it is impossible to answer*. In such cases the noun which precedes *possible* or *impossible* must be the object of the infinitive. We cannot say *a situation possible to arise*, where the noun is the subject of the infinitive.

post-

(prefix) *Postgraduate* and *postscript* are written as one word, but in most other words in which it occurs the prefix is hyphenated: *post-war*, *post-operational*.

post mortem

Grammatical purists insist that *post mortem* should be written as two words when used adverbially (*an examination post mortem*), but hyphenated when an adjective or a noun: *a post-mortem examination*; *to conduct a post-mortem*. It is, however, acceptable modern practice to write just one word *postmortem* in all positions. A recent extension of the meaning of the word ('an examination of some thing that did not work, to discover the causes of failure') is slightly informal:

□ They held a *postmortem* on the plan to increase output by 15%.

postpone

See **cancel/postpone**.

postscript

PS (the abbreviation of *postscript*) is an afterthought added to the bottom of a letter which has already been finished and signed. If a second postscript is added, the abbreviation *PPS* is used.

□ *PS* Stephanie sends her regards.

□ *PPS* Don't forget to tell Tony to come in and see us next time he's in Colchester.

Postscripts should be avoided in business correspondence.

potent/potential

Potent means 'strong, powerful': *a potent influence for good.* *Potential* means 'that could be, but is not yet': *a potential leader, a potential source of wealth.*

practicable/practical

1 Usage The two words are sometimes confused. *Practicable* means 'such as can be carried out'. *Practical* means (a) 'carried out in practice', as *a practical joke, the practical application of one's knowledge* (b) 'suited, or adapted, to the prevailing circumstances', as *a practical suggestion,* ie one which has regard to an existing situation and is made in the light of it. *A practicable suggestion* (one which could be carried out) might not, in certain circumstances, be a *practical* one. (c) 'not theoretical, concerned with action or actual conditions not with ideas':

□ The practical sessions are in the afternoon, the lectures in the morning.

(See also **impracticable/impractical.**)

2 Practically *Practically,* in the sense of 'almost', is permissible, but the adjective *practical* cannot be used in the same way. Thus, we may say *The match is practically over,* but not *This is the practical end of the match; he is practically an imbecile,* but not *a practical imbecile.*

practice/practise

The difference of spelling has nothing to do with the kind of *practice,* whether medical, legal or otherwise; it is purely grammatical, and depends on the part of speech. The noun is spelt with a *c,* the verb with an *s.* (The Americans, however, use the *c* for both.)

Note the two adjectival uses: *a practice match* (a match played for practice), but *a practised speaker* (the participle used adjectivally). Here are a few more pairs which follow the same rule: *advice/advise, device/devise, licence/license, prophecy/prophesy.*

pray/prey

When addressing God we *pray.* A hunted animal is *prey*: *The lion devoured its prey.*

precede

Note spelling. *Precede, preceded* and *preceding* all have only one *e.*

precedence/precedent

Precedence means 'priority'. Something has or takes *precedence* over something else:

□ When allocating Government funds, *precedence* must be given to health, education and housing.

A *precedent* is something which has taken place in the past and which is used as a guideline for a present course of action. We set, create or establish a *precedent* for something:

□ The judge's lenient decision has created an unfavourable *precedent* for the future.

precipitate/precipitous

Precipitate means 'hasty; done without proper consideration':

□ Recent Chinese aggression in Vietnam is regarded as *precipitate* by many Western nations.

Precipitous means 'steep':

□ Many mountaineers have lost their lives on the *precipitous* slopes of Everest.

preface

(verb)

□ He *prefaced* his remarks *with* a reference to the recent death of the chairman

□ He *prefaced* his remarks *by* referring to the recent death of the chairman.

With before a *noun*, *by* before a *gerund*. *By*, however, is used after a passive voice, even though a noun follows:

□ His speech *was prefaced by* a reference to . . . .

prefer

Prefer is normally followed by *to*, not *than*:

□ I *prefer* coffee *to* tea

□ She *preferred* sewing *to* knitting

□ We *prefer* going by car *to* travelling by train.

The difficulty arises when infinitives are involved. We cannot say *She preferred to sew to to knit*. In such cases we use *rather than*, but never *than* alone.

Here is an incorrect use: *Which do you prefer most?* Literally, *prefer* means 'to place before the other(s)'. It is therefore an absolute term, and cannot be modified by *more* or *most*.

Past tense and past participle are spelt *preferred*. For the general rule, see **spelling 6**, and **refer**.

preferable
One thing is *preferable* to another. *More preferable* and *most preferable* are incorrect. (See **prefer**.)

prejudice
A prejudice *in favour of* or *against*; prejudiced *in favour of* or *against*.

preoccupied
The preposition is *with*, not *by*.

preposition
1 Position There is no rule forbidding the use of a preposition at the end of a sentence. Sometimes it is the only possible place for it:

☐ Where has this bus come *from*?

☐ Who is that letter *for*?

☐ My little girl has no one to play *with*.

A writer must use his discretion and sense of style. Sometimes the preposition is best placed before the word it governs, sometimes at the end of the sentence or clause.

2 With objective case In English all prepositions govern the objective case:

☐ *For us* who can remember the England of pre-war days this book will have a special appeal (not *for we*)

☐ *To us* English the pace of American life seems very fast (not *to we* English).

There is a tendency to use *we* + noun in every position. It is clearly wrong in *none of we girls*. A simple test is to omit the noun – no one would ever say *none of we*.

If the preposition governs two co-ordinated pronouns, both must be in the objective:

☐ Most of the work will fall upon you and *me* (not upon *you and I*).

☐ Between *you and me* (not *you and I*).

This is a particularly common instance. For further examples, see **pronouns** and **me**.

3 Using the preposition twice Be on guard against using the same preposition twice in the sentence, usually the result of using a preposition before the word it governs, and at the end of the sentence as well:

☐ The car *in* which they came *in*

☐ The instrument *with* which he did it *with*.

prerequisite

See **perquisite/prerequisite.**

prescribe/proscribe

A doctor *prescribes* treatment or medicine, and an examining body *prescribes* certain books to be studied: a government *proscribes* (ie places outside the protection of the law) persons and practices it regards as undesirable.

press

A capital letter should be used when referring to newspapers and magazines in general:

☐ Several MPs complained that the election date should have been announced to Parliament before the *Press* was informed.

pretence/pretension

Pretence means 'the act of pretending, deception': *She made a pretence to faint. Pretension* is a claim:

☐ I make no *pretension* to scholarship

☐ His *pretensions* are quite without foundation.

The common American spelling of the first word is *pretense.* The second word is formal.

preventative/preventive

There is no difference of meaning. The latter is more frequent, whether as noun or adjective, though the former is sometimes used, more especially as the noun.

previous

The idiomatic constructions are *the previous day, the day previous, two days previous to Christmas, two days previously* (adverb), *previous to going* (not *previously*).

prey

See **pray/prey.**

principal/principle

Whatever the part of speech, if the sense is 'chief' the spelling is *principal*: *the principal reason, the principal of a college*; the *principals* in a choir, orchestra or cast of a play; *principal* as opposed to *interest.*

Principle means 'a fundamental law governing one's conduct, natural phenomena, the functioning of a piece of mechanism, etc': *do a thing on principle*; *act against one's principles*; *a person without principles*; *the principle of gravitation*; *an invention that works on the same principle as the old-fashioned water wheel.* It is scarcely credible, but nevertheless true, that an Education Committee in the north of England once advertised a course at one of its technical colleges on *Principals of Mining*.

principal parts

These are the main inflected forms of a verb, from which other inflections may be worked out. In this book, they are the third person singular of the present tense, the present participle, the past tense and the past participle. Often the past tense and the past participle are the same, and so they are not stated separately; for example, the principal parts of *die*: *dies*, *dying*, *died*. Similarly, the present participle is not given when it is derived regularly, for example, the principal parts of *sink*: *sinks*, *sank*, *sunk*.

proceed/process

(verb) *Proceed* means 'to go forward, or continue on one's way'. *Process* means 'to walk in procession'. Another verbal use is a coinage by conversion of the noun: to *process* foods, materials, etc.

professional

See **amateur/amateurish**.

programme

This is the traditionally correct spelling in British English. The American spelling *program* is becoming widely used in the heavily American-influenced area of the *computer program*.

prohibit

Prohibit a person *from doing* (not *to do*) something. *Prohibit* his *doing* it is also sometimes heard, and seen in print, but it is better avoided.

Prohibit can also, of course, take a noun as its object:

□ An order *prohibiting* the movement of cattle

□ An Act which *prohibits* unofficial strikes.

In the same way it may take a gerund provided the gerund is used in a general sense: *to prohibit the parking of cars in specified areas.*

prompt/promptly

The idiomatic constructions are (a) we shall start *promptly*, (b) we shall start *promptly* at 7.30, and (c) we shall start at 7.30 *prompt*.

pronouns

The subject pronouns (*I*, *you*, *he*, *she*, *it*, *we*, *they*) should be used in subject position and the corresponding objective forms (*me*, *you*, *him*, *her*, *it*, *us*, *them*) in direct object position and after prepositions. It is amazing, however, how frequently even well-known authors do not follow this rule:

□ The only thing which makes *you and I* individuals is our brains. (Barbara Cartland, *Evening Standard*)

□ Then they collected Norman . . . and took him home, leaving George and *I* in a state of gloomy suspense. (John Mortimer, *Rumpole of the Bailey*)

□ Yes, everything comes to *he* who waits. (*The Listener*)

□ . . . Joseph McCarthy charged Secretary of the Army, Robert T Stevens, with trying to blackmail and smear *he* and his loyal staff. (*Guardian*)

The phrase *you and I* in particular is becoming almost a fixed expression and is widely used incorrectly: *Between you and I* . . . . (See also **as 1**, **as well as 3**, **between 1**, **me**, **preposition 2**, **they**.)

prophecy/prophesy

Prophecy is the noun, *prophesy* is the verb.

See also **practice/practise**.

proportion

1 Usage Strictly speaking, *proportion* means the relation of a part to the whole in one case, as compared with a similar relation in another case. Thus if a person with an income of £5000 a year saves £500 of it, and another person with an income of £10,000 saves £1000, they both save the same *proportion* of their income. If the latter saves £1200 as against the former's £500, then he saves a *greater proportion*. But popular usage has extended the term to mean the part in relation to the whole, or the total, without any implication of a comparison with other cases:

□ Only a small *proportion* of the candidates failed to complete the paper

□ What *proportion* of the members are manual workers?

□ There was a high *proportion* of women amongst the audience.

This extension we may accept (though the last example is very vague, since we do not know what proportion was expected); but we should not go any further. Two misuses in particular should be avoided:

a The use of *a proportion* in the sense of 'a few, a part, a number or an amount':

□ At every election *a proportion* of ballot papers are spoiled

☐ *A proportion* of the money raised will be retained to meet expenses
☐ We always expect *a proportion* of the goods to remain unsold.
Even allowing for the extended use of the word noted above, one might ask, what proportion? (See also the comment at **per cent/percentage 2**.)
b The use of *the greater proportion* when all that is meant is 'the greater part', 'the greater number', or even 'most':
☐ *The greater proportion* of the audience consisted of children
☐ *The greater proportion* of the land is still uncultivated.
2 With preposition to The correct preposition to follow *proportion* is *to*, not *with*:
☐ in proportion *to*/out of all proportion *to* the work involved.
3 The verb proportion *Proportion* may be used as a verb, provided there is the sense of varying the amount in order to keep the same relation between two things in all cases concerned: *to proportion the payment to the work done* or *to proportion the tax to the value of the goods*. It should not, however, be used merely in the sense of 'to share, or share equally': *to proportion the food out amongst the members of the party*.

proportional/proportionate
Proportional is usually used before a noun: *a proportional amount, proportional representation. Proportionate* is used after a verb or noun: *his share of the profits was proportionate to the money invested*; *a reward proportionate to the effort*. Both are followed by *to*.

pros and cons
From the Latin *pro* (for) and *contra* (against). When we *weigh (up) the pros and cons*, we consider the arguments for and against the situation before coming to a decision:
☐ We cannot possibly decide whether to invest the money without first considering *the pros and cons*.

proscribe
See **prescribe/proscribe**.

prosecute
See **persecute/prosecute**.

protagonist
Wrong use:
☐ He was a staunch *protagonist* of all good causes.

Protagonist does not mean 'a fighter for' (as though it were the opposite of *antagonist*); it means 'one who plays a leading part'. The *protagonists* of a movement are the prominent figures in it. The word comes from Greek, and means, literally, 'the actor who takes the leading part in a play'.

Another mistake sometimes made is to use the word as though it meant 'the earliest advocate of, or fighter for, a cause', a meaning perhaps suggested by a mistaken analogy with *prototype*:

□ Mrs Pankhurst was one of the leading *protagonists* of women's suffrage.

In any event, the adjective *leading* is unnecessary with *protagonist*; by definition a *protagonist* plays a leading role.

proverbial

□ We were up with the proverbial lark.

The proverbial so and so has become a cliché. Do not use it. Of course, there is no objection to such expressions as *proverbial wisdom* (the wisdom expressed in proverbs), *proverbial expressions* (expressions which have become proverbs).

provocative

See **evocative/provocative**.

purely

For its position in a sentence, see **particularly 1**.

purge

□ Sixty Pound a Week Typist *Purged*

□ *Purged* Alderman appeals to Minister of Health. (newspaper headlines)

Anyone who used this piece of modern political jargon should remember that literally the word means 'to rid of impurities'. It is therefore the party or organisation that is *purged*, not the persons who are expelled from it.

purport

This word is formal as a noun and verb.

1 Noun The *purport* of a letter or document is its apparent meaning or signification. The word does not suggest either that the apparent meaning is true or that it is not.

2 Verb

a Can be used only in the active voice:

□ The letter *purports* to be a copy of one received by him on 11 June (not *is purported to be*).

b *Purport* cannot have a personal subject unless the word itself is followed by *to be* with a complement. We cannot say *They purported to have confidential information*; but:

□ They *purported to be* messengers from the king

is accepted usage.

c Only the present participle can be used adjectivally to qualify a noun preceding it: *a letter* purporting (not *purported*) *to come from his father*.

purpose

Note the constructions *on purpose* (not *of purpose*), but *of set purpose, to some/no/little purpose, with the purpose of* + gerund, *not to the purpose* ('irrelevant'). The formal verb *to purpose* ('to intend') may be followed by an infinitive or a gerund.

purposely/purposefully/purposively

Purposely means 'intentionally'. *Purposefully* means 'in a determined manner; as if animated by a strong purpose':

□ They set about the task *purposefully* and without delay.

Purposively means 'in such a manner as to achieve an end or purpose': *Studies which are purposively directed*. This last word is not very common.

q

quay

So spelt, although it is pronounced the same as *key*. The plural is *quays*.

query

Do not use this verb as a synonym for *ask*:

□ 'Can we rely upon your help?' he *queried*.

Its only legitimate meaning is to question in the sense of 'to cast doubt upon': *I am inclined to query the accuracy of that statement*.

question mark

A punctuation mark (?).

It is used at the end of direct questions:

□ 'May I come with you tomorrow?'

It is not used after indirect questions:

□ She asked if she could have a glass of water.

It is used after constructions such as *I wonder whether* . . . where the sentence has the force of a request:
□ I wonder whether I might borrow your dictionary? (meaning 'Will you lend me your dictionary?')
This is also the case even when the grammatical form is that of a statement, but the rising intonation pattern used in speech would indicate a question: *You've not seen her since Thursday?*
(See also **suppose/supposing**.)

question tags
Short questions added to a statement to invite agreement from the person addressed. A negative statement is followed by a positive question tag:
□ You didn't steal that money, *did you*? (The answer *no* is expected in agreement.)
A positive statement is followed by a negative question tag:
□ You stole that money, *didn't you*? (The answer *yes* is expected in agreement.) (See **aren't I**?)

questionnaire
Note the double *n*.

quicker
(adverb)
1 Quicker or more quickly? The normal comparative is *more quickly*, but when we are thinking of length of time rather than speed the tendency is to use *quicker*:
□ As we get older the years seem to pass *more quickly* (the speed of their passing),
but:
□ The train will get you there *quicker* than the bus (ie in a shorter time).
2 Quicker or sooner? *Quicker*, used in this sense, differs from *sooner* in that *sooner* refers merely to a point of time, *quicker* to length of time. If train and bus arrive at the same time one will not get us there any *sooner* than the other, but it may get us there *quicker*.
3 Exceptions Sometimes, even where speed is concerned, *quicker* is to be preferred to *more quickly* as it sounds better:
□ I cannot walk *any quicker* than that.
Any more quickly than that would sound awkward and cumbersome. (See also **adverb and adjective?**)

quit

Past tense is *quitted*, past participle is *quit*. The sense is 'to go away; leave', as in:

☐ The boss told the clerk to *quit*.

Quit in the sense of 'give up, leave off' is an Americanism which is now heard in spoken British English.

To be quits (even) is an accepted colloquialism.

quite/quiet

These words are often confused. *Quiet* means 'silent; noiseless' (*He lives in a quiet country road.*) *Quite* has two meanings: 'completely, entirely' and 'fairly, rather'.

1 Quite + adjective or participle It has the sense of 'completely, entirely' when used with adjectives and participles which have a sense of finality in their meaning: eg *excellent*, *right*, *wrong*, *impossible*, etc. It would not usually be possible to put *very* before these words. If the adjectives used with *quite* have no such absolute quality, the meaning is 'fairly, rather': eg *good*, *happy*, *pleased*, *disappointing*, etc. *Very* would be permissible in these cases. Consider these two sentences:

☐ That picture is *quite* (absolutely) beautiful

☐ The picture was *quite* (fairly) nice.

2 Quite + verb The same differences of meaning apply here also:

☐ I didn't *quite* (completely) understand what he said

☐ I would *quite* like (would like fairly well) to go to the cinema.

3 Quite + adverb The sense here is always 'fairly':

☐ The house is *quite* close to the station. It won't take you long to walk.

4 Quite + a + noun An Americanism. This is acceptable in spoken English but should not be used in written work:

☐ That's *quite a* car you've bought

☐ He grows all his own vegetables. He's *quite a* gardener, you know.

Sentences with this construction are generally appreciative, but may be said in an ironic way:

☐ Have you met Elsie? She's *quite a* girl.

5 Quite + adjective + noun This construction may be used in written contexts. *Quite* here means 'fairly':

☐ It was *quite* an enjoyable film

☐ He's *quite* a skilful player.

6 Quite so This is an affirmative response to a remark, meaning 'certainly, that's right', in somewhat formal style. The one word *Quite* may also be used:

☐ 'I love Saturdays, there's always so much to do.' – '*Quite so.*'

Quite so may also be used to show irony. It is not very common these days.

quiz

Quiz was once a verb, meaning 'to make a person look foolish', or 'to pull one's leg'; then it meant 'to pry into the affairs of others', or 'to question a person in order to get from him information without his realising it'. Contemporary usage is as follows:

1 As a verb, meaning 'to test the knowledge of':

☐ The Chairman *quizzed* the participants in the competition.

It is a journalistic misuse where the meaning is 'question' or 'interrogate':

☐ The police *quizzed* the suspects for several hours.

2 As a noun, meaning 'a panel game on radio or television', 'a test of knowledge played for fun among friends'. But the journalistic use of this word as a synonym for *questionnaire* is incorrect:

☐ Trade Unions to Get *Quiz* on Unofficial Strikes.

quotation

1 When to quote Quote only if there is a point in doing so. Quotation for quotation's sake, or merely to display one's knowledge or erudition, is a literary sin.

2 Quote correctly If you are not sure of a quotation, verify it; and be particularly careful about well-known quotations, for sometimes the well-known form is an incorrect form. Coleridge did not write:

☐ Water, water everywhere,
And not a drop to drink,

but '*Nor any drop* to drink', and Milton did not speak, in *Lycidas*, of 'fresh *fields* and pastures new', but 'fresh *woods* and pastures new'. C P Scott's famous dictum was not 'Comment is free, *news* is sacred' (the form in which it is frequently quoted), but '*fact* is sacred'. Lord Acton did not say 'All power corrupts', but 'Power *tends* to corrupt', which is a rather different thing. Shakespeare, according to Ben Jonson, had *small* (not *little*) Latin and less Greek, and Napoleon's boast was that 'the word *impossible* is not in my vocabulary'. To substitute 'in the dictionary', as is often done, misses the point and makes the statement not only false but absurd. James Thomson wrote 'Britannia, rule the waves' (either an exhortation or a wish), not 'Britannia *rules* the waves'; Macbeth determined to make assurance *double* (not *doubly*) sure, and dared Macduff to *lay on*, not to *lead on*, while his wife urged him to screw his courage to the *sticking place*, not the *sticking-point*. Kipling wrote 'The female of the species is more *deadly* than the male', not 'more dangerous', and Pope that 'a little *learning* is a dangerous thing' (not *a little knowledge*).

The best way to verify a quotation is, of course, to turn to the work from which it comes. Failing that, there are various dictionaries of quotations. The best-known are Bartlett's *Familiar Quotations* and *The Oxford Dictionary of Quotations*. *The Penguin Dictionary of Quotations*, though not so comprehensive, includes quotations from recent works which are not found in the others. Some rather obscure quotations, which have become clichés, will be found in Eric Partridge's *Dictionary of Clichés*. For the Bible, Shakespeare and some of the major poets, concordances exist.

3 Check the source If an author or source is given, see that the information is correct.

4 Quote honestly Do not use a quotation to prove something that its author never intended it to, or give its meaning a 'twist' to make it suit your own purpose. And remember that the meaning of a quotation may be changed or misrepresented if it is taken apart from its context. Thomas Gray did not declare that 'ignorance is bliss', but that:

□ Where ignorance is bliss
'Tis folly to be wise

– a very different idea.

5 Quotation marks No quotation marks are needed when what is actually a quotation is presented as an original observation and then referred to its author:

□ The paths of glory lead but to the grave, Gray tells us

□ Fools rush in where angels fear to tread, as the poet Pope reminds us.

6 Verse quotation A verse quotation consisting of a complete line should not be incorporated in the text, but set on a line of its own. If it consists of more than one line it must be set out in the correct metrical form. It must not be quoted as though it were prose. No inverted commas are required.

7 Omissions If words are omitted from a quotation, indicate the omission by a *hiatus* (a series of three dots).
(On minor points concerning the use of inverted commas for quotations, see **inverted commas 2**. See also **colon 5**.)

quotation marks
See **inverted commas**.

r

race
Wrong use:
□ The British are a humane *race*.
The British are not a race. Substitute *nation* or *people*. A *race* is a group of people, usually consisting of several nations, all of whom possess certain physical characteristics in common. Thus the British, Germans, Dutch and Scandinavians all belong to the same race. It is, of course, correct to speak of a *race of giants*, *a race of dwarfs*, or *a race of pygmies*.

raise/rise
Raise is transitive (ie it must have an object), *rise* intransitive. We *raise* prices, *raise* money, etc, but prices *rise*.
Principal parts: *raise, raised, raised*; *rise, rose, risen*.
A person whose wages are *raised* gets a *rise*, not a *raise*. (*Raise* is standard in America.) *Raise* in England is not used as a noun, except in a few place names, like *Dunmail Raise*.
Raised, in the sense of 'brought up' (*Raised in a small Lancashire mill town, he went to London at the age of eighteen*) is accepted in America. In British English it has a definite transatlantic flavour.

rapt
See **wrapped/rapt**.

rarely
□ It is very *rarely* that opportunity knocks twice.
Since it is here anticipating the noun clause 'that . . . twice', we might expect the adjective *rare* to occur with the verb (which would be perfectly correct in this sentence) but the adverb *rarely* is also idiomatic in such sentences. There are the parallel cases of

seldom and *not often* (both adverbial), which are similarly used. *Rare*, and not *rarely*, is essential however, when *for* + an infinitive follows instead of a noun clause:

□ It is very *rare* for a dog to live for twenty years.

Rarely if ever, *rarely or never*, but not *rarely or ever*.

raspberry

Note the unpronounced *p* in the spelling.

raze

See **erase/raze**.

re

Use no full stops. *Re* means 'about, regarding'. Apart from its use in legal documents, it should be confined to formal headings of official or business letters: *re John Smith, deceased*; *re The Fisher Charity*. It is normally written without a capital letter in this usage, even initially. Do not use it in a sentence:

□ I am writing to you *re* the repairs recently carried out at 15 Blackstone Road

□ *Re* your letter of 27 July, we write to say . . . .

Use *about*, *regarding* or *with reference to*.

reaction

Should be used of a person only when it is meant to express a sudden, almost automatic, response:

□ Her *reaction* to the terrible news.

As a synonym for *opinion*, *view*, *impression*, it is a piece of jargon. Do not say 'Listen to this letter and tell me your *reaction*' if you mean 'Tell me your opinion of it' or 'Tell me what you think of it'; if, however, a strong show of feeling were anticipated, the use of the word would be justified.

reason

An example of incorrect use:

□ *The reason* for the delay is because we have had difficulty in obtaining materials.

The reason . . . is because is always incorrect. Amend to *The reason is that* . . . . Alternatively we may retain *because* and re-word the first part of the sentence:

□ The delay has arisen because . . . .

Similarly incorrect are *the reason is because of*, *the reason is due to*. The delay is due to our having difficulties in obtaining materials. The *reason* for the delay is not due to that; that *is* the reason.

Another wrong use:

☐ *Because* you hadn't a ticket is no *reason* why you should be refused admission.

Amend to:

☐ *The fact* that you hadn't a ticket,

or:

☐ You shouldn't have been refused admission merely because you hadn't a ticket.

receipt

Do not speak of a *receipt* for making jam, cakes, etc. The correct word is *recipe* (though *receipt* was used in this sense in older English). A *receipt* is a written statement that money or goods have been received.

reciprocal

See **mutual/reciprocal**.

recommend

Note the spelling. The word has only one *c* but a double *m*.

recourse

See **resort/recourse**.

redolent

Followed by *of*, not *with*.

refer

In the past tense, past participle and present participle, the *r* is doubled: *referred*, *referring*. Similarly, *concur*, *confer*, *defer*, *demur*, *infer*, *prefer*. (See **spelling 6**.)

For use in sentences such as *Referring to your letter of 3 August, the goods have been dispatched today*, see **-ing 3**.

reference/testimonial

An open letter testifying to a person's character, abilities, suitability for a post, etc, should not be called a *reference* but a *testimonial*. A *reference* is a confidential document, addressed to the prospective employer, which the candidate does not usually see. A *referee* is the person to whom the employer writes for information.

reflexive pronouns

See **-self, -selves**.

refrain

Wrong use:

☐ The writer has *refrained* from the temptation to condemn merely on moral grounds.

Resisted should have been used. *Refrain from* can be followed only by (a) a gerund in the active voice (*refrain from doing something*), and (b) a noun with an active sense (*refrain from theft*, *from crime*, etc). It cannot take a noun, like *temptation*, which is passive in sense. We *refrain* from doing something which we are tempted to do; we *resist* the temptation to do it.

refute

Incorrect use:

□ What the Tories are really saying here is that health service workers should not have the right to strike like any other workers. That I totally *refute*.

Refute does not mean 'disagree' or 'challenge' but 'prove wrong': *refute a statement*, *refute an opinion*, *refute an opponent*, etc.

regard

1 Have regard to 'Take into consideration':

□ In planning the syllabus we must *have regard to* the needs of those students who are taking the commercial course.

This phrase is only found in more formal contexts.

2 Have regard for 'Show consideration for':

□ He *has no regard for* other people.

3 With regard to 'Concerning':

□ *With regard to* the point you have just raised, I will have the matter investigated.

4 Without regard to 'Without considering or taking into account':

□ He always does what he thinks right, *without regard to* the consequences.

5 As regards 'With reference to, about' (mainly used in official correspondence):

□ *As regards* the request you make in your letter, we have given the appropriate file to Mr Smith.

6 Give one's regards to 'Pay one's respects':

□ *Give my regards to* your parents.

7 With kind regards The formal ending of a letter to a friend or acquaintance.

Register Office

The office where births, deaths and marriages are registered, and where civil marriages take place. *Registry Office* is now also widely used.

regretful/regrettable

Wrong uses:

□ Drunkenness '*Regretful*'. (headline, *East Anglian Daily Times*)

□ . . . it was a popular question, done well. *Regretfully*, however, there were candidates who wrote the story of the book, often slipping in a final, relevant paragraph at the end. (*Associated Examining Board's Reports of Examiners*)

In both of the above examples, the misuse of *regretful* and *regretfully* is *regrettable. Regretful* can only be applied to people. It means 'full of regret' or 'sad', as in *We said goodbye to our friends, regretful that we had to leave and would probably never see them again. Regrettable* is applied to things and means 'to be regretted', as in *The low success rate in the summer examinations is regrettable.*

The words needed in the headline and the AEB report are *regrettable* and *regrettably* respectively.

Note the single *t* and single *l* in *regretful*, and the double *t* in *regrettable.*

For the rule in this latter word, see **spelling 6**.

rehabilitate

The word is fast becoming a piece of official jargon for *repair* or *restore*:

□ A grant of £500 was made towards the *rehabilitation* of the church at Dover. (from a Free Church weekly)

It should not be used in this sense. Its strict meaning is 'to restore a person (or a group of persons) to a position of respectability or usefulness': the *rehabilitation* of a person discharged from prison, the *rehabilitation* of disabled persons, etc. It may legitimately be extended to an organisation or an institution (eg the *rehabilitation* of a club or a dance hall which has fallen into disrepute), but not to a building which has fallen into disrepair or suffered material damage.

relation/relationship/relative

1 Relation and relationship These both express the idea of a connection between one thing, or person, and another:

□ Doctors think there is a *relationship/relation* between smoking and cancer.

2 Relation and relative *Relation* can also mean *relative*. However, because *relation* and *relationship* are often interchangeable, it is perhaps better to use *relative* when speaking of one's uncles, aunts, cousins, etc. We would say 'Is he a *relative* of yours?' and 'What is his *relationship* to you?'

We speak of *rich* (or *poor*) *relations*, but *elderly relatives*.

relatively

Relatively should not be used as a synonym for *rather* or *fairly*. A *relatively* short distance is not a fairly short distance, but one that is short *as compared with*, or *in relation to*, another. A person who has to make a daily journey of ten miles to his work may not think it a short one, but it may be *relatively* short if most of his colleagues have to come twenty-five or thirty miles. (See also **comparatively**.)

relevant

'Having a bearing on the matter in question': *the relevant information, the relevant facts, the relevant documents, the relevant parts of the letter*. Book reviewers, theatre critics, etc, often misuse it to mean 'modern' or 'of contemporary social significance', as here:

□ This is a very *relevant* production, with its twin themes of the alienation of black youth and the hostility of middle class response.

rent

See **hire/rent**.

replace

Care is needed with prepositions. When *replace* is active it has for its object the name of the thing that is replaced, followed by *with*:

□ We are *replacing* all the old typewriters *with* new ones.

When the verb is passive, with the thing that is *replaced* as its subject, *by* is used:

□ All the old typewriters have been *replaced by* new ones.

But in a passive sentence where it is necessary to use *by* to denote an agent, *with* must be used before the name of the thing that is substituted:

□ All the old typewriters have been *replaced by* the management *with* new ones.

(See also **substitute**.)

replete

This word is sometimes incorrectly used as in this sentence from *Screen International*:

□ Leslie Pound, *replete* with family . . .

Replete does not mean 'together with' or 'complete with', but 'full of; containing as much as possible'. After a good Christmas dinner, one feels *replete* with food.

require

1 The active voice When used in the active voice, *require* cannot be followed by an infinitive which has as its subject the subject of *require* itself: *You require to have a University degree for a post of that kind.* The correct alternatives are:

□ You *require* a University degree

□ You *need to have* a University degree.

It is perfectly idiomatic, however, if the infinitive has a subject of its own:

□ We *require* you to have a University degree

□ The law *requires* all parents to send their children to school until the age of sixteen.

This, changed into the passive voice, gives *You are required to have a University degree*; *all parents are required by law to send their children to school until the age of sixteen.*

2 The passive voice The passive voice of *require* cannot be followed by a passive infinitive: *The money is required to be paid by Saturday next.* The two acceptable constructions are:

□ We *require* the money *to be paid* (active voice of *require* + passive infinitive)

□ 'You *are required to pay* the money' (passive voice of *require* + active infinitive).

resign

One *resigns* a position, *resigns from* an organisation, and is *resigned to* one's fate or to a situation which one accepts because there is no escape from it.

resort/recourse

The idiomatic constructions are *resort* to compulsion, *have recourse* to compulsion, but not *have resort* to. We do something *as a last resort*, not *as a last recourse.*

respective/respectively

The legitimate uses are (a) to express an exact correspondence or relationship between the individual members or items of two series or sequences:

□ John and James went to Harrow and Rugby *respectively* (ie John went to Harrow, James went to Rugby)

(b) in a distributive sense, as:

☐ Three Directors of Education explained how the problem was being dealt with in their *respective* areas (ie A in his area, B in his area, and C in his).

The following exemplify some incorrect uses:

1 The meeting was addressed by Smith, Jones and Brown *respectively*.
(Here the intended meaning is presumably 'in that order'; but that is not the meaning of *respectively*.)

2 The members took their *respective* seats.
(Here *respective* adds nothing to the meaning of the sentence.)

3 Each of the delegates gave his *respective* views.
(When *each* is used, *respective* is merely tautological.)

4 We all have a right to our *respective* opinions.
(*Respective* is here wrongly used as a synonym for *own*.)

5 *Vanity Fair*, *The History of Henry Esmond*, and *Bleak House* were written by Thackeray and Dickens *respectively*.
(Of course, what the author of the sentence meant was that the first two were written by Thackeray and the third by Dickens; but to express this notion by *respectively* will not do. The reader will, no doubt, guess that two of the works must have been written by one of the novelists, but how can he tell which two, and which novelist?)

6 He was a Fellow of the Royal Historical Society and of the Royal Society of Literature *respectively*.
(Here *respectively* seems to be used in the sense of *both*.)

7 We have interviewed the four applicants *respectively*.
(It is difficult to know quite what *respectively* means here. 'In turn'? 'Individually'? 'All four applicants'?)

restaurant

A French borrowing. Note spelling.

restive/restless

Restive means 'unwilling to accept control or discipline'. *Restless* means 'unable to rest; never still'.

revenge

See **avenge/revenge**.

reverend/reverent/revered

1 **Definitions** *Reverend* means 'worthy of reverence'; *reverent* 'showing reverence': *reverent forms of worship*; *revered* 'accorded great reverence': *a much revered man*.

2 Reverend *Reverend* (often abbreviated to *Rev*) is prefixed to the name of a clergyman or minister; but it should never be prefixed to the surname alone: *the Rev J G Elton, the Rev John Elton, the Rev Mr Elton, the Rev Dr Elton,* etc, but not *the Rev Elton.*

3 Plural form Since *reverend* is an adjective, strictly speaking there is no plural form of it; but *the Reverends J C Smith and S L Brown* is frequently seen in print, and may be regarded as accepted usage.

rhetorical question

A question, often asked for effect, to which an answer is not expected:

□ 'What does all this mean? Let me tell you . . . .'

□ 'Who was the person who made all these election promises and broke every one? The Prime Minister.'

This stylistic device is often overworked and, like the exclamation, should only be used sparingly and with caution. Its effect is then all the greater.

rhyme

This is the normal British English spelling. See **rime/rhyme**.

rhyming slang

Slang is by definition colloquial, and so should be generally avoided in written English, except for special effect. *Rhyming slang* is one type of slang which was very popular earlier in the century but is no longer productive. It originated in the Cockney practice (Cockneys are inhabitants of London's East End) of using a rhyming phrase (or abbreviated form of it) in place of the actual words: *plates* (plates of meat) for 'feet'; *titfer* (tit for tat) for 'hat'; *rosie lee* for 'tea'; *apples and pears* for 'stairs'; etc. A few common examples such as these are widely known, but best avoided.

Right Honourable

(Abbreviated to *Rt Hon*) Used of members of the Privy Council (which includes Cabinet Ministers and ex-Cabinet Ministers), peers and peeresses, the children of those peers above the rank of Viscount, and certain Lord Mayors; but it is incorrect to prefix it to the office of all Lord Mayors. (See **Lord Mayor/Lady Mayoress** and **honorary/honourable.**)

right/rightly/rights

1 Rightly For the adverb, *rightly* must always be used when it modifies a whole sentence or expresses an opinion on the fact stated in the sentence:

□ They *rightly* refused the offer
□ He declined to answer the question, and *rightly* so
□ Quite *rightly*, she referred the complaint to the manager.
When it is merely the verb of the sentence that is modified, *rightly* again is necessary if the adverb precedes the verb:
□ She had not been *rightly* informed.
When the adverb follows the verb *rightly* and *right* are often equally acceptable (*If I remember right* and *If I remember rightly*), but when the meaning is 'in such a way as to produce a *right* result', only *right* is possible:
□ I seem unable to do it *right*
□ This machine won't work *right*
□ You haven't added the figures up *right*
□ I can never spell that word *right*.
2 Right meaning 'very' *Right* in the sense of *very* is archaic, though it is still heard in regional speech: *He was a right clever person*; *it's right warm today*.
3 Right now *Right now* and *right away* (meaning 'immediately') are Americanisms, now recognised in British English.
4 Set a thing to rights *Set a thing to rights* is accepted colloquially, but *by rights* is incorrect, though frequently heard in speech. The correct form is *by right*:
□ *By right*, the house should have belonged to his brother (not *by rights*).
5 In political contexts *right* is spelt with a capital in the phrase *the Right*, but *right-wing politicians* (small *r*). (See **capital letters 7**.)

rime/rhyme

The *rhyme* in poetry. A nursery *rhyme*. Coleridge called his well-known poem *The Rime of the Ancient Mariner*, and when the full title is quoted the word must be so spelt, but otherwise use *rhyme* for a poem. The verb *to rhyme* is spelt in the same way. *Rime* is American usage. It is also the word for a 'hoar frost'.

rise/arise

A person *rises* from his chair or his bed, *rises* at 7.30, *rises* in the world, *rises* to the occasion, etc. The sun, the temperature, the barometer and prices all *rise*, while an aeroplane *rises* into the sky. *Rise*, that is to say, is the word that is used when the meaning is 'getting, going or coming up'.
Arise means 'to come into being'. A quarrel, an argument, a

difficulty, a doubt, a question, a storm, an awkward situation *arise*. *A wind arose* (suddenly blew up), but *The wind rose to gale force* (increased in velocity or intensity).

In older English *arise* was often used where today we should use *rise* or *rise up*: *My lady sweet, arise*; *I will arise and go to my father*. But except in verse this is now archaic.

(On *rise* and *raise*, see **raise/rise**.)

risqué

'Verging on impropriety, slightly dirty': *a risqué story, a risqué joke*. Do not confuse this word with *risky* (meaning 'potentially dangerous'). Note the acute accent.

road

When the word is part of the proper name of a thoroughfare, write it with a capital (*Euston Road*, *Westbourne Road*, etc). A small letter is, of course, needed when road is not part of the name, as *the London road* (the road leading to London).

We may speak either of *a shop in Edgware Road*, *a flat in Bayswater Road* or *. . . in the Edgware Road*, *. . . in the Bayswater Road*, etc. The use of the article in this way is quite common in London, but is practically unknown elsewhere. (It is never used before Street, except for *the High Street*. We cannot speak of *the Oxford Street*, *the Bond Street*.)

role/roll

Wrong use:

□ Guyana Sect Death *Role* May Top 800. (headline, *The Daily Telegraph*)

For a list of names, *roll* is the correct word. A *role* is a part in a play: *Who will play the role of Hamlet?* Some people still spell it *rôle*, with a circumflex, recalling its French origin.

roughage

Roughage is vegetable fibre or the coarse part of grain which, taken as a foodstuff, ensures that the digestive system works correctly. This is the only possible meaning of the word but, because of its association with 'rough', it is frequently misused. The following examples are taken from the *Guardian*. The first is from a cricket commentary:

□ One explanation was that Lever's delivery might have struck *roughage* caused by the bowler's footmarks.

The term required here is *rough ground*.

□ If you have patented any technique for the *roughage* of urban life, please let . . . us know.
This should be *difficulties*.

rouse/arouse

Rouse means, primarily, 'to wake one from sleep':
□ He gave instructions that he was to be *roused* at six o'clock.
From this literal sense it is applied figuratively to awakening any power, quality or attribute that is thought of as being dormant: *rouse* one's anger, spirits, energies; *rouse* one to action.
Arouse means 'to give rise to, bring into being, cause to arise': *arouse* criticism, comment, fears, suspicion, interest, opposition, resentment, etc. *Rouse* may be used both transitively and intransitively; *arouse* transitively only.

ruminate

Animals which do this chew their cud. People *ruminate* only in the figurative sense of the word, that is they 'chew over' decisions, questions, events, etc. To *ruminate* means 'to meditate on, reflect on'.

rural/rustic

Rural is the neutral term, and is contrasted with *urban*: *a rural life, a rural scene, rural areas. Rustic* suggests a certain quaintness, simplicity or crudity: *rustic characters, rustic speech.*

S

sabbath

Spelt with a small *s*. Use the word only when the religious character of the day is to be stressed: *sabbath observance, sabbath breakers, working on the sabbath.* For all other purposes use *Sunday*. The word was originally, of course, applied to the Jewish holy day, which is Saturday.

said

The adjectival use of *said* in expressions like *the said Henry Jackson* is accepted in the language of legal documents, but elsewhere it is out of place, except as a humorous device. (Compare **aforesaid**.) In prose the inverted formula *said Mrs Jones* should be used only within or after a passage of direct speech, never before it. Popular journalism has started using sentences like:

☐ *Said* the Headmaster, 'We are very proud of Tony's achievement.'

This should not be copied. In verse, however, it is accepted.

sake

1 Usage Normally there is no plural: *for everyone's sake, for the children's sake, for Tom and Mary's sake, for our sake* (not *sakes*); but *for all our sakes, for all their sakes* is allowable, though *for the sake of us all* and *for the sake of them all* is to be preferred.

2 Apostrophe *Sake* is usually preceded by the possessive: *for God's sake, for heaven's sake*, etc, but *for goodness sake* (with no apostrophe *s*) has become traditional, and we say *for conscience' sake* (note the apostrophe in the written form) because it sounds better. *For Tom and Mary's sake* when the two persons are thought of together (eg as man and wife, or as brother and sister), but *for Tom's and Mary's sake* when they are thought of separately.

salubrious/salutary

Salubrious means 'producing physical health': *a salubrious spot, not a very salubrious atmosphere. Salutary* means 'beneficial morally': *a salutary lesson, a salutary experience.*

same

☐ Complete the enclosed form and return *same* without delay.

A piece of commercial jargon, which should be avoided. Use *it* (or *them* if plural).

The same can be followed by both *as* and *that. As* must always be used when resemblance is in question:

☐ She has the same fair hair and blue eyes *as* her mother had

☐ This coffee is *the same as* we had at Mrs Dawson's,

but *that* is permissible when identity is indicated:

☐ He was wearing *the same* coat and hat *that* he had on when we met him five years ago.

Wrong uses:

☐ He speaks with a slight lisp, *same* as his brother

☐ Why don't you walk to work of a morning, *same* as me?

Amend to *the same as*, or *like.*

sanction

One important sense of the word is 'penalty', 'act of retribution or punishment', as in:

□ *Sanctions* against Rhodesia were never very successfully sustained.
Sometimes writers confuse this word with another:
□ Later he foresaw possible *sanctuaries* in the form of withheld grants and subsidies . . . . (*Daily Mail*)
A *sanctuary* is a sacred place of refuge.

sat

□ She was *sat* by the fire reading a book.
Very common, even amongst well-spoken people, in certain districts, but not accepted as correct in Standard English. Amend to *was sitting* or *was seated*. The same applies to *He was stood at the door* (see **stood**) and *He was laid on the couch*, neither of which is accepted as Standard English (except, of course, as a passive voice). (See also **lay/lie** and **participles 4**.)

satire/satyr

Satire is the literary form, *satyr* the mythological creature, half man and half goat.

scarcely

1 Scarcely . . . when *Scarcely* is followed by *when*, not *than*:
□ We had *scarcely* set out *when* it began to pour with rain.
2 Without scarcely
□ He escaped *without scarcely* a scratch.
Incorrect, since *without scarcely* is a double negative. The alternatives are *without a scratch* and *with scarcely a scratch*.

scarify

□ The road to it [the house], particularly the last part, is *scarifying*, but it's well worth it when you get there. (Noël Coward, *Pomp and Circumstance*)
Scarifying is used here in the sense of 'scaring, frightening or terrifying'. This is strictly a misuse, but one which is common. To *scarify* has no connection whatever with *scaring*; it means 'to lacerate or tear ruthlessly'. *Scarifying* criticism of a work of literature or of a person's conduct is criticism which, figuratively, tears it to pieces.

sceptic/septic

A *sceptic* is one who is inclined to disbelief: *septic* is an adjective meaning 'infected, affected by poisoning of the blood'. The latter is sometimes mis-spelt *sceptic*.

schedule
Note the initial consonant sequence: *sch.*

scholar
Years ago this word was frequently used instead of *pupil.* This old use still lingers on in certain parts of the country, but today *scholar* should only be used to refer to a person of great learning. A schoolchild is not a *scholar*, he is a *pupil.* (See also **student.**)

school
On whether to say *go to school* or *go to the school*, see **the 7**.

scot-free
So spelt: not *scott*. A *scot* was the name of an old tax, so that *to get off scot-free* originally meant to get off without having to pay the tax. Today it means 'to get off without punishment; escape punishment'. The compound has a small *s*, not a capital, and is spelt with a single *t*.

Scotch/Scottish/Scots
The *Scots* (or *Scotch*?) themselves are less particular than the English in the matter of these three words. The following recommendations are based upon what seems to be present-day practice in England:

1 Noun For the noun denoting the people use *Scots*, not *Scotch*: and similarly *Scotsman*, not *Scotchman.* The famous express train is often incorrectly referred to as 'The Flying Scotchman'.

2 Adjective For the adjective, use *Scottish* when the thing to be described is part of, situated in, native to, or otherwise closely associated with Scotland: *the Scottish universities, the Scottish Highlands, the Scottish herring industry, a Scottish accent.*
Scotch is used when the adjective is thought of as denoting a kind rather than the place of origin: *a Scotch terrier, Scotch mist*. The noun following *Scotch* often denotes produce of Scotland: *Scotch whisky, Scotch wool, Scotch plaid, Scotch tweed, Scotch eggs, Scotch pancakes*.

scull/skull
Scull (verb) means 'to row a boat'.
Skull (noun) is the bones of the head.

seasonable/seasonal
In England, wet, windy weather is *seasonable* in March (ie it is what we expect at that time of the year). The use of this adjective has been extended to mean 'coming at the right time'; we speak of

seasonable help, encouragement, advice, etc.
Seasonal means 'depending on the seasons', 'varying with the seasons'. Harvesting and fruit-picking are *seasonal* activities; the making and selling of Easter Eggs and Hot Cross Buns is also *seasonal*.

seeing
For use in such sentences as *Seeing it is your birthday, you may stay up an hour later tonight*, see **-ing 3**.

seize
Note spelling. See **spelling 1**.

seldom
1 Use after a verb *Seldom* is an adverb. We may say *I seldom go to London*, but not *My visits to London are seldom*, for here we are treating the word as a predicative adjective. It can be used after a verb in this way (and then as an adverb) only in the following types of construction:
a After It is After *It is* (*was*), and followed by a that-clause in apposition to the anticipatory pronoun *it*:
□ It is *seldom* that we get such an opportunity as this.
b In a relative clause In a relative clause that refers back to the whole notion expressed in a preceding clause of time:
□ When she lost her temper, which was *seldom*, . . .
□ Whenever I take a day off from work, which is *seldom*, . . .
c In a parenthetic clause In a parenthetic clause referring back to the entire notion expressed in a preceding adverb clause of time:
□ Whenever I take a day off from work, which is *seldom*, ...
2 To modify seldom *Seldom* is a negative word meaning 'not often' and should not, therefore, be modified by another negative. In this incorrect sentence from the *Daily Telegraph*, *less* is a negative modifying *seldom*:
□ I would feel more charitably disposed to them all if some of the Middle Eastern ones were *less seldom* found . . . trying to stuff 14 unpaid-for cardigans up their burnouses.
Amend to *less often*.
Note the phrases *seldom if ever* and *seldom or never* (but not *seldom or ever*).

-self, -selves
1 Usage The pronouns ending in *-self* and *-selves* may be either reflexive or emphasising. The forms are *myself*, *yourself*, *himself*,

herself, itself, oneself, ourselves, yourselves, themselves. Note the spelling *oneself* (not *one's self*). *One's self* does exist, but it is not the personal pronoun. It is a psychological term which means 'one's essential personality'.

2 Hisself and theirselves These are incorrect.

3 Never as subject A *-self* pronoun cannot be used alone as the subject of a verb.

□ *The manager himself* is attending to the matter

is correct, as here *himself* stands in apposition to *manager*, but not *Himself is attending to the matter, Myself heard him say it*, etc. In certain cases, however, the subject may be omitted if it is understood from a previous clause:

□ He is always urging others to take risks, but never takes them *himself.*

The remarks in the foregoing paragraph apply to normal modern English prose. In Ireland *himself* is sometimes used colloquially as an emphatic subject, to denote a person of some importance, often the master of the house: *Himself* will see you in a moment. But this is a special case.

4 Unnecessary use Avoid the pointless or unnecessary use of the emphasising pronoun. There is a point in using it in *I saw it myself,* but not in *I think myself that we ought to reconsider the matter.*

5 To use or omit? There are one or two expressions in which the *-self* pronoun (in this case a reflexive) can be either used or omitted:

□ He knows how to behave (*himself*)

□ She wouldn't trouble (*herself*) to do it

□ He will worry (*himself*) about trivialities.

The use of the reflexive pronoun makes it more vivid and personal, and perhaps more forceful.

6 -self: pronoun or personal pronoun? In some cases the *-self* pronoun competes with the simple personal pronoun:

□ This tax will fall very heavily on people like you (or *on people like yourself*).

Both are correct; the difference is one of viewpoint. *You* represents the second person as he is seen by the speaker, *yourself* as he is seen or thought of by himself. When A refers to B as *you*, he is presenting the situation as he (A) sees it; when he refers to him as *yourself* he is asking him to look at it from his own (B's) point of view.

7 My-, your-, her- not to be detached *My-*, *your-* and *her-* cannot be detached from the rest of the word and made to qualify a noun and a co-ordinated *-self*. *Kind regards to your mother and self* is incorrect. Say *Your mother and yourself* or *Yourself and your mother* (but not *Yourself and mother*). *Your good self* and *your good selves* are pieces of deplorable business jargon which no self-respecting company should allow to appear in its correspondence. Even worse, and bordering on an illiteracy, is *your goodself*.

semicolon

A punctuation mark (;).

1 Usage It separates two clauses not joined by a conjunction, which are syntactically independent but which are closely connected in thought:

☐ He's a clever fellow; even his enemies admit that

☐ You couldn't expect it to last very long; it was too cheap.

2 Comma or semicolon? Sometimes it is hard to decide whether to use a comma or a semicolon. The sense we wish to express is the best guide. Generally the semicolon, being a heavier punctuation mark than the comma, throws more emphasis on the words that follow it. Compare these sentences:

☐ He gave his promise, but I didn't suppose he would keep it

☐ He gave his promise; but I didn't suppose he would keep it.

☐ I knew he would fail, and he did

☐ I knew he would fail; and he did.

3 Other use It separates items in a list where commas are ineffective because they have been used within the items themselves:

☐ To avoid sunburn you need: a big, shady sun-hat; a good, protective, cream; a cool, cotton shirt as a cover-up; and self-discipline not to stay out in the sun too long.

sensual/sensuous

Sensual means 'appealing to the senses or bodily appetites' (usually with a pejorative connotation): *sensual pleasures*. *Sensuous* means 'appealing to the senses of sight, taste, smell, etc' (generally used approvingly): *the sensuous imagery of Keat's poetry*.

septic

See **sceptic/septic**.

serial

See **cereal/serial**.

sew/sow

Sew (with needle and cotton), *sow* (seeds). The principal parts are *sews, sewed, sewn* and *sows, sowed, sown* (or *sowed*) respectively.

Sow is often used figuratively (*sow dissension, sow the seeds of discontent*), *sew* rarely so.

Sow is a noun meaning 'a female pig'.

sewage/sewerage

Sewage is the waste matter carried off in sewers; *sewerage* is the network of sewers, the system of drains: *The sewerage of the district has become inadequate.*

Shakespearian

This spelling is to be preferred to *Shakespearean.*

shall/will

See **will and shall/would and should**.

shambles

☐ After the robbery, the inside of the house was a *shambles.*
This word has come to mean a scene of ruin, confusion or disorder. The correct meaning is a *slaughter-house.* The extended use seems to have arisen from World War II, when a heavily bombed district was described as a 'shambles' (ie a large number of people were killed). The word was then applied to the material destruction that was caused, and later was extended to a mere state of disorder, without any suggestion of destruction. Possibly the spread of the new meaning has been helped by the fact that, in its original sense, the word is now unused. Even a slaughter-house is now an *abattoir*. The original sense is archaic; the present sense is informal.

shew

At one time this was the accepted spelling for the verb, *show* being reserved for the noun. It is no longer used. Use the spelling *show* for both noun and verb.

should

See **will and shall/would and should**. On the use of *should* or *ought to*, see **ought 4**.

shine

In most senses, the past tense and past participle are *shone*:

☐ The sun *shone* today

☐ He *shone* the torch in my eyes.

But in the sense 'to polish; make bright by polishing', the past tense and past participle are *shined*:

☐ We *shined* our shoes before going out into the rain.

shrunk/shrunken

Shrunken is an adjective, used before a noun: *a small, shrunken body*. *Shrunk* is the past participle: *The garment has shrunk in the wash.*

shy

The comparative and superlative of the adjective, meaning 'timid', are spelt *shyer* and *shyest*. The derived noun is *shyness*. The gerund of the verb *to shy*, meaning 'to move away in fear or alarm (of a horse)', is *shying*, but the past tense is *shied*.

sic

A Latin word meaning 'thus'. In English its only legitimate use is as an interruption in a quotation from or a transcription of a document where some obvious error of spelling or fact occurs:

☐ On p 15 of the guidebook we read that 'on the outskirts of the village is an old cottage which is supposed to have been the home of Adam Bede, in George Elliot's [sic] novel of that name'.

The author of the sentence is, in effect, saying, 'Yes, I know that George Eliot spelt her name with only one *l*, but the mistake is not mine or the printer's. I am quoting it exactly as it is given in the guidebook.'

sick

See **ill/sick**.

siege

Note the *ie* in the spelling. For the general rule, see **spelling 1**.

signal

As an adjective, means 'outstanding, conspicuous': *signal success, a man of signal virtues*. The verb meaning 'to pick out from amongst many', or 'to cause to stand out clearly from amongst others' is *single out*, not *signal out*.

simply

For its position in a sentence, see **particularly 1**.

simultaneous

See **instantaneous/simultaneous**.

since

(expressing time)

1 Usage Normally *since* is preceded by a verb in the perfect tense, and followed by a word or expression denoting a point in past time:

☐ We have lived here *since* 1968

☐ I have not seen him *since* last Saturday.

If *since* introduces a clause, then the verb of this clause must normally be in the past tense:

☐ I have not seen him *since* he left school.

There are, however, two exceptions to this:

a When the sentence is concerned with the total amount of time, counting from the point in the past up to the present, *since* is preceded by a present tense (usually *is*):

☐ It *is* thirty years *since* the war ended

☐ It *must be* almost five years *since* we last met.

b *Since* is followed by a perfect tense instead of the past when the reference is to the beginning of something that has persisted ever since, and that still persists:

☐ *Since* I have been at this school we have had three headmasters

☐ He has never been to see me *since* I have been ill.

Since I was would imply that I am no longer at the school and no longer ill. It is incorrect, however, to say *It is three years since I have seen him.* This falls under **a** above, and *since* must be followed by the past tense *saw*.

2 Since and ago Wrong use:

☐ It is ten years *ago since* my brother left for America.

Since reckons from a point of time in the past up to the present; *ago* reckons from the present back to the past. The two, therefore, cannot be combined. (See **ago**.)

3 Ever since *Ever since* is two words, not one.

singular or plural verb?

Usually it is not difficult to know whether we should use a singular or a plural verb, but there are a few words, expressions or constructions over which writers may hesitate. The chief of these are listed below.

1 Other references On **anyone**, **each**, **either**, **every**, **everybody** **everyone**, **none**, **nobody**, see the word in question. On singular or plural verbs with collective nouns like *committee*, *board*, *staff*, etc, see **collective nouns**. For nouns ending in *-ics* (as *ethics*, *physics*, *economics*), see **mathematics**.

2 There The formal subject *there* usually takes a verb agreeing in number with the 'real' subject that follows (*There is good reason*; *there are many reasons*); but there are exceptions. (See **there**.)

3 The anticipatory subject it The anticipatory subject *it* in such sentences as:

□ *It* is the early bird that catches the worm

always takes a singular verb itself, even though the complement that follows it is plural (eg *It is the children that we have to consider*); but when it is qualified by a relative clause with *which*, *that* or *who* as a subject, the verb of this relative clause agrees in number with the preceding complement:

□ It is his *manner* that *annoys* me
□ It is his *manners* that *annoy* me
□ It is *John* who *is* to blame
□ It is *John and Charles* who *are* to blame.

4 Two singular subjects co-ordinated by and Normally, of course, two singular subjects co-ordinated by *and* take a plural verb (*Milk and butter have gone up in price*); but if the two co-ordinated terms represent a single idea, a singular verb is used:

□ The tumult and the shouting *dies*
□ All coming and going *was* forbidden
□ Screaming and shouting *was* heard coming from the hall.

5 Singular and plural subjects co-ordinated by or When there are alternative subjects co-ordinated by *or* or *nor*, one singular and one plural, the verb agrees with the one which immediately precedes it:

□ Neither the child nor her companions *have been heard* of since
□ Either the children or their friend *has taken* the book.

(See also **agreement of verb and subject**.)

6 A number of Though grammatically singular, *a number of*, when it means *several* or *many*, is treated as plural and takes a plural verb:

□ A number of people *were* present.

But:

□ The number of people present *was* greater than we expected,

since here number has the more definite meaning of a numerical total. (See also **number 1**.)

7 More than one Conversely, though *more than one* is notionally plural, it is treated as singular:

□ More than one person *is* involved in this
□ There *is* more than one possible explanation.

8 The greater/greatest part *The greater/greatest part* is singular when it refers to amount or quantity, plural when to number:
□ *The greater part* of the land *is* uncultivated
□ *The greater part* of the apples *are* bad.
9 Expressions like two weeks Expressions like *two weeks, ten pounds, five miles*, are singular when they are thought of as denoting a single amount or distance:
□ Two weeks *is* a long time when you are ill in bed
□ Ten pounds *is* not much for all the trouble we took.
10 So many pounds' worth of With the expression *so many pounds' worth of*, followed by a plural noun, we must have regard to the context and the precise idea to be expressed. If the *noun* is the significant word, then the verb agrees with that, and is plural; if the *value* is the significant fact, then the verb is singular, to agree with *worth*:
□ Nearly *a thousand pounds' worth of* cigarettes *were* stolen (here we think of the cigarettes, not the worth of them, being stolen); but:
□ There *is* nearly *a thousand pounds' worth of* cigarettes on that shelf (here it is the value that we have in mind).
11 One of When *one of*, followed by a plural noun, is the subject, the actual subject word is *one*, and the verb must be in the singular:
□ *One of* the doors *is* damaged (not *are* damaged).
12 One of + plural noun + relative clause Mistakes are very frequent when *one of* + a plural noun is followed by a relative clause:
□ This is one of the rooms that was damaged in the fire
□ He is one of those persons who always thinks he is right.
Both sentences are wrong. The antecedent of *that* and *who* is not *one*, but *rooms* and *persons* respectively. It is therefore *plural*. Amend to . . . *that were damaged in the fire* and . . . *who always think they are right*. But:
□ One of the documents which *is* of special interest is a fifteenth-century charter
is correct, for here the relative clause does qualify *one*, not *documents*: it is this one that is of special interest.
13 What *What* may also give difficulty. As a relative pronoun it may represent a singular ('that which' or 'the thing which') or a

plural ('those which' or 'the things which'). When used as a subject it takes a singular or plural verb accordingly:
□ I can see *what appears* to be a ship on the horizon
□ We can see *what appear* to be camels.
When a whole clause beginning with *what* is the subject of a verb, should the verb be singular or plural?
□ *What* caused the accident *was* (or *were*?) two stones which had been placed on the lines
□ *What* the children liked most *was* (or *were*?) his jokes.
Of course, when the complement is singular there is no difficulty (*What I should like most for a birthday present is a camera*); it is with a plural complement that doubt arises.
If the sentence can be remodelled on the *it . . . that* pattern, then a singular verb should be used:
□ It was two stones that caused the accident;
hence:
□ What caused the accident *was* (not *were*) two stones
□ It was his jokes that the children liked most;
hence:
□ What the children liked most *was* (not *were*) his jokes.
It and *that* combine to make *what* (singular).
But:
□ What appear to be specks on the moon's surface *are* really large craters,
since here *what* is plural ('those things which'). (See also **what 1**.)
14 Other cases On singular or plural verbs in inverted constructions like *as was the case*, *as were our intentions*, and on *than was/were*, see **as 5**, and **than 3**.

sink
The principal parts are *sinks*, *sank*, *sunk*. See also **sunk/sunken**.

skilful
One *l* in the middle. Adverb: *skilfully*. Americans prefer *skillful* and *skillfully*. (For the general rule, see **spelling 3**.)

skull
See **scull/skull**.

slander
Spoken defamation; *libel* is written. See **libel**.

slant
In the sense of 'bias; point of view; one-sided view or presentation'

(*give a particular slant to a story*) a piece of American slang which has been taken up by some British speakers and journals. It is now accepted colloquially.

slink

The past tense and participle is *slunk*, not *slank*.

slovenly

An adjective. Do not say *She dresses very slovenly*, or *He did his work very slovenly. She is slovenly in her dress* and *He did very slovenly work* are correct, but for the adverb a phrase must be used: *in a slovenly manner*.

slow

Go slow is an accepted idiom. The normal adverb is *slowly*, and the comparative *more slowly*, but we say:

☐ The car went *slower* and *slower* until it came to a standstill.

(See **adverb or adjective?**)

smelt

Smelt or *smelled*? See **past tense and participle: regular or irregular form?**

so

1 So or So that? It is incorrect to introduce a clause expressing purpose by the one word *so*:

☐ He saved up his money *so* he might go abroad for his holiday.

So that is required.

2 So as Equally incorrect is *so as he might go abroad. So as* is followed by an infinitive: *so as to do it, so as to go abroad, so as not to be seen*, but *so that he might do it, so that they might not be seen*, etc.

3 So that *So that* may also introduce a clause of result; in this case it should be preceded by a comma:

☐ He injured his foot, *so that* he was unable to play in the match.

(No comma is needed before a clause of purpose.) However, it is more common to find *so* rather than *so that* in clauses of result:

☐ He injured his foot, *so* he was unable to play in the match.

4 To do so *To do so* may be used as a 'substitute verb', to avoid repeating a verb used previously, but the verb it replaces must be in the active voice; it cannot replace a passive:

☐ He was asked to move to another seat, but he refused *to do so*

is correct; here *to do so* replaces the active infinitive *to move*. The following, however, is incorrect:

☐ The flowers in the park must not be gathered. Anyone found *doing so* will be prosecuted.
Here the active *doing so* (which is intended to stand for *gathering them*) refers back incorrectly to the passive *must not be gathered.*
5 So-called Hyphenated when used before a noun, as a compound adjective (*a so-called statesman, the so-called Reformation, the so-called Catholic church*); two words when used as a participle preceded by adverb:
☐ He was *so called* after his father
☐ Our cat Snowy – *so called* because of his white fur – caught his first mouse last week.

solidarity/solidity
We cannot speak of the *solidarity* of a wall. The word needed would be *solidity* which means 'solid quality'.
Solidarity is unity which arises from shared interests, ideals or feelings. Unions speak of *solidarity* in a strike and *solidarity* is important for an army on active service.

sort
1 These sort and those sort *These sort* and *those sort* are usually condemned on the ground that a plural demonstrative adjective is combined with a singular noun, but they are frequently heard in speech and sometimes found in print:
☐ With *those sort* of people one must be plain, or one will not be understood.
They are today almost as well accepted as the alternatives *those sorts of people, people of that sort* and *that sort of person.*
2 What sort of The objection made to *what sort of a . . . ?* is identical to that raised to *what kind of a . . . ?* (see **kind**), namely that there is no need of the article. But, as with *kind*, there is room for the construction with and without the article:
☐ *What sort of* musician is he?
inquires about the kind of instrument he plays or whether he is in an orchestra, band or group.
☐ *What sort of a* musician is he?
inquires about his capabilities, whether he is a good or bad musician.

sow
See **sew/sow**.

speaking
For use in such sentences as: *Speaking of novels, what was the title of the one you recommended to me?*, see **-ing 3**.

specially
See **especially/specially**.

speed
(verb) *We sped along*, but *speeded* when the meaning is 'went at an excessive speed':
□ Because he had speeded through the police radar trap at 80 mph, he was fined £100.

spelling
English is not an easy language to spell because it is not phonetic. It is possible to supply some guidance, however, and below is a list of spelling rules to take away some of the mystery.
1 ie or ei? *i* comes before *e* except after *c* when the sound is *ee*, as in *brief, fierce, field*. In *ceiling* and *perceive*, the *e* comes first. In *beige* and *reign*, the sound is not *ee*. Exceptions: *seize, weird*.
2 When y changes to i When adding a suffix to a word ending in *-y*, the *y* is changed to an *i* only if the preceding letter is a consonant, as in: *lovely/loveliest, ready/readiness, tidy/tidiness, lady/ladies*. In *essay/essays*, there is a preceding vowel. Exceptions: when adding *-ing*, the *y* is always kept to avoid having a double *i*: *try/trying, worry/worrying*; for *shyer, shyest*, etc, see **shy**.
3 When double l becomes single l When words ending in double *l* are used to form compounds, the double *l* becomes single, as in: *hopeful* (*hope* and *full*), *always* (*all* and *ways*), *welfare* (*well* and *fare*), *skilful* (*skill* and *full*), etc. Exception: *stillness*.
4 When a silent e is dropped When a suffix beginning with a vowel is added to a word ending in a silent *-e*, the *e* is dropped, as in: *loving, liked, sensible*. In *hateful, senseless, lovely*, the suffixes do not begin with a vowel. Exceptions: *likeable, sizeable*.
When a suffix beginning with a vowel is added to a word where there is a final *-e* preceded by a soft *c* or *g*, the *e* is retained, as in: *manageable, peaceable*.
Also there is an increasing tendency to write *aging* rather than *ageing*, *waging* rather than *wageing*, etc. *Singeing* must always be so spelt, however, to avoid confusion with *singing*.
5 Doubling of consonant before suffix When a suffix beginning with a vowel is added to a word of only one syllable which contains

one vowel followed by a single consonant, the consonant is doubled, as in: *shop/shopping/shopped, bat/batting/batter, shut/shutter, swim/swimmer/swimming.*

6 Doubling of consonants in words of more than one syllable In words of more than one syllable where the last syllable is stressed and contains a single vowel followed by a single consonant, the consonant is doubled when a suffix beginning with a vowel is added, as in: *prefer/preferred, compel/compelling.* (For other examples, see **refer**.) In *appeal/appealed*, there are two vowels. In *report/reporter* there are two consonants. In *consider/considering*, the last syllable is not stressed.

Where stress patterns vary in related words, spelling varies in accordance with the above rule, as in: *prefer, preferred, preferring, preferable, preference.*

Exceptions in British English: *travelled, worshipped, kidnapped.*

7 When c takes k When adding a suffix beginning with *i*, *e* or *y* to a word ending in *-c*, add a *k* to keep the *c* hard, as in: *picnic/picnicking, mimic/mimicked, traffic/trafficker.*

8 When adding ly When adding *ly* to words which end in *-le*, drop the *le*, as in: *ably, comfortably, gently.*

9 When g takes u When there is a hard *g* sound before an *i* or an *e*, the *g* must be followed by a *u*, as in: *guile, vogue, guitar, guess, tongue*. Exception: *guard.*

10 For notes on the spelling of plurals, see **plural forms**.

spelt

For the past tense and past participle, use either *spelled* or *spelt*. See **past tense and participle: regular or irregular form?**

spendthrift

Wrong use:

☐ . . . in the light of the council's financial cut-backs, councillors are being asked to become more *spendthrift* in their expenses. (*Bracknell Times*)

The use of *spendthrift* in this sentence is incorrect for two reasons. First, it is a noun but the writer has used it as an adjective; second, it means a person who spends money lavishly, but the councillors were presumably being asked to economise.

spilt

Spilt or *spilled*? See **past tense and participle: regular or irregular form?**

spiritual/spirituous

Spiritual is 'of the human spirit, not body'. *Spirituous* corresponds to 'spirit in the sense of a liquid containing alcohol': *spirituous liquors. Spirituous* is not a very commonly used word.

spirt/spurt

A liquid either *spirts* or *spurts* (the second spelling is more common); a runner *spurts* and puts on a *spurt.*

split infinitive

Because a Latin infinitive is one word, and so impossible to split, the English infinitive, which happens to be two words, should similarly not be split. So runs the argument of nineteenth-century pedants. The simple answer is that English is not Latin, and is in no way obliged to follow its rules.

None the less, the influence of these older grammarians remains strong, so it is perhaps best to adopt the policy of not splitting infinitives where possible. There are many cases, however, where to place the adverb anywhere else than between the stem of the verb and the prefixed *to* would destroy the sense or produce an awkward sentence: *to really enjoy oneself, to fully understand something, to better equip oneself for one's task, to openly admit something, to partially damage something, to strongly criticise a person,* etc. National newspapers do not hesitate to split infinitives:

☐ The Channel Tunnel Refuses To Just Lay Down and Die. (headline, *Guardian*)

Note also in this example the incorrect use of *lay.*

(See **lay/lie**.)

spoiled/spoilt

When *spoil* means 'to rob, ravage, lay waste', the past tense and past participle are *spoiled.* When it means 'to mar (partially damage) or ruin', usage is not fixed, but the general tendency is to use *spoiled* for the former and *spoilt* for the latter:

☐ A shower of rain *spoiled* our day's outing

☐ Her essay was *spoiled* by careless mistakes

☐ The dinner was completely *spoilt*

☐ The bad egg *spoilt* the cake.

(See also **past tense and participle: regular or irregular form?**)

Spoilt is also the usual spelling for the use before a noun: *a spoilt child, spoilt ballot papers.*

spoliation

So spelt: not *spoilation*. The word does not mean spoiling in the sense of damaging, but of plundering. It is a formal word.

spurt

See **spirt/spurt**.

stable

See **static/stable**.

stanch/staunch

For the verb either spelling may be used, but the second is more usual, especially in British English: *to staunch the flow of blood.* The adjective is always *staunch: a staunch supporter, a staunch friend.*

Standard English

In this book, the term means usages of grammar and vocabulary accepted by educated, careful writers of English prose. In more general terms, *Standard English* cuts across dialectal boundaries, is neutral in style (not very informal or very formal) and is usually concerned with non-specialist subject matter.

It also refers in a wider sense to the spoken language, where standard pronunciation is termed RP (Received Pronunciation). Weekly magazines such as *The Economist* are good models, but the most copied and accepted model of all for over 50 years has been the BBC. Not surprisingly, therefore, *BBC English* has become synonymous with *Standard English.*

It is worth noting that there is no body which decides on the acceptability of a word, as does the Académie Française in France. Because there is no standardisation by official action, it is sometimes difficult to know the exact status of a phrase or word. This is particularly true since standards change; what is informal to one generation, to be used only in speech with one's friends, may well be perfectly acceptable *Standard English* to the next, to be used in all written contexts. As there is more agreement and less variation in the written *Standard English* of educated users, it has been the accepted norm for this book.

start

See **begin/commence/start**.

starved

Dialectal uses:

□ You look *starved*: come near the fire and warm yourself

☐ We can't hold the meeting in this room; it's so cold that we shall be *starved.*
This use of the word (meaning 'feel, or be, very cold') is now dialectal. The only meanings of *starve* recognised by Standard English are (a) 'die of hunger', (b) 'be very hungry':
☐ We're *starving*: we haven't eaten for the last twelve hours,
and (c) 'provide with insufficient food':
☐ She was so mean that she *starved* herself and her family.
This, of course, gives rise to the metaphorical use: *starved of affection*; *to starve the mind.*

static/stable

Static means 'not moving, unchanging, still': *a static situation. Stable* means 'firm, well established, enduring, steady': *a stable home background, a stable Government.*

stationary/stationery

Stationary (adjective) means 'not moving':
☐ Passengers must not get off the train until it is *stationary.*
Stationery is writing materials:
☐ The letter should be typed on Departmental *stationery.*
In distinguishing between these words, it may help to realise that a *stationer* (a man who sells writing materials in a *stationer's*) is similar in form to *baker, greengrocer,* etc, who sell their goods in a *baker's,* a *greengrocer's.* We would never write *bakary* or *greengrocaries,* so we do not write *stationary.*

status quo

Formerly the only correct meaning was 'the previous position' (the complete phrase is *status quo ante bellum* meaning 'the state in which things were before the war'). Nowadays, it can also be used to mean 'the present position'; hence we can either *restore the status quo* (the previous position) or *preserve the status quo* (the present position).

staunch

See **stanch/staunch.**

stay

See **stop/stay.**

stimulant/stimulus

Coffee is a *stimulant*; it contains caffeine which increases mental activity. Any drink or drug which 'stimulates' bodily or mental energy is a *stimulant.*

A *stimulus* is something which stirs feeling or thought and moves us to action. If a child is encouraged in his schoolwork, the encouragement is often a *stimulus* to try harder.

stood

□ He was *stood* in the doorway/on the hearth-rug.

In Standard English this can only be a passive, meaning that he had been placed there, though in regional usage it is frequently heard in the speech of even educated persons in an active sense. Correct to *standing*. (See also **sat**, **lay/lie** and **participles 4**.)

stop/stay

It is common to hear the informal *stop* for the Standard English *stay* in such sentences as:

□ She was *stopping* with her aunt

□ I shall *stop* at a hotel.

Use *stay* when the sense is 'remain' (*Stay where you are*) or 'reside temporarily' (with a person or at a place): *stay at a farm, stay with friends, stay in Paris for a few days.*

It is quite correct, however, to use *stop*, followed by words denoting a period of time, if the meaning is 'break a journey':

□ The coach will *stop* in Leicester for an hour to allow passengers to have lunch.

straightaway

One word, not two.

straightforward

One word, not two.

strata

A plural noun. The singular is *stratum.* (See **data**.)

streamline

In its technical sense, it means 'to alter the shape of something (a car or boat) so that it minimises resistance to the flow of air, water, etc'. Recently, however, the use of the word has been extended to non-concrete nouns to mean 'make more efficient by simplifying' (eg plans, arrangements, factory production, etc).

stride

(verb) Past tense *strode.* The past participle *stridden* is archaic and has been replaced by *strode.*

strike

Past tense *struck*, past participle *struck* and *stricken.* Generally, *struck* as a past participle is used when the meaning is 'to hit hard physically':

☐ He was *struck* on the head with an iron bar;

stricken is used with afflictions or illnesses: *stricken* by grief, sorrow, etc; *stricken* with fever.

strive

Past tense *strove*, past participle *striven.*

student

Someone who attends an institute of higher education (a technical college, polytechnic or university). There is a growing tendency to use *student*, instead of *pupil*, for those studying in secondary schools. (See also **scholar**.)

stupefy

Note the spelling, with the medial *e*, not *i*.

sty/stye

A pig *sty*, but a *stye* on the eye. Plurals, *sties* and *styes* respectively.

subconscious/unconscious

Unconscious means: (a) 'without consciousness':

☐ The boxer was still *unconscious* two months after the fight.

(b) 'unaware of one's surroundings, or of what is taking place, although fully conscious':

☐ He was so interested in his book that he was quite *unconscious* that the train had reached Birmingham.

Subconscious is used of impressions made upon our mind, of which we are unaware but which may nevertheless influence our motives and our conduct:

☐ Advertising is immoral when it is designed to appeal to the *subconscious* mind and not to our powers of reason.

Note carefully the spelling, in particular the medial *s*.

subjunctive

A manner in which a verb is expressed. It expresses a state, event or act as possible, conditional or wished rather than as actual (compare **indicative**). It survives in a few inflections and in some expressions. The third person singular present has the subjunctive forms: if *he have*, lest *he go* (contrast indicative *he has*, *he goes*), and the present and past tenses of the verb *to be* has: If *I be*, if *I were* (contrast indicative *I am*, *I was*). It also remains in some formulaic expressions such as *Far be it from me; if I were you;*

come what may. The subjunctive can be used to indicate shades of meaning (see **as if/as though**), but it is falling into disuse, and other forms are often used instead (see **lest**).

subpoena

A legal document requiring a person to appear in a law court. It is an awkward word to convert into a verb. The difficulty is in attaching endings. Write *subpoena-ed, subpoena-ing*. As a verb, it means to summon anyone to attend a court of justice under penalty for disobedience.

subsequent

The preposition that follows *subsequent* is *to*. See **consequent on/ subsequent to**.

substitute

Wrong use:

☐ All the old typewriters are being *substituted* by new ones.

Write instead . . . *are being replaced by new ones*, or *new ones are being substituted for the old*. A *substitute* is something that takes the place of another thing; the verb therefore means 'to put in place of'. (See also **replace**.)

such

An adjective clause following *such*, or a noun qualified by *such*, is introduced by *as*:

☐ *such a spectacle* (or *a spectacle such*) *as* I had never seen before.

For result, *as* is used when an infinitive follows, *that* when a clause follows:

☐ I am not *such* a fool *as* to believe that

☐ There was *such* a noise *that* we could not hear ourselves speak.

By strict grammatical rule *such as* should be followed by the subject case (*People such as he are not to be trusted*), since it is really a clause where the verb is understood but not written (*such as he is*); but when it refers back to an antecedent in the objective case, the pronoun following *such as* is often put in the objective case also:

☐ I dislike people *such as him.*

Such as he, short for *such as he is*, would be very formal here. Similarly:

☐ It is too expensive for people *such as us.*

Be careful of the placing of the qualifying construction *such as*.

The following comes from an examination essay:

☐ Some countries have no sea coast, *such as* Austria.

But Austria is not a sea coast. Obviously, *such as Austria* should have followed *countries. Such as* should be placed immediately after the word it qualifies. Avoid expressions of the type *if such is the case, if such should happen.* Use *this* or *that.*

suchlike

Used as a pronoun (*apples, pears and suchlike*) the word is colloquial. Used adjectivally (*Avoid pork and suchlike indigestible foods*) it is, today, generally replaced by *other* or *similar. Other suchlike* is tautological.

suddenness

Note the double *n* in the spelling.

suffer

A person suffers *from* (not *with*) indigestion.

sufficient

In spoken English and informal written style, use *enough* wherever possible:

☐ Have you *enough* money?

☐ We have *enough* food to last us three days.

Unlike *enough, sufficient* cannot be used as a noun. Do not say *I have said sufficient about that. Have you had enough?* is better than *Have you had sufficient?*, but the latter may be accepted if a noun (eg *food*) is understood after it.

Amply sufficient is incorrect, and *sufficient enough* tautological.

summer

Summertime is the summer season; *summer time* is the system of time, one hour in advance of Greenwich time, in use during the summer months. It is often written with capitals (*British Summer Time*) or as an abbreviation (*BST*). (Compare *GMT* under **meantime/meanwhile**.)

summon/summons

A *summons* is served *on* a person or he is served *with* a *summons.* A person receives a *summons* to appear before a court of law, a *summons* to the telephone or a *summons* to the bedside of a sick friend or relative, etc. In other words, in whatever sense it is used, the noun is always *summons.*

As a verb, *summons* can be used only in the judicial sense of 'to serve with a summons'. A person is *summonsed* (served with a summons), and we threaten to *summons* him (to have a summons served on him). *Summon* must always be used when it means 'order or request to appear'. A person is *summoned* to appear before a court of law, *summoned* before his superior, *summoned* to a meeting, *summoned* to the telephone, etc. There is an obvious difference of meaning between the two sentences

□ He *summoned* the waiter

and:

□ He *summonsed* the waiter.

sunk/sunken

Sunk is a participle, *sunken* an adjective. A person has *sunken* eyes or cheeks, but a well is *sunk*, and a ship *has sunk*. The past tense of *sink* is properly *sank*.

□ The ship *sank* in a very few minutes

□ Her heart *sank* at the thought

□ The waves soon swamped the small boat and *sank* it.

superior

1 *Superior* is followed by *to*, not *than*.

2 No comparative or superlative *Superior* (like its opposite *inferior*) is an absolute term. We cannot speak of something being *more superior*. Just as *superior* cannot have a comparative, so it cannot have a superlative. We cannot say *This is the most superior of the three*; but there is no objection to *He is a most superior person* when *most* is not really a superlative, but an adverb of degree, meaning 'very'.

3 Much or very? One thing is *much* (not *very*) *superior* to another, but we may speak of a *very superior* person, or say that he thinks himself *very superior*. When used in this way, *superior* has largely lost its comparative sense.

superlative degree

See **comparatives**. On use of *the* with superlatives, see **the 5, 6**.

supersede

Note spelling.

suppose/supposing

1 Usage *Suppose*, not *supposing*, should be used to express an imaginary condition, ie as an approximate equivalent of *if*:

□ *Suppose* (not *supposing*) you won first prize, what would you do with the money?

Supposing is a participle, and is generally used to introduce a reason:
□ *Supposing* the man to be injured, they sent for the ambulance.
It may also be used to state a pre-supposed condition on which a statement is based, or a question asked. The meaning is 'on the assumption that':
□ *Supposing* everyone who accepted the invitation actually comes, there will be just under two hundred guests
□ *Supposing* no unforeseen delays occur, how long would the work take?
2 Suppose as question Formally *I suppose* is a statement, but it sometimes has the force of a question, in which case it seems legitimate to use a question mark:
□ I *suppose* they know how to find the house?
Similarly, a suggestion introduced by *suppose* may be given a question mark if it has an interrogative import:
□ *Suppose* we have a round of golf?
(See also the remarks on *wonder* under **question mark** and **wonder 2b**.)

surnames

A *surname* is the family name of the father. Surnames come from many sources. Below is a list, following Maciver's classification in *New First Aid in English*, of some of them:
1 Surnames from christian names *Alexander*, *Graham*, *Allen* and *Francis* are all common surnames. Many family names are formed by adding the words 'son of' to an existing christian name. The prefix 'son of' differs in form from country to country in the United Kingdom and Ireland:
a Ireland The prefix *Fitz* ('son of') is sometimes added (*Fitzpatrick*, *Fitzwilliam*), but more commonly 'son of' is shown by *Mc*: *McAdam*, *McNeil*. Many Irish surnames begin with *O'* (from *Ogha* which means 'grandson of') because, years ago, it was the grandfather who was considered head of the family: *O'Connor*, *O'Reilly*, *O'Brien*.
b Scotland *Mac* ('son of') is commonly found: *MacDonald*, *MacGregor*, *MacDougall*.
c Wales Here, *ap* or *ab* meant 'son of'. Eventually, the prefix was shortened to *p* or *b*: *Broderick*, *Pritchard*. Welsh surnames were also formed by adding *s* to existing Christian names: *Davies*, *Phillips*, *Roberts*, *Williams*.

d England In England, the suffix *son* meant 'son of', so we have *Adamson, Richardson, Williamson.*

2 Surnames from animals and birds *Fox, Hogg, Lamb, Lyon, Drake, Nightingale, Wren.*

3 Surnames from occupations *Baker, Cook, Farmer, Miller, Shepherd, Smith, Taylor.*

4 Surnames from places *Burns, England, Forest, Ford, Hill, Mills, Park, Wood.*

5 Surnames from physical and mental qualities *Bright, Good, Hardy, Little, Noble, Short, Small, Young.*

6 Surnames from colours *Black, Brown, Grey, Green, White.*

surprise

☐ I shouldn't be *surprised* if it doesn't snow.

The negative, to express the idea that the speaker thinks it may snow, is illogical, but has come to be accepted colloquially. The more logical *I shouldn't be surprised if it snows* is still correct, however. (See also **double negative**.)

When *surprised* means 'taken by surprise', or 'caught unawares', it is followed by the preposition *by*:

☐ The intruder was *surprised by* the police;

when it means 'filled with surprise' it takes *at*:

☐ I *was surprised at* his conduct.

susceptible

Susceptible to means 'sensitive to, easily affected or influenced by'. Thus we say a person is *susceptible to* colds, to flattery, to feminine charms, etc.

Susceptible of means 'admitting of' (used after a noun or verb only). So we say something is *susceptible of* proof, of verification, of demonstration, of two interpretations. *Susceptible to* should not be used in the sense of 'frequently or easily displaying', as:

☐ She is *susceptible to* fits of melancholy

☐ He is *susceptible to* outbursts of temper.

swap

Slang, meaning 'exchange'; sometimes spelt *swop.*

swat/swot

Swat means 'to kill (a fly, etc) with a flat object'. *Swot* means 'to study hard (for an examination)'. The latter, of course, is colloquial, if not actually slang. It is derived from *sweat.* The noun *a swot* has a derogatory suggestion that the verb has not.

sweat/sweated
See **past tense and participle: regular or irregular form?**

swell
The past tense is *swelled* and the past participle normally *swollen*, but *swelled* is used as the past participle when the sense is 'increased numerically' or 'increased in amount':
☐ Our numbers were *swelled* by the arrival of a party from Birmingham
☐ Several large donations have *swelled* the fund considerably.
To say that our numbers were *swollen* or that the fund was *swollen* would suggest that they were greater than was good or desirable. *Swollen*, therefore, has more of a negative connotation.

swingeing
Note the medial *e*. *Swingeing* means 'very great; severe' and is used especially when referring to financial matters: *swingeing cuts in public expenditure.*

swot See **swat/swot**.

sympathy/sympathise
We *have sympathy for* a person who is in trouble (ie feel pity), *have sympathy with* him or with his views when we are in partial agreement. *Sympathise* always takes *with*:
☐ I can *sympathise with* anyone who has migraine, for I suffer from it myself
☐ While we *sympathise with* you in the views you express, there is little we can do to help.
The adjectives *sympathetic* and *unsympathetic* both take *to*. (See also **empathise**.)

t

tall/high
Tall refers to height from base to top, in proportion to breadth: *a tall person, a tall tree, a tall spire, a tall lamp standard.*
High refers to distance above – usually, though not always, above the ground or the floor: *a high hill, a high window, a high roof.*
A building may be described as *tall* by a person who looks at it from the ground and sees it towering above him, but anyone who

climbs to the top storey climbs to the top of a *high* building, since in this case it is merely the distance that is in question.
A tall order, *a tall story* are accepted colloquial idioms.

target

□ Our *target* is £1000

□ We have set ourselves a *target* of a hundred new members by the end of the year.

A very much overworked metaphor whose use has many traps for the careless. In popular jargon targets are *set*, *raised*, *lowered*, *reduced*, *increased*, *passed*, *achieved*, *beaten* – in fact anything but *hit*. Be careful of mixed metaphors, such as:

□ We should set ourselves a *target* and pursue it vigorously. (from a Sunday newspaper)

and the words of a senior official in the National Coal Board, who:

□ would use every weapon in the armoury to carve out and hold a *target* of two million tons of coal a year.

(See also **mixed metaphor**.)

tariff

Note spelling: one *r* and double *f*.

tautology

The use of words which are unnecessary because they repeat an idea which has already been expressed in the same sentence:

□ He drew a round circle on the paper.

Circles are always round, so the word *round* is redundant and should be omitted.

□ There was a tiny little kitten in the basket.

Tiny expresses how small the kitten was, so *little* adds nothing to the sentence. Here is an example from the *Sunday Times*:

□ He can take you through the steps of the Hustle, the Funky Robot, the Bump and (a new innovation) the Spank.

An *innovation* is something new that has just been introduced; it cannot, therefore, be used with the word *new*. The Spank can be described either as 'a new dance' or as 'an innovation'; it cannot be both.

teach

See **learn/teach**.

teach school

An Americanism. British English would simply say *She's a (school) teacher*.

teenager

Now Standard English.

teens

No apostrophe: *A girl in her teens.*

televise

Must be so spelt, not *televize.*

television

Television is the name of the system of broadcasting pictures. The apparatus on which the picture is received should strictly be referred to as a *television set*, not a *television.* However, modern usage accepts *Have you got a television?* as well as *Have you got a television set? Telly* is a colloquial abbreviation found in speech or informal writing.

In the phrase *on the television*, it is now more common to omit the definite article:

□ Did you see the Prime Minister *on television* last night?

temporal/temporary

Temporal means 'having to do with time': *a temporal clause* is another name for an adverb clause of time. It is often used as the opposite of *spiritual*, as in the expression *Lords Temporal and Lords Spiritual*, the Lords *Temporal* being the Peers, and the Lords Spiritual the Bishops. Compare also:

□ His [ie the king's] sceptre shows the force of *temporal* power. (Shakespeare, *The Merchant of Venice*)

Temporary means 'lasting, or intended, for a short time only': *a temporary post, a temporary building, temporary measures.*

Be careful of the spelling of the adverb from *temporary*; it is *temporarily.*

tend

Wrong use:

□ Her life was spent *tending to* the sick and the wounded.

Tend, in this sense of the word, is a transitive verb: *attending to the sick*, but *tending the sick.*

term

(verb) *The play may be* termed *a tragi-comedy* – not *termed as* a tragi-comedy.

terminal/terminus

Usually an air *terminal*, but a railway *terminus.* The plural of the latter can be *termini* or *terminuses.*

terrible/terribly
See **awful/awfully**.

testimonial
See **reference/testimonial**.

than

1 Usage Be careful of the case of pronouns after *than*. There is always an ellipsis, and the test is to supply the 'understood' words:

☐ You can do it better than I (can)
☐ You like him better than I (do)
☐ You like him better than (you like) me
☐ That is a task for you rather than (for) me
☐ He is two years older than I (am)
☐ You, rather than I, should have the reward (short for *rather than I should have it*).

(See also **me**.) After a few common verbs (*be, seem, became* etc) followed by an adjective, the objective case is, however, often used where prescriptive grammar would require the subject case:

☐ His wife was several years younger than him.

This may be accepted.

2 Than what

☐ It is warmer today *than what* it was yesterday
☐ The trip cost us more *than what* we expected.

Omit *what*. In such sentences the clauses of comparison are short for *than it was warm yesterday* and *than we expected it to cost us*. *What* is, however, correctly used in the following sentence:

☐ Nothing could give me greater pleasure *than what* you have just told me.

Here *what*, being a combination of *that which*, serves as both the subject of the understood verb *does* and the object of *have told*. (See also **what**.)

3 Than with inverted construction

☐ There were more people present than *were* expected,
if the sentence is short for . . . *than there were people expected*.
☐ There were more people present than *was* expected,
if it stands for *than it was expected there would be*. In all the following only the singular verb is correct:
☐ There were more casualties than *was* reported (short for *than it was reported there were*),

☐ More middle-aged persons suffer from heart trouble than *is* generally realised,
☐ The really serious cases are fewer than *has* been suggested.
On possible mistakes in the number of the verb when *than* introduces an inverted construction like *than was the case*, *than were our intentions*, see also **case 1**.

thank you

Always two words, except where it is used as a compound adjective: *a thankyou letter*. Informally, it may also be a noun:
☐ Your father deserves a special *thankyou* for increasing your pocket money.

that

1 As a relative pronoun As a relative pronoun, *that* may be used to refer to persons as well as to things; we may quite well speak of the man *that* built the house. *That* can introduce only defining clauses, never non-defining. Normally, therefore, it must not be separated from what comes before by a comma. In this respect it differs from *which* and *who*. We cannot say:
☐ Sheffield, *that* is a large industrial city in South Yorkshire, is famous for its cutlery.
In such clauses only *which* is possible.
Only *that* is idiomatic when the clause qualifies an introductory *it*:
☐ *It* is his rudeness *that* I object to.

2 When to omit that
☐ Name any book *that* you like.
Correct, if it is meant to exclude books that we don't like; but if the intended meaning is 'any book you like to name', irrespective of whether you like it or not, then *that* should be omitted.

3 When that does not refer back
☐ The more *that* I tried to pacify him, the angrier he became
☐ The sooner *that* we start, the sooner we shall arrive
☐ The further *that* we went, the worse the road became
☐ The older *that* we get, the wiser we become.
From all these sentences, and from all others of the same type, *that* should be omitted. It does not refer back to anything, and hence has no place in the syntax of the sentence.

4 That as an adverb of degree The use of *that* as an adverb of degree, instead of *so*, in constructions of the type:
☐ It was *that* dark we could scarcely see in front of us

is dialectal. Equally non-standard are such informal expressions as *that much, all that far*.

the

1 Usage The definite article may legitimately be used with a singular noun as a 'generic singular', ie a single one of a species or a group taken to represent the whole, as:

☐ The camel is the ship of the desert

☐ The tiger and the cat belong to the same family of animals

☐ The child is father of the man.

It must be remembered, however, that all pronouns and possessive adjectives that refer back to a generic singular must themselves be singular. Because a generic singular has a plural idea, it is very easy to slip into such errors as the following:

☐ The plight of the agricultural labourer was even worse than that of the town worker. *Their* wages were low, and if *they* lost *their* job *they* were turned out of *their* cottages.

Correct to *his* and *he*.

2 Two nouns co-ordinated by and When two nouns are co-ordinated by *and*, the article is not repeated before the second one if the two are thought of in conjunction, as:

☐ The King and Queen have visited the exhibition

☐ The girls and boys in the junior class,

but if the two are thought of separately then it is better to use the article before each one:

☐ God sends his sunshine on *the* just and *the* unjust alike.

This, however, should not be regarded as a rigid rule. We clearly must speak of *the Prime Minister and the Foreign Secretary*, as we must of *the Queen and the Duke of Edinburgh*, but it is not incorrect to say:

☐ *The* Conservatives and Liberals are both opposed to the suggestion,

though many might prefer a repetition of the article.

It is always necessary to repeat the article if the combination is preceded by *both*:

☐ *Both the* Conservatives and *the* Liberals have decided to oppose the measure

☐ *Both the* boys and *the* girls did well in their examinations

☐ The proposals have now been accepted by *both the* employers and *the* workers.

After *or*, the article must be repeated if *or* denotes an alternative:
☐ Do you support the Conservatives *or* the Socialists?
☐ I do not know whether I prefer the blue *or* the green dress.
3 The before a comparative *The* before a comparative is normal idiom in such expressions as *The sooner the better*; *the more the merrier*; *the longer I live, the more cynical I become.*
4 The meaning 'in virtue of this', 'on this account' It may also be used before a comparative to point backwards or forwards to something which will explain the reason for the excess denoted by the comparative, or which at least has a bearing on it:
☐ I am *the more inclined* to believe him because he has nothing to gain by concealing the truth
☐ We were none *the wiser* for his explanation
☐ If a person was reputed to be rich, she was *the more disposed* to excuse his faults.
The in such sentences means 'in virtue of this' or 'on this account'.
5 The before comparative and superlative adjectives *The* is, of course, normal before any adjective of both the comparative and the superlative degree when a noun is felt, if only vaguely, to be understood after it:
☐ Of the two courses you suggest, the second would be *the more acceptable*
☐ Of the three boys, John was *the eldest*
☐ Which way is *the shortest*?
Most and *least* are found both with and without *the*, even when a noun is actually expressed after them:
☐ Of all the people we have been discussing, he has *the least cause* to complain
☐ The competitor who gets *the most points* wins the prize.
In both the sentences the article could be omitted, but its use renders the application more specific by singling out the one in question from the others, where the construction without the article takes it in conjunction with the others.
6 The before superlative adverbs Superlative adverbs may also be preceded by *the*, though again the sentence would generally be quite idiomatic without it:
☐ The person who works the hardest should receive the greatest reward

☐ Which of these flowers do you like the best?
☐ Families without children have to wait the longest for a council house.

7 Go to school or go to the school? With expressions like *go to school, go to church, stay in hospital,* as opposed to the same phrases with *the,* the article is used when the reference is to the building, and omitted when the reference is to the purpose or the function of the building, or to the characteristic activity associated with it. We go to school to learn or to teach, go to church or chapel to worship, go to prison as a punishment. We go to *the* school, church, chapel or prison if we merely visit the place on business. The list of phrases in which the omission of the article is idiomatic is, however, limited. We cannot say that a business man 'goes to office'; it must always be 'go to *the* office'; and although a student goes to college, until recently he always went to *the* university. Now *go to university* is current.

8 Before bishop, headmaster, etc With words like *bishop, archbishop, secretary, headmaster, mayor,* the article is used when the person himself is referred to:
☐ Mr Jackson, *the* Headmaster of Deerwood School.
In some types of journalistic writing, *the* is omitted:
☐ Mr Len Murray, TUC general secretary, spoke on the subject of union reform.
This practice is best not copied.

9 The in titles On *the* in the names of periodicals and in the titles of literary works, see **titles**, and for *the Edgware Road* as an alternative to *Edgware Road*, see **road**.

theirs

No apostrophe.

thence/thither

These adverbs are rarely used in modern English. The principal sense of *thence* is 'from there':
☐ I went to Stratford first and *thence* to Scotland.
Thither is a similarly uncommon adverb meaning 'to there', and they are often confused:
☐ There is a Naturist Foundation at Orpington that I wanted to visit . . . and *thence* I made my way. (*Observer Magazine*)
The correct word here would be *thither*. (See also **hence/hither** and **whence/whither**.)

there

(formal subject) The rule is that normally the verb agrees with the 'real' subject that follows:

☐ *There are* some apples in that bowl

☐ *There is* a lamp on that table;

but a singular verb is used, even if a plural noun or pronoun follows, when:

1 The plural form denotes a single sum or amount:

☐ *There is* five pence to pay

☐ *There is* only another four kilometres to go.

2 A combination of two or more nouns represents a single idea:

☐ *There was* much coming and going

☐ *There is* duck and green peas for dinner.

3 The reference is to a situation in its entirety:

☐ *There is* my wife and family to consider

☐ *There is* only two packets of butter and some tea left

There are is equally acceptable here.

4 The verb is thought of as applying to each term in a list successively and separately:

☐ *There is* John, James, Alec . . . .

Note that no matter whether the 'real' subject that follows is first, second or third person, *there* always takes a third person verb:

☐ *There is* only me to be served now.

(See also **agreement of verb and subject**.)

For possible misuse in such sentences as *Not being stamp collectors, there was nothing in the exhibition to interest us*, see **-ing 1**.

therefore

It means 'for that reason', or 'because of that':

☐ He has transgressed, therefore he must be punished.

The normal position of *therefore* is at the beginning of a clause, and its function is that of what we may call a conjunctive adverb. In this position it is not followed by a comma; to use one, indeed, would be incompatible with its conjunctive function, since a conjunction joins, whereas a comma separates. If, however, it is placed within a clause it becomes parenthetic, and may have a comma both before and after it:

☐ If, therefore, we wish to put the matter to the test . . . .

they

On the common, but incorrect, use of *they* with **anyone**, **each**, **everybody**, **everyone** and **nobody**, as well as with the generalising personal pronoun **one**, see under these words.

□ If anyone is to blame, it's they

is correct from the point of view of strict grammar, but most people would say *It's them*, and this is quite acceptable. (See also **me** and **pronouns**.)

thing

An over-used word. Many writers use *thing* when they cannot be bothered to find a more exact word:

□ He gave me a *thing* for scraping off the old paint (a tool).

□ It was a good *thing* he didn't have far to travel (Fortunately . . .)

thither

See **thence/thither**.

tho'

Sometimes *tho*. Not accepted English spellings. Always write *though*. *Altho* and *altho'* are similarly incorrect, except in letters to friends and personal notes.

though/although

1 On the abbreviated spellings *tho* or *tho'*, *altho* or *altho'*, see previous entry.

2 No difference in meaning There is no difference of meaning. *Although* is felt to be stronger than *though* and is therefore more frequently used at the beginning of a sentence, and internally when emphasis is desired:

□ He insisted on doing it, *although* I warned him not to.

3 Even though We may say *even though*, but not *even although*.

4 Though meaning 'but' *Though* is also used in preference to *although* when it has a meaning close to that of the co-ordinating conjunction *but*:

□ There are several theories about how the treasure came here, *though* we cannot go into them now

□ I have not yet verified the information, *though* I think it is correct

□ No one is infallible, *though* there are some people who think they are.

It is just possible that *although* might be used instead of *though* in all of these.

5 At the end of a sentence When the word is put at the end of the sentence, *although* is out of the question; only *though* is idiomatic:
□ There is an interesting story about how the treasure came to be buried here. We can't go into that now, *though*.

thrash/thresh

The two words are the same by origin, though usage has differentiated them. A person is *thrashed*, corn is *threshed*. The latter is restricted to agricultural contexts; the former is more widely used and has metaphorical applications. One *thrashes* out a problem, and a football team *thrashes* its opponents (gives them a sound beating).

thrice

Now archaic. See **once/twice/thrice**.

thrive

In present-day usage the past tense and the past participle are *thrived*. *Throve* and *thriven* are archaic.

through

Avoid the spellings *thro'*, *thro* and *thru* except in very informal writing.
□ Congress at Davos, Switzerland, August 8th *through* August 13th 1980.
This American use of *through* to denote a period of time, inclusive of both dates given, is not yet British English. This usage does, however, have the advantage of meaning unambiguously 'up to and including' the dates mentioned. The simple preposition *to* that British English uses can sometimes be unclear as to whether the final date is to be included or not.

thus

When *thus* means 'in this way' and is used before a participle, care is necessary to ensure that the noun or pronoun to which it refers really was the person (or thing) that acted 'thus'. The following sentence is, therefore, incorrect:
□ All his money was taken away, *thus* rendering him penniless.
According to the syntax of the sentence, *rendering* refers to *money*. But did his money render him penniless? Amend to either *All his money was taken away and he was thus rendered penniless* or *They took all his money away, thus rendering him penniless.*

tight/tightly

In the following sentences *tight* is correct:

□ Don't tie the bandage too *tight*
□ See that the lid is screwed down *tight*
□ Her dress was drawn in *tight* at the waist
□ She clasped the child *tight* against her body.
In such sentences *tight* is not an adverb, but an adjective used as a complement of result: the sense is 'so that it is/was *tight*'. Note a similar use of *loose* and *firm* in the sentences *The nut worked loose*; *allow the mixture to stand till it sets firm. Tightly* is an adverb of manner:
□ He held me *tightly* by the arm.
Tight, not *tightly*, is used before a present participle to make a compound adjective, as *a tight-fitting suit*. This is consistent with similar combinations with other words as the first element: paint that dries quickly is *quick-drying paint*, and traffic that moves slowly is *slow-moving traffic*.
(See also **adverb or adjective?**)

till/until

There is no difference of meaning: which of the two is used in a particular context seems to be determined largely by considerations of rhythm or **euphony**, though there is a tendency to use *till* for a point of time and *until* for duration of time. Thus:
□ Don't do anything further *till* you hear from me
□ We didn't get home *till* ten o'clock
□ The fruit will not ripen *till* we get more sun
□ You must stay in bed *until* your temperature is normal
□ She lived with an aunt *until* she married
□ We shall have to stay here *until* help arrives
Until is also more usual:
1 At the beginning of a sentence:
□ *Until* we know the facts, we can do nothing further
□ *Until* he was sixteen, he had never been away from his native village.
2 When result, not merely time, is expressed:
□ The frog inflated himself more and more, *until* finally he burst
□ They frittered their money away, *until* they had only a few pence left.
There is no justification whatever for the spelling '*til*.

time and again

Idiomatic, though *time and time again* is, perhaps, more usual.

times

In Shakespeare's time, in our grandparents' time (not *times*), but *olden times, past times, these times, such times as these, good times and bad times, modern times.*

The twice-times table, though illogical, is as accepted as *the two-times table.*

On *three times heavier, many times bigger, ten times larger*, etc, see **comparatives 2**.

tire

(of a vehicle) American spelling. See **tyre**.

titillate/titivate

The two words are sometimes confused. *Titillate* means 'to tickle' (figuratively), 'to excite a pleasant feeling or sensation': *to titillate one's appetite.*

Titivate means 'to smarten up'. It is generally used half humorously, as in the expression *to titivate oneself.*

titles

1 To write or print titles In print the titles of literary works, periodicals, etc are usually set in italics. In writing or typescript they may be underlined (the equivalent of italics in print) or placed in inverted commas, but both methods must not be used together. We may write either 'Paradise Lost' or *Paradise Lost*, but not '*Paradise Lost*'. The advantage of underlining is that it allows inverted commas to be used for secondary titles, ie the titles of chapters, poems, essays, etc within the main work:

□ Browning's 'Andrea del Sarto' first appeared in the volume *Men and Women*, published in 1855.

If the title of the individual poem, essay or article is the only one mentioned, then, within that context, it is a main title, and should be underlined.

(See also **italics** and **underlining**.)

2 First lines If, as with most hymns and some poems, the work is referred to by its first line, it should be given inverted commas, as a quotation, not underlined:

□ The author of 'Nearer, my God, to Thee' was Sarah Flower Adams.

3 Periodicals With periodicals it is usual to exclude an initial *the* from the italics (or inverted commas):

□ He was reading the *Daily Express*.

Exceptions include *The Times* and *The Economist*, who insist on its inclusion. But even with these it must be excluded when it belongs, not to the title of the periodical, but to a noun that follows the title:

☐ The *Times* leading article which we have been discussing is very thoughtful.

(See also **the**.)

4 The article in literary works For literary works (books, plays, poems, essays, etc) the article should normally be included:

☐ Hardy's *The Trumpet-Major*

☐ Anthony Trollope's *The Warden.*

But it may be necessary, for reasons of **euphony**, to omit an article, either definite or indefinite, if the title is preceded by a possessive adjective or the possessive of the author's name. We should, for instance, normally speak of 'Gibbon's *Decline and Fall of the Roman Empire*', though the actual title of the work is *The Decline and Fall of the Roman Empire*, and we would never write 'my *A Dictionary of Slang and Unconventional English*'. However, if we risk ambiguity, the article should be kept. We could not speak of 'Hardy's *Pair of Blue Eyes*', for (to the ear, at least) this would attribute the blue eyes to Hardy. We should have to say 'Hardy's *A Pair of Blue Eyes*'.

5 The Bible, etc No italics or inverted commas are used for the Bible, for the names of its individual books, or for the sacred writings of the well-known non-Christian religions: the Koran, the Vedas, the Talmud. The article is written with a small letter. The derived adjective *biblical* is also written with an initial small letter.

6 'Substitute titles' When a work is popularly known, not by its actual title, but by a personal name with which it is always associated (eg Hansard, Wisden, Bradshaw, Old Moore), so that the name becomes a 'substitute title', it should not be italicised or placed in inverted commas. But when initials are used as an abbreviated form of title for well-known works, these should be italicised: *DNB* (*The Dictionary of National Biography*), *TLS* (*The Times Literary Supplement*), *COD* (*The Concise Oxford Dictionary of Current English*), *OALDCE* (*The Oxford Advanced Learner's Dictionary of Current English*), *LDOCE* (*The Longman Dictionary of Contemporary English*).

7 Periodicals in the possessive When we have to write the possessive case of the name of a periodical, the *'s* should be included in the italics
☐ in the *Guardian's* opinion
☐ in the *Spectator's* view.

too

Only too true, only too pleased, etc are acceptable colloquially, but *It's too good of you* should be avoided when the meaning is 'very good of you'.
Too gives the sense of an understatement in colloquial phrases such as:
☐ He wasn't *too* pleased (meaning 'He was rather annoyed'),
☐ He's not *too* badly off (meaning 'He's in a comfortable financial position'),
☐ It isn't *too* warm today (meaning 'It's chilly').
For its position in a sentence, with the meaning of 'also', see **particularly 3**.

tortious/tortuous/torturous

Tortious means 'constituting a tort (ie a civil wrong)'. *Tortuous* means 'winding': *a tortuous route, a very tortuous chain of argument. Torturous* means 'inflicting torture'. *Tortuous* is the most common word of the three.

trade union

So spelt. The plural is *trade unions*, not *trades unions*; but *The Trades Union Congress.*

traffic

The present participle and gerund of the verb are spelt *trafficking*; past participle *trafficked.*

transpire

A common mistake is to use *transpire* as though it meant 'occur' or 'happen':
☐ Many a quarrel has *transpired* through idle gossip.
It does not mean this. Nor is it synonymous with 'prove to be' or 'turn out':
☐ To the delight of us all it *transpired* that the weather was fine, so the fête could be held after all
☐ The driver of the vehicle *transpired* to be drunk.
It means 'to come to light':
☐ As a result of the inquiry it *transpired* that no proper accounts had been kept for the past three years.

transport/transportation

In British English *transportation* is generally reserved for the one-time punishment of criminals by sending them to penal settlements overseas: *transportation for life*. Americans also speak of the *transportation* of goods, luggage, passengers, etc, but British English generally uses *transport* for this sense:

□ motorways to facilitate the *transport* of goods between large cities

□ large tankers for the *transport* of oil

□ vans specially constructed for the *transport* of perishable foods.

travel

In British English the *l* is doubled before a suffix which begins with a vowel symbol: *travelled, travelling, traveller*. The Americans only use one *l*. (See **spelling 6**.)

triumphant/triumphal

Triumphant is often used where *triumphal* should be used: *triumphant* means 'victorious': *the triumphant army*; *to emerge triumphant from a conflict*.

Triumphal means 'concerned with the celebration of a triumph or a victory': a *triumphal* march, hymn, arch, procession, etc.

try

Try and do something. It expresses greater urgency or determination than *try to do*.

twice

See **once/twice/thrice**.

two words or one?

See **one word or two?**

tyrannise

Tyrannise over people, not *tyrannise them*. Perhaps the tendency to make the verb transitive has arisen through confusion with *terrorise*.

tyre

The accepted spelling in British English, though in the USA usually *tire*.

U

ult

□ Your letter of 29th *ult*.

A now old-fashioned piece of business jargon, meaning 'last month', as *inst* means 'this month' and *prox* 'next month'. Do not use these, either in business letters or elsewhere. Name the month.

'un

Colloquial for *one*. Usually written with an apostrophe (*a good 'un, a wrong 'un*), though strictly there is no justification for it, since there is no omission. An argument for retaining the apostrophe is that the word would look strange and unfamiliar without it.

un-

(prefix) There is no strict rule about hyphenation. Generally, in established combinations the prefix and the 'base' word are written as one: *unusual, unimportant*. A hyphen must be used when the 'base' word begins with a capital, as *un-Christian, un-English, un-American*, etc. (See **hyphen 1**.) When in doubt, consult a dictionary.

In combinations where *non-* as well as *un-* is possible, *un-* generally has a negative import, and means 'the opposite of', while *non-* means 'other than': *an un-Christian act, un-Christian conduct*, but *non-Christian religions*.

unanimous

Wrong use:

□ The proposal has my *unanimous* support.

Amend to *wholehearted*. *Unanimous* can be used only when a number of people are all in agreement. A motion is passed *unanimously* only when everyone present votes in its favour. If no votes are cast against it but a few people abstain from voting, it is not correct to say that it is passed *unanimously*, or that the vote is *unanimous*. The correct term in such circumstances is *nem con* (short for the Latin, *nemine contradicente*, meaning 'no one speaking against').

unaware(s)

Unaware is the adjective:

☐ They were *unaware* of what was happening.
Unawares is the adverb:
☐ He came upon me *unawares*.
In a sentence such as the following it is the adjective that is required:
☐ She arrived home *unaware* of the surprise that awaited her.
It would be incorrect to use *unawares*, since the word refers back to *she*, not to the verb *arrived*. Only *unaware* (the adjective) can be followed by *of*. *Unawares* is more formal than *unaware*.

under
See **above/over**.

underline
☐ I should like to *underline* what the last speaker has said.
Permissible in rather informal style, but *emphasise* is better.

underlining
The only really legitimate use of underlining in longhand or typescript is to represent italics in print. (See **italics** and **titles 1**.) In personal letters it may occasionally be used to emphasise, or draw special attention to, certain words or phrases, but it is inadvisable to employ it for this purpose in more formal writing.

undoubtedly
So spelt, not *undoubtably*.

undue/unduly
To show undue concern; *to be unduly pessimistic* are correct; they mean 'more concern than is necessary', 'more pessimistic than one need be'. But:
☐ There is no need for *undue* pessimism
and:
☐ We should not be *unduly* pessimistic
are mere tautology, since what, in effect, they say is 'There is no need for more pessimism than there is need for', 'We should not be more pessimistic than we should be'. Do not say *It is not unduly late* if you mean merely 'It is not very late'.

uninterested
See **disinterested/uninterested**.

unique
Wrong use:
☐ *Books of the Times* is *so unique*, we're surprised we didn't think of it sooner! (advertisement, *New York Review of Books*)

A thing is either *unique*, or it is not. *So unique, very unique, rather unique, most unique* are all incorrect. *Almost unique* is allowable. There cannot be degrees of uniqueness. *Time* magazine quotes this beautiful example of breaking the rules:
☐ Lafayette's most unique restaurant is now even more unique.
Let us hope the food is better than the grammar. (Compare **perfect**.)

university

We *go to university, go to college, go to church,* not *to the university, to the church,* etc, unless we are being specific about the building (*He goes to the college at the end of Lambourne Road.*)
(See **the 7**.)

unlawful/illegal

See **lawful/legal** and **illegal/illegitimate/illicit**.

unlike

See **like**.

unloose

Though, logically, to *unloose* should mean the opposite of to *loose*, it is accepted as a synonym: *unloose the dog, unloose one's shoelaces.* Neither word is as common as *undo, untie* or *unfasten.*

until

See **till/until**.

unto

No longer used, except in verse.

unwieldy

So spelt, not *unwieldly.* It means 'difficult to handle, or manage' and comes from the verb *to wield.* An *unwieldy* sword was one which was difficult to wield, on account of its size or weight. The word is still used literally, of material things, but by an extension of meaning we can speak of *an unwieldy organisation,* etc.

up to date

Until recently the phrase was hyphenated when used, either before a noun or after a verb, as a compound adjective: *an up-to-date edition, an edition which is not very up-to-date.* No hyphens when the expression is used as an adverbial or adjectival phrase:
☐ *Up to date,* we have collected just over fifty pounds
☐ The book has been revised and brought *up to date*
☐ We have now got the accounts *up to date.*
Today the hyphens may be omitted in all uses.

upstair/upstairs

Originally *upstair* was the adjective, *upstairs* the adverb, and this distinction is still made by some: *an upstair room, an upstair window, go upstairs.* Generally, *upstair* has now dropped out and *upstairs* is used for both parts of speech. The same is true for *downstair* and *downstairs, oversea* and *overseas.* Compare **-ward/-wards.**

urban/urbane

Urban means 'of the town': *urban development. Urbane* means 'courteous in manners; refined'.

use

(noun)

☐ This is no *use* to me

☐ Is this any *use* to you?

These are accepted as idiomatic, and most people would, in fact, use them in preference to the more formally correct *of no use, of any use. Of* must, however, always be used if *use* is not preceded by a word qualifying it:

☐ It's no *use* to me, but may be *of use* to someone.

used to

1 Usage Note spelling – *I* used *to do it* (past tense), not *I use to do it.*

a *Used to* refers to an habitual or lengthy action in the past and is followed by an infinitive:

☐ I *used to live* in Manchester

☐ I *used to enjoy* rich food

☐ I *used to go* for a walk every morning.

b The negative almost always in speech and in much written work is *didn't use*; the form *used not* is generally restricted to more formal styles:

☐ He *used not* to have any friends.

c The interrogative is:

☐ *Did you/Didn't you use* to swim regularly?

2 Used meaning 'accustomed' *Used* in *to be used to* is an adjective meaning 'accustomed to', and is followed by a noun or a gerund:

☐ I *am used to* a solitary life

☐ I *am not used to* living in a crowded flat

☐ Are you *used* to snowy weather?

Where habitual or repeated activity or occurrence in the past is concerned, *would* is sometimes used:
□ Every Christmas Day we *would* attend a church service before dinner. After a huge meal, we *would* exchange presents.
Where there is no sense of repetition or habitual action, *would* cannot be used. We cannot, for instance, replace *used to* by *would* in such sentences as *I used to live in Manchester*; *he used to be much better off than he is now.*
The use of *would* exemplified above has a counterpart in the present tense in a similar use of *will*:
□ She *will come* home from work, have her tea, and sit watching television until about ten o'clock.

utilise

Often used incorrectly as here:
□ Electricity can be *utilised* for a number of purposes.
Utilise is not a synonym of *use*. It means 'to put to a useful purpose, or find a use for, something that would otherwise be wasted'. In certain industries by-products which formerly were regarded as refuse, and treated accordingly, are now *utilised*.

V

v

(abbreviation)
□ Manchester United *v* Liverpool.
Pronounce *versus* (the full word for which it stands), not *vee*. An alternative form of the abbreviation is *vs*.

vacation

In British English this word is mostly applied to the weeks when the law courts and universities are not working: *the Christmas vacation, the Easter vacation, the long/summer vacation.* Schools have *holidays*, not *vacations*, when they are closed for their normal activities.
In another sense of these words, British people have *holidays* at the seaside, in the mountains, abroad, etc; Americans have *vacations*. When the British are *on holiday*, the Americans are *on vacation* (or even *vacationing*!).

various

Wrong uses:

□ We tested *various* of the samples, but none proved satisfactory

□ *Various* of his friends advised him against taking that course.

Various can be used only as an adjective, and cannot be followed by *of*. The alternatives are *his various friends*, *various friends of his*, *several of his friends*.

venal/venial

Venal means 'dishonest; for payment'. It may be applied to a person who, for instance, uses his influence to dishonest ends for money (*a venal politician*); or to his conduct (*venal conduct*). *Venial* is applied to a fault, an offence, etc and means 'pardonable, excusable'.

verify/corroborate

To *verify* means 'to ascertain whether or not something is true': *to verify a person's story*, *verify one's facts*. But if the truth of one story is borne out by another, the second story does not *verify* the first; it *corroborates* it.

very/much

Very is used before adjectives and adverbs, *much* before participles when they retain their verbal function:

□ This picture has been *much* admired, *much* criticised, *much* discussed.

But when a participle is used adjectivally it takes *very*:

□ I am *very* concerned about his health

□ He is *very* interested in stamp collecting

□ We are *very* pleased to hear of your success.

(See also **much 1**.)

via

Use only for the route, not for the method of transport:

□ From Liverpool to London *via* Crewe,

but not *via train*, *via the Canadian Pacific Railway*, *via British Airways*.

viable

Does not mean 'able to be used as a thoroughfare' (a *viable* route) or 'workable, practicable' (a *viable* scheme), but 'capable of maintaining life' (a *viable* foetus) in medicine. Outside its strict medical sense it may be used figuratively for new-born states or communities, in the sense of 'capable of evolving and existing without outside help', but if there is any doubt about its correctness or suitability it had better be avoided.

vicious/viscous

Vicious means 'characterised by vice or evil conduct'. *Viscous* means 'of a thick, runny consistency, like honey or oil'.

vicious circle

A situation in which one evil produces another, which in its turn aggravates the first, which then reproduces the second, and so on. For example, rising prices lead to demands for higher wages, higher wages cause prices to rise still further; this leads to more demands for wage increases, which once again raises prices.

view

The constructions are (a) *in view of* + noun (*In view of the gravity of the situation*), (b) *with a view to* + noun or gerund (*With a view to easing the difficulties*), and (c) *with the view of* + gerund (*With the view of ascertaining the facts*).

In view of expresses reason; *with a view to* and *with the view of* denote purpose. *With a view to* takes a gerund and not an infinitive:

□ He gave up general practice and went into hospital work, *with a view ultimately to become* a consultant.

Amend to *with a view to ultimately becoming a consultant.*

In view of is followed by a noun or pronoun, not by a noun clause. It is true, we can say *In view of what has happened*, or *In view of what you tell me*, but here the clause introduced by *what* is not a noun clause, but an adjective clause containing its own antecedent. *What* means 'that which'.

viewpoint

At one time an Americanism, but now accepted in British English. (On the confusion between *view* and *viewpoint* or *point of view*, see **point of view**.)

virtuosity

The skill of a *virtuoso*; he is someone with a wide knowledge of the arts, or a collector of fine paintings or antiques, or, more commonly today, an extremely gifted musician.

virtuoso

See previous entry.

vis-à-vis

So spelt. A formal preposition, meaning 'with regard to'.

viscous

See **vicious/viscous.**

visit/visitation

Americans *visit with* friends: in Britain we merely *visit* them. *Visitation* is not used of ordinary visiting, but only of (a) a formal visit, in an official capacity: *The Governors' annual visitation of the school*; *the visitation of the sick* (by a clergyman), and (b) visiting in the sense of 'afflicting':

□ The frequent *visitation* of Eastern cities by plague.

viz

The abbreviated form of the Latin, *videlicet*, meaning 'namely, that is to say'. Do not use *viz* unless a full explanation follows, as:

□ The person responsible for the selection of the books, *viz* the librarian.

If only examples are given, then *eg*, not *viz*, is required. (See also **eg/ie.**)

In reading *viz* aloud, say 'namely'. In print it is not italicised.

vowel

Vowels are sounds, not letters. There are only five letters of the alphabet (a, e, i, o, u) to represent the vowel sounds in English, although there are many more than five vowel sounds. The same written symbol may represent more than one vowel sound: contrast, for instance, the sound represented by *u* in *cut* with that in *put*. Conversely, the same vowel may be represented by two different symbols (as in *son* and *sun*, *park* and *clerk*). Sometimes two symbols are written to represent a single vowel (as in *caught* and *tease*). The entry **spelling** gives some of the main connections between sound and spelling. (See also **a/an.**)

W

wait/await

1 Await + object *Await* must have an object; it cannot be used intransitively, nor can it be followed by a preposition. We cannot say *I will await here* or *Await for me at the main entrance*.

2 Await and wait for *Await* and *wait for* are not generally interchangeable. We *wait for*, not *await*, a person or a thing:

□ I am *waiting for* my wife
□ We were *waiting for* the bus
□ *Wait for* me near the ticket barrier.

We *await* some happening, occurrence or development:

□ We must *await* his decision
□ They were eagerly *awaiting* the announcement of the results
□ We *await* your reply with interest.

Await may, however, have a personal object when it means 'to be in store for', or 'lie in wait for':

□ A fortune *awaits* the person who discovers a cure for the common cold
□ On arrival at his hotel he found a telegram *awaiting* him
□ Little did they realise what a surprise *awaited* them at home.

Await is more formal in style than *wait for*.

waive/wave/waver

Waive is not to insist on a right or privilege:

□ In the divorce proceedings, Mr Simpson *waived* his parental rights.

Wave means 'to gesture; move from side to side':

□ Come to the door and *wave* goodbye.
□ He *waved* the flag energetically when the Queen passed by.

Waver means 'to hesitate; become uncertain':

□ The choice was not an easy one to make and he *wavered*
□ When he saw the sea below him, his courage *wavered* and he refused to jump.

want

(verb)

1 Want and need The basic distinction between *want* and *need* is that whereas *need* denotes a necessity, *want* expresses a desire. Many things that we *want* we do not necessarily *need*, and sometimes what a person *needs* he may not *want*. There is an obvious difference between:

□ He *needs* every penny he can get

and:

□ He *wants* every penny he can get.

Since a lack of something implies (to some extent, at least) a need of it, and since a desire may be prompted by a genuine need, *need* and *want* often overlap. There are obvious cases, like those given in the examples above, where the two are not interchangeable, but there are others where either could be used. We may divide them into two classes:

a where *need* can be interchanged with *want* in the sense of 'desire':

☐ Do you know of anyone who *wants/needs* a gardener?

Here *want* means more or less the same as 'require'.

b Where *need* can be interchanged with *want* in the sense of 'lack', or something approaching it:

☐ That dress *needs/wants* washing

☐ What you *need/want* to put you right is a good holiday.

Want suggests that the need is an urgent one, which should be satisfied or attended to.

When the need is belittled, or represented as trivial, the tendency is to use *need*, not *want*:

☐ My house *wants* painting from top to bottom,

but:

☐ All it *needs* is a coat of paint.

2 Want meaning 'lack' Another meaning of *want* is 'to lack; be deficient in':

☐ Her father left her a considerable fortune, so she shouldn't *want* for money

☐ He is *wanting* in common sense.

This use is rather formal.

3 Want to *Want* is used in conjunction with an infinitive in sentences conveying advice, censure, warning, etc:

☐ You *want to* watch that fellow, or he'll cheat you

☐ You think you've got some fine roses, but you *want to see* mine.

-ward/-wards

These are suffixes which indicate direction: *backward/backwards*, *forward/forwards*, *westward/westwards*, etc. Today, many people do not distinguish between the two forms. Originally, though, *-ward* was adjectival in use: *a forward movement*, *a westward direction*, *a downward glance*, and *-wards* was used adverbially: *to lean backwards*, *to throw a ball upwards*, etc. The *-wards* form is less frequently used in America, even adverbially.

Some expressions, however, are established and never change: 'Forward!' (command to an army, etc); *to come forward* ('to present oneself': *Several people have come forward with offers of help*); *to put forward* a suggestion, an idea, etc; *a backward child*; *backwards and forwards*:

□ The pendulum swings *backwards and forwards*.

Compare **upstair/upstairs**.

waste/wastage

Wrong use:

□ The management complained about the *wastage* of electricity caused by lights being left on when rooms were not in use.

The word required is *waste*. *Wastage* means 'loss due to evaporation, decay, leakage, etc'. The daily *wastage* of water from a reservoir is that which is lost through more or less unavoidable causes. The following, from the *Birmingham Post*, also illustrates the correct use:

□ Only about thirty-four per cent of boys and seven per cent of girls leaving school, enter apprenticeships or learnerships in skilled occupations. There is a considerable *wastage* among those who do.

wave

See **waive/wave/waver**.

waver

See **waive/wave/waver**.

-wear

Footwear and *underwear* have become accepted, but *neckwear* (collars, ties, scarves, etc) and *headwear* (hats) should not be used in ordinary English. Common two-word combinations with *-wear* are: *men's wear*, *ladies' wear*, *children's wear*.

wed

Except in a few colloquial phrases like *newly-weds*, *wedded bliss*, etc, the word is now dialectal or journalistic: *Millionaire Weds Shop Girl*. Use *marry* instead. On *wed* or *wedded*, see **past tense or participle: regular or irregular form?**

weird

Note spelling; see **spelling 1**.

welcome/welcomed

Welcome is an adjective, *welcomed* a participle: *a welcome guest*, *a welcome change*, *a most welcome suggestion*. It is mainly after a verb that confusion sometimes occurs:

□ Anyone who cares to come will be *welcome* (not *welcomed*), but:

□ The guests were *welcomed* by the chairman.

In America, anyone begging another person's pardon may receive the reply, *You're welcome*. This is less common in Britain.
Welcome to + infinitive or noun:
☐ You're *welcome to* come in and have some tea (I'd be happy to give you tea);
☐ He's *welcome to* the car (I'm happy for him to take it).

well/good
When prefixed to a participle to make a compound adjective, the word generally used is *well*: *well-spoken*, *well-read*, *well-behaved*. *Well* is also the usual prefix for a pseudo-participle (ie a noun with *-ed* or *-ing* added to it, so that it is made to appear a participle). Thus a person with good intentions is *well-intentioned*, and one with good manners is *well-mannered*; but a person with good looks is *good-looking*, possibly because *well-looking* might suggest that he was looking *well* (ie in good health). In general, *well* (adverb) is used with verbs and adjectives, *good* (adjective) is used with nouns.

wet/wetted
Wet is the usual form of the past tense and past participle when the 'wetting' is not a deliberate act:
☐ The heavy rain *wet* us through.
☐ That slight shower has scarcely *wet* the soil.
Wetted is more usual for something that is done deliberately:
☐ He *wetted* his handkerchief in the stream
☐ She *wetted* the stamp before trying to remove it from the envelope.
(See also **past tense and participle: regular or irregular form?**)

what
1 Difficulties of number When *what* means 'that which' it is singular and takes a singular verb: when it means 'those which' it is plural and takes a plural verb:
☐ We shall not need any more bread; *what* we have *is* quite sufficient
☐ You need not get any more stamps; *what* we have *are* quite sufficient.
When a noun clause beginning with *what* is the subject of a verb which is followed by a plural complement, there is a temptation to make the verb plural; but this is incorrect. It must be singular, since the noun clause represents a single idea:

□ *What* we need *is* more helpers (not *are*: what we need means 'our need'),
□ What interested the children most *was* the monkeys (not *were*),
□ What proved his undoing *was* the lies he told.
A useful rule of thumb is, if the clause introduced by *what* could be converted to a question, to which the sentence as a whole is the answer, then use a singular verb: *What interested the children most?* – What *interested the children most* was *the monkeys*.
(See also **singular or plural verb? 13**.)

2 What with the same as *The same as what* is correct when *what* means 'that which' and is fully pronominal:
□ *What* he says now is not *the same as what* he told me last night.
But when it is semi-adjectival, and refers back to a definite antecedent, it is better omitted:
□ He is wearing the same suit as he wore last Sunday (not as *what* he wore last Sunday).
When *the same* is adverbial, and means 'in the same way' or 'just as', *what* should never be used:
□ Do it *the same as what* I do
□ He is tall and stout, just *the same as what* his father was.
In both these sentences omit *what*.

3 What have you *What have you*, in the sense of 'anything else you like to think of' is not accepted English, and should not be used in serious speech or writing: *Pears, apples, bananas and what have you.*

4 Than what On *than what* in such sentences as *He is older than what I am*, see **than 2**.

whatever/what ever

See **ever/-ever 3**.

whence/whither

1 Whence A question word and conjunction, now little used, meaning 'from what place':
□ *Whence* did he come?
□ I do not know *whence* he came.
Since *whence* means 'from what place', it is incorrect to say *From whence did he come?*

2 Whither *Whither* is archaic for 'to what place'. It is best not used. In the following incorrect example it should be replaced by *where*:

☐ The meeting almost foundered on the rocks of Capri, *whither* I had landed. (*The Observer*)

(See also **hence/hither** and **thence/thither**.)

whenever/when ever

See **ever/-ever 3**.

whereabouts

When used as a noun, either singular or plural is acceptable:

☐ His *whereabouts is/are* unknown.

Even if the reference is to several persons, each with a different whereabouts, a singular verb is still possible:

☐ She has a brother and two sisters, but their *whereabouts is/are* unknown.

wherever/where ever

See **ever/-ever 3**.

wherewithal

In its original sense of 'means', the word is archaic. Today, *the wherewithal* ('money') is colloquial:

☐ I haven't got *the wherewithal* to go out tonight.

Note that it is always used with the definite article.

which

1 Which and what As an interrogative pronoun or adjective, *which* differs from *what* in that it selects from a number of alternatives (though the precise number may not be known to the speaker), whereas *what* is general, and does not take alternatives into account. '*Which train are you going by?*' implies that the speaker has in mind several possible trains; '*What train are you going by?*' merely asks for the time of the train, and gives no indication that the speaker has any notion of the trains that are available.

2 As a relative pronoun As a relative pronoun, *which* must be preceded by a comma if it is non-defining, but no comma must be used if it is defining, ie if it selects a particular one, or particular ones, from amongst others:

☐ The house which was burgled is the one at the corner (defining),

☐ That house, which was built in 1780, has an interesting history (non-defining).

(See also **comma 5**.)

3 Which meaning 'and this' Normally *which* should have a specific word as its antecedent, but it is permissible to use it to introduce

a continuative clause, when it refers back to the entire notion of the previous clause:
□ I said he would withdraw his support at the last moment, *which* is just what happened.
In such sentences *which* means 'and this'.
4 But which and and which *But which* and *and which* need watching. Since *but* and *and* are co-ordinating conjunctions they must join two words or word-groups of the same kind. When, therefore, they are followed by an adjective (relative) clause introduced by *which*, they must be preceded by another adjective clause of the same type, and the two must have the same antecedent:
□ This passage refers to a situation *which* is superficially calm and tranquil *but which*, in effect, is far from what it seems.
A frequent mistake is to use *and* or *but* to join an adjective clause introduced by *which* to a totally different kind of construction:
□ The envelope with a foreign stamp on it, *and which* you promised to give me . . . (adjective phrase and adjective clause).
□ A house containing six large rooms, *and which* has a garden at the back . . . (participial construction and adjective clause).
This does not mean, however, that if the second of the co-ordinated clauses begins with *which*, the first must also begin with *which*. The following are quite idiomatic:
□ Improvements that everyone would like to see, but *which* no one is willing to pay for
□ The place where he lived as a child, and to *which* he always hoped to return.
The three essential conditions are that both must be adjective clauses, both must be defining or both non-defining (a defining clause cannot be co-ordinated with a non-defining or vice versa), and both must qualify the same antecedent.
There is no objection to sentences where the second *which* is understood but not expressed:
□ That is a place *which* many people have seen but few can describe.
5 On *whichever* or *which ever*, see **ever/-ever 3**.

while/whilst

1 Whilst *Whilst* is less frequently found in Standard English than *while*. It remains common in many dialects.

2 While *While* may legitimately be used in the sense of 'although':
□ *While* I sympathise with you, I am afraid there is little I can do.
The clause which it introduces must always precede the main clause. It is sometimes found also as a substitute for *and*:
□ His eldest son became a barrister, the second entered the Church, *while* the youngest made the army his career.
This, however, does not mean that *while* can always be used in this way:
□ White outfought Ritchie in nearly every round, and the latter bled profusely, *while* both his eyes were nearly closed at the end.
This is not acceptable. Perhaps the writer used *while* to avoid repeating *and*, but still it does not sound right. As a general rule, *while* should be used to co-ordinate only when there is a kind of parallelism between the two clauses, as there is in the previous example. As *while* contrasts when it is used in place of *although*, so it compares when it replaces *and*. But even so, it is advisable not to use it if it might lead to ambiguity:
□ The vicar conducted the service *while* the Archdeacon preached the sermon.
3 While meaning 'until' In certain dialects there is a use of *while* in the sense of 'until':
□ I did not get home *while* eight o'clock
□ They have invited us to stay *while* next Sunday,
but though it was at one time more widely used (there is an example of it in Shakespeare's *Macbeth*) it is no longer recognised as correct in Standard English.
4 Awhile and a while When the expression is preceded by a preposition, two words must always be used:
□ Let us stay here for *a while* (not for *awhile*).
5 For *while* and *wile*, see **wile/while**.

whisky/whiskey
Prefer the first spelling, which is always used by Scottish distillers, though the Irish and Americans use the second.

whither
See **whence/whither**.

Whitsun
Whitsun and *Whitsuntide* are both used for the season (the latter is perhaps commoner in the northern parts of England than in the southern), but *Whitsun Sunday* and *Whitsun Monday* are not

correct: they should be *Whit Sunday* and *Whit Monday. Whit week* and *Whitsun week* are, however, both allowable. As an alternative to *Whit Sunday* there is *Whitsun Day*, which is also permissible. These words are now rapidly disappearing from use now that the Government has renamed the Whit holiday the 'Spring Bank Holiday'.

who/whom

1 **Who and whom for persons** *Who* and *whom* are normally reserved for persons, but they may be used of animals when they are thought of in a semi-personal way (*My dog, who is getting old now*) and of countries when the people rather than the territory are referred to: *India, who feels very strongly on this matter.*

2 **Who and whom as relative pronouns** As relative pronouns, *who* and *whom* are preceded by a comma when they introduce a non-defining clause, but the comma must not be used when the clause is a defining one.

(See **comma 5** and **which 2**).

3 **Who as subject, whom as object** *Who* is used for the subject and the complement of a verb:

☐ My father, *who* works in a bank, is retiring soon.

☐ My father, *who* is sixty next year, works in a bank.

Whom is used for the object and when governed by a preposition:

☐ The man *whom* you rescued from the sea has recovered

☐ The newspaper editor, *to whom* we all owe so much, is leaving the company.

But in questions introduced by an interrogative pronoun which is governed by a preposition which comes at the end of the sentence, it is more usual to use *who*:

☐ *Who* is that letter from?

☐ *Who* was this poem written by?

In spoken English or colloquial written style, *who* is now almost universally used. But even here, *whom* must always be used after a preposition at the beginning of a sentence:

☐ *To whom* do I send it?

4 **Who/whom in relative clauses** A frequent source of trouble is sentences of this type:

☐ The person *who* (or *whom*?) we thought was guilty proved to be innocent

□ The man *who* (or *whom*?) we feared we had injured proved to be unharmed.

The temptation is always to use *whom*, presumably because it is felt that the word is the object of *thought* and *feared* (or whatever verb takes their place in other sentences); but it is not. In the first sentence it is the subject of *was guilty*, hence *who* is correct, and in the second the object of *had injured*, hence *whom* is required. *We thought* and *we feared* have the force of parentheses, and could be moved to another part of the sentence: *the person who was guilty, we thought*; *the man whom we had injured, we feared* . . . Even *The Times Literary Supplement* had this sentence:

□ The German people, *whom* Hitler had determined should not survive defeat, did in fact survive.

Obviously *who* should have been used, since it is the subject of *should not survive*. And the *Sunday Times* made the same mistake in this headline:

□ The entire Magazine, except Lifespan, is devoted this week to 100 men and women *whom* Sunday Times writers and expert consultants believe will be making headlines in the Britain of the 1980s.

Again, *who* should have been used as it is the subject of *will be making*. When it goes with an infinitive, however, *whom* is always required:

□ The person *whom* we thought to be guilty.

If there is any doubt, a useful test is to substitute the personal pronoun *he* or *him*; if *he* would be used, the correct relative is *who*, if *him*, it is *whom*:

□ We thought *he* was guilty (therefore *who*),
□ We feared we had injured *him* (therefore *whom*),
□ We thought *him* to be guilty (therefore *whom*).

5 Questions A similar difficulty may arise with questions:

□ *Who* (not *whom*) do you think she is?

since it is the complement of *is*, not the object of *do think*; but:

□ *Whom* do you think we saw?

because it is the object of *saw*.

6 Whom is never indirect object *Whom* is not used as an indirect object. We do not say *The boy whom I gave the book*, or ask *Whom did you give the book?* It must be *to whom* (or the preposition may be placed at the end).

7 The verb after who *Who* is the same number and person as its antecedent, and takes its verb accordingly:

☐ It is *I who am* to blame.

The rules regarding the use of the co-ordinating conjunctions *and* and *but* before *who* are the same as those for *which*: see **which 4**.

whodunit

A crime story, usually one concerned with a murder, in which the interest is in establishing the identity of the criminal. Now an accepted noun which has gained literary status. No question mark should be used. The word is made up by phonetic imitation of *who done it?*, uneducated usage for *who did it?*

whoever/who ever

(On the correct use of each, see **ever/-ever 3**.)

Whoever is used for the objective as well as the subject case:

☐ We shall invite *whoever* we please.

This is also extended to *who ever*:

☐ *Who ever* shall we ask?

whose

1 With impersonal things It is correct to use *whose* of non-personal and inanimate things:

☐ a lake *whose* surface sparkled in the sunlight

☐ houses *whose* trim gardens seemed to indicate the characters of their owners.

2 Whose and who's Care should be taken not to confuse *whose* with *who's* (meaning 'who is' or 'who has'), a mistake that is easily made as, like *its* and *it's*, they are pronounced the same. Even the journalists of *The Times Educational Supplement* are not always so careful as they should be, as this headline shows:

☐ *Whose* Afraid of the Big Bad Comprehensive?

And here is the mistake the other way round from *The Observer*:

☐ I relished the anticipation of clever people, cleverly swapping anecdotes, cleverly punning, cleverly imitating others, indiscreetly prognosticating who'd get *who's* job.

wile/while

(verb) To *wile* (meaning 'to trick') a person into doing something, but to *while* away ('pass, fill in') the time. Today, *wile* is most commonly found as a plural noun, *wiles*, meaning 'cunning'.

will and shall/would and should

1 I shall and I will There once was a rule that *shall* expressed simple futurity in the first person singular and plural (*I/we shall*) and *will* in the second and third persons (*you/he/she/it/they will*). To express volition, a determination to do something, exactly the reverse was true. There is the story of two men who fell off London Bridge into the Thames. One shouted out, 'I *shall* drown, no one *will* save me.' The other said, 'I *will* drown, no one *shall* save me.' Which one wanted to commit suicide? Assuming that both retained a memory of a traditional training in grammar in such extreme circumstances, it was the second.

Today, this distinction is rarely made. This is partly a result of the running together of *I will* and *I shall* in speech into the single form *I'll*. This meant that people were often unsure which form they were using, and the uncertainty spread to the written language. Further, American English and Scottish long ago gave up the distinction and their influence has spread in Britain.

2 Shall in questions Although *will* is very common to express futurity for all persons (as well as to express volition), *shall* is not wrong in the first person singular and plural. Indeed, it *must* be used in questions: *Shall I?* and *Shall we?*;

□ *Shall* I come at four o'clock?

□ *Shall* we see you at the party tonight?

Will I? would be incorrect here and *Will we?* marginally acceptable.

3 Would and should instead of 'will' and 'shall' *Would* and *should* are sometimes used instead of *will* and *shall* in requests and suggestions. Being more remote, they suggest a certain degree of reluctance, hesitancy or deference:

□ *Would* you lend me 50 pence?

□ *Should* I ask her to tea?

4 Should or would in a suggestion A suggestion requires I *should* (or I *shouldn't*) not I *would* (or I *wouldn't*):

□ I *shouldn't* do that, if I were you.

But the expression of determination or resolution needs *would*:

□ Even if I were well off I *wouldn't* pay that price for a suit.

I shouldn't do that, if I were you means merely 'I should refrain from doing that', but *I wouldn't do that, if I were you* means 'I should refuse to do that'.

5 Abbreviated forms The abbreviated forms are *'ll* for *shall* and *will*:

□ *I'll* meet you at 7.30.

The negative contractions are *I won't* and *I shan't*.
As an abbreviation of *would* and *should*, use *'d*, not *'ld*: *He said* he'd *be there*, not *He said he'ld be there*.
It is standard practice to use full forms in most written contexts. Contractions may appear in informal letters, dialogues, etc.
6 On *will* in habitual sense, see **used to 2**.

winter/wintry
See **autumn/autumnal**.

woe betide
This expression is used both for wishes and statements, in the past as well as in the present:
☐ *Woe betide* anyone who offends him
☐ *Woe betide* anyone who offended him.

woman
See **lady/woman**.

Women's Lib
Abbreviation for Women's Liberation Movement. American English is certainly more affected than British English. It remains to be seen if a pressure group can change the patterns of existing usage. For advice on specific issues, see **Ms**, **chairman**, **he or she**, **his or her** and **gender in nouns**.

wonder
1 As a noun In such expressions as *It's a wonder*, *no wonder* (short for *It is no wonder*), *wonder* is a noun meaning 'a matter for wonder' or 'something to be wondered at'. It is followed by a noun clause in apposition to it, specifying the thing or the fact that is regarded as the wonder. In statements, the clause is generally not introduced by *that*:
☐ *It's a wonder* he wasn't killed
☐ *No wonder* they were annoyed.
In questions also, *that* may sometimes be omitted, but it is generally used:
☐ What *wonder* that we missed the way?
☐ Is it any *wonder* (that) she is always in debt?
Small wonder, which has a mild exclamatory force, is usually followed by *that*:
☐ *Small wonder* that they refused the offer!
A wonder may also be followed by a conditional clause:
☐ It will be *a wonder* if he is punctual,

or by an indirect question denoting the thing that arouses the wonder:

□ It has always been *a wonder* to me how he manages to live/ where he gets his money from.

In sentences of the last type, *a wonder* means 'something that provokes wonder or curiosity'.

2 As a verb As a verb, *wonder* is used with two different meanings:

a In the sense of 'to marvel'. When it has this meaning it is followed by a noun clause having the form of an indirect statement and specifying the fact that excites the wonder. Again, in statement sentences there is no introductory *that*:

□ I *wonder* he wasn't killed

□ I don't *wonder* you were anxious about their safety.

But *that* is generally used when the sentence is an interrogative one:

□ Do you/can you *wonder* that no one trusts him?

b In the sense of 'to ask oneself' or 'be curious about'. When the verb has this meaning it is followed by an indirect question in the form of a noun clause:

□ I *wonder* where they have gone

□ I *wonder* what we had better do,

or an infinitive:

□ I *wonder* what to buy my father for Christmas

As with other indirect questions, there is normally no question mark at the end of the sentence, but one is permissible if the *I wonder* . . . formula is felt to be a courteous substitute for an interrogative:

□ I *wonder* whether you could lend me 50 pence?

□ We *wondered* whether we might beg a lift in your car?

Compare **suppose/supposing 2**.

3 Shouldn't wonder + subjunctive Strictly speaking, a conditional clause which follows *shouldn't wonder* requires the subjunctive:

□ I *shouldn't wonder* if they *came* after all

□ I *shouldn't wonder* if they *were to come* after all,

but very frequently the indicative (*if they come*) is used in writing as well as in speech.

4 Double negative The double negative in sentences of the type: *I shouldn't wonder if she hasn't missed the train* (suggesting that she probably has) is indefensible from a grammatical point of view, but is accepted by usage.

5 Wonder whether

□ I *wonder whether* it wouldn't be better to see him personally rather than to write to him.

The negative is correct. It corresponds to the direct question *Wouldn't it be better?* suggesting that it would. This, of course, does not exclude the use of the positive indirect form *whether it would*. The difference is that the positive form leaves the question undecided, and waits for an answer or for suggestions, whereas the negative form suggests the speaker's own answer.

worship

Note spelling of *worshipped, worshipper*. Similarly *handicap, handicapped*; *kidnap, kidnapped*. American English uses one *p*. (See also **spelling 6**.)

would

See **will and shall/would and should**. On *would* in habitual sense, see **used to 2**.

wouldn't know

The use of *I wouldn't know* when all that is meant is 'I don't know' is absurd but must be accepted as idiomatic.

wrapped/rapt

Wrapped means 'enclosed by some kind of wrapper', as *wrapped in tissue paper, wrapped in a cloth*.

Rapt means absorbed (in), carried away (by): *rapt in his studies, a rapt expression of countenance, rapt attention*. The noun *rapture* comes from the same root.

Note the metaphorical use of *wrapped*: a subject is *wrapped* in mystery (not *rapt*, which is hardly ever used figuratively).

Xmas

Do not use this spelling. If you come across it in writing or in print, pronounce it *Christmas*, not *Ex-mas*. The initial symbol is not the English letter *X*, but the Greek *chi*, the first letter in the Greek word for *Christ*. It occurs in many Greek words, and is usually rendered into English by the 'hard' *ch*, pronounced as *k*.

y

yet

Yet in the sense of 'still' (*Are you here yet?*) is archaic or dialectal. *As yet*, which means 'as the position is at present', should not be used if the simple *yet* will suffice, as it would in such sentences as:

□ We have not *as yet* received his reply

□ I have not had a chance to read the letter *as yet*

□ Eight and twenty years I've lived, and never seen a ghost *as yet*. (H G Wells, *The Red Room*)

As yet implies a certain element of expectancy, or looking forward; it is therefore justified in a sentence like the following:

□ We have received only two applications for the post *as yet*.

The suggestion is that the present position is not expected to be the final one.

you

As a generalising personal pronoun, *You don't have to be brilliant to get ahead*, see **one**.

your/you're

Remember that, although these two words are pronounced alike, *your* is the possessive adjective and *you're* is the contracted form of *you are*. The two are sometimes confused, as on the child's greetings card which read *For you're 7th birthday*. Similarly, this example from the *Guardian*:

□ Do you really need a new car with 50,000 miles in it before anything goes wrong if *your* 65 and average 5,000 miles a year?

yours

No apostrophe. *Yours* is a possessive pronoun, not a possessive adjective. It cannot, therefore, be used to qualify a noun. Its adjectival counterpart is *your*. We cannot say *Yours and my interests*. The alternatives are *Your interests and mine* or *My interests and yours*. Never write *your's*.

Appendix

Plurals of commoner foreign words and some English words

An asterisk denotes that the word in question is dealt with in the main part of the book.

For the general rules regarding plurals of words ending in *-y* and in *-o*, the plurals of compound nouns and the plural forms of proper names, see **plural forms** in the main part of the book.

abacus – abaci
addendum – addenda
agenda* – agendas
alga – algae
alto – altos
alumnus – alumni
analysis – analyses
antirrhinum – antirrhinums
antithesis* – antitheses
apex – apexes (or *-ices*)
aphis – aphides
appendix* – appendices (to books, etc)
appendix* – appendixes (anatomical)
aquarium – aquaria (or *-iums*)
archipelago – archipelagos
armadillo – armadillos
autobahn – autobahns
automaton – automata
axis – axes
ay – ayes (*The Ayes have it*)
bacillus – bacilli
bacterium – bacteria*
bamboo – bamboos
banjo – banjos (or *-oes*)
basis – bases
beau – beaux
bonus – bonuses
buffalo – buffalo (or *-oes*)
bus* – buses
cactus – cacti
calix – calices
cannon* – cannon (or *-ons*)
canto – cantos
cargo – cargoes
cherub – cherubs, cherubim
chipolata – chipolatas
commando* – commandos
concerto – concertos
contralto – contraltos
conversazione – conversazioni
corps* – corps
corrigendum – corrigenda
coup d'état – coups d'état
crematorium – crematoria
crisis – crises
criterion – criteria*
crocus – crocuses
crux – cruces
cupful – cupfuls (see **-ful***)
curio – curios
dado – dadoes
datum – data*
desideratum – desiderata
desperado – desperadoes
dictum – dicta
dodo – dodos

domino – dominos (cloaks)
domino – dominoes (the game)
dwarf – dwarfs
dynamo – dynamos
echo – echoes
effluvium – effluvia
elf – elves
embargo – embargoes
emporium – emporia
encomium – encomiums
enigma – enigmas
equinox – equinoxes
erratum – errata
Eskimo* – Eskimoes
euphonium – euphoniums
facsimile – facsimiles
factotum – factotums
fait accompli – faits accomplis
falsetto – falsettos
fish* – fishes (or *fish*)
flamingo – flamingoes
focus – focuses (*foci* in scientific contexts)
folio – folios
formula – formulae (or *-as*)
forum – forums
fresco – frescoes
fulcrum – fulcrums
fungus – fungi
gas – gases
genius – geniuses
genus – genera
geranium – geraniums
gladiolus – gladioli
graffito – graffiti*
grotto – grottoes
gymnasium – gymnasiums (but *gymnasia* for the German High Schools)
halo – haloes
handful – handfuls (see **-ful***)
handkerchief – handkerchiefs
harmonica – harmonicas
harmonium – harmoniums
hero – heroes
hippopotamus – hippopotamuses (or *-mi*)
hoof – hoofs (occasionally *hooves*)
hors-d'œuvre – hors-d'œuvre
hydrangea – hydrangeas
hypothesis – hypotheses
igloo – igloos
ignoramus – ignoramuses
impetus – impetuses
impresario – impresarios
index* – indices (mathematical)
index* – indexes (to books, etc)
innuendo – innuendoes
isthmus – isthmuses
kilo – kilos
laburnum – laburnums
lacuna – lacunae (or *-as*)
larva – larvae
lasso – lassos
lay-by – lay-bys
libretto – libretti (or *librettos*)
linoleum – linoleums
loofa – loofas (sometimes spelt *-fah*(*s*))
Lord Justice – Lords Justices
Lord Lieutenant – Lord Lieutenants
Lord Mayor* – Lord Mayors (similarly Lady Mayoresses)
maestro – maestros
magneto – magnetos
mango – mangoes

manifesto – manifestoes
Maori – Maoris
matrix – matrices
mausoleum – mausoleums
maximum – maxima
medium – media*
medium – mediums (spiritualist)
memento – mementoes
memorandum – memoranda
menu – menus
Mikado – Mikados
minimum* – minima
minus – minuses (for the sign)
momentum – momenta
mongoose – mongooses
mosquito – mosquitoes
mother-in-law – mothers-in-law (see **in-law***)
motto – mottoes
mulatto – mulattos (*-oes*)
mummy – mummies
narcissus – narcissi (or *-uses*)
nasturtium – nasturtiums
nebula – nebulae
negro – negroes
no – noes (*The Noes have it*)
nostrum – nostrums
nucleus – nuclei
nuncio – nuncios
oaf – oafs
oasis – oases
octavo – octavos
octopus – octopuses
omnibus* – omnibuses
oratorio – oratorios
pagoda – pagodas
parenthesis* – parentheses
parvenu(e) – parvenu(e)s (the *e* for the feminine)
peccadillo – peccadillos
pendulum – pendulums
pergola – pergolas
phenomenon* – phenomena
phobia – phobias
photo – photos
piano – pianos
piccolo – piccolos
pick-me-up – pick-me-ups
plateau – plateaux (or *-s*)
plus* – pluses (the sign)
Poet Laureate – Poets Laureate
polyanthus – polyanthuses
portfolio – portfolios
portico – porticoes
portmanteau – portmanteaus (or *-eaux*)
potato – potatoes
premium – premiums
prima donna – prima donnas
prospectus – prospectuses
proviso – provisos
purlieu – purlieus
quarto – quartos
quiz* – quizzes
quorum – quorums
quota – quotas
rabbi – rabbis
radio – radios
radius – radii
referendum – referendums (or *-da*)
rhino – rhinos
rhinoceros – rhinoceroses
rhododendron – rhododendrons (or *-dron*)
rhombus – rhombuses
roebuck – roebuck
roof – roofs

rostrum – rostrums
rota – rotas
rotunda – rotundas
saga – sagas
salmon – salmon
salvo – salvoes
sanatorium – sanatoria (occasionally *-iums*)
sari – saris
scarf – scarfs (or *scarves*)
scenario – scenarios
schema – schemata
scherzo – scherzos (or *-zi*)
seraglio – seraglios
seraph – seraphs (in biblical contexts *seraphim*)
serf – serfs
series – series
serum – serums
shako – shakos
shampoo – shampoos
sheaf – sheaves
sheriff – sheriffs
siesta – siestas
silo – silos
simile – similes
sinus – sinuses
ski – skis
solarium – solariums (less frequently *-ia*)
solo – solos
soprano – sopranos
spatula – spatulas
species – species
spectrum – spectra
spermatozoon – spermatozoa
sphinx – sphinxes
spoonful – spoonfuls (see **-ful***)
staccato – staccatos
stadium – stadiums
staff – staffs
stamen – stamens
stand-by – stand-bys
stanza – stanzas
stiletto – stilettos
stimulus* – stimuli
stratum – strata*
studio – studios
stylo – stylos
stylus – styluses
subpoena* – subpoenas
substratum – substrata
surplus – surpluses
syllabus – syllabuses
symposium – symposia
synopsis – synopses
tableau – tableaux (sometimes *-s*)
taboo – taboos
talisman – talismans
tango – tangos
tattoo – tattoos
taxi – taxis
terminus* – termini (also *-uses*)
terra-cotta – terra-cottas
thesis – theses
tiara – tiaras
timpano – timpani
tiro – tiros (see also *tyro*)
tobacco – tobaccos
toga – togas
tomato – tomatoes
tornado – tornadoes
torpedo – torpedoes
torso – torsos
trade union* – trade unions
trapezium – trapeziums
trauma – traumas
tremolo – tremolos

trio – trios
triumvir – triumvirs (or *-viri*)
trousseau – trousseaus (or *-eaux*)
tuba – tubas
tumulus – tumuli
turf – turfs
two – twos
tympanum – tympana
tyro – tyros
ultimatum – ultimatums
Utopia – Utopias
vacuum – vacuums (but *vacua* in scientific contexts)
veranda – verandas
vertebra – vertebrae
veto – vetoes
virago – viragos
virtuoso* – virtuosi
virus – viruses
vista – vistas
volcano – volcanoes
volte-face – volte-faces
vortex – vortices
wharf – wharfs (sometimes *wharves*)
will-o'-the-wisp – will-o'-the-wisps
yogi – yogis
zero – zeros
zoo – zoos